Iréne de Brice

Contributions by Vivia Astraia, Louisa Wargo and Maricel Flores Díaz

HANDS OF WONDER

CONTEMPLATIVE ART MEDITATIONS™

Visit www.puraprana.com to

DISCOVER | INSPIRE | CREATE

Connect at

 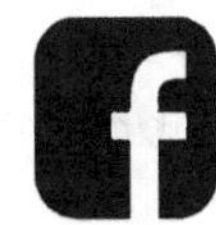

@puraprana /puraprana

#puraprana
#handsofwonder
#anewkindofcoloringbook

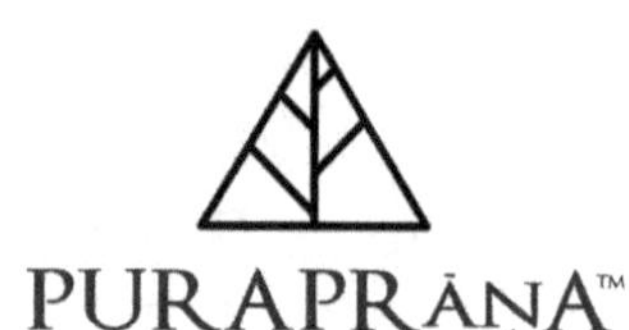

First Edition - 2016, ISBN: 978-1541331334
Second Edition - 2019, ISBN: 978-0692173886

To order wholesale contact elevate@puraprana.com

**Created with love on Taíno territory,
currently known as Saint Thomas, United States Virgin Islands**

Seneca Kakona

To all the people who believed in this project, thank you for shining your light.
For all who will touch the pages of this book,
let's be the beacons of love and hope this world so desperately needs.

CONTENTS

WELCOME 1
THIS BOOK & HOW TO USE IT 2

SACRED PRACTICE 4
Mapping Your Contemplative Practices 5
Contemplative Art & Creative Alchemy As Meditation 11
Creating Space To Practice 11

CREATIVE SELF-CARE 16
Integrating Personal Creative Self-Care Into Your Sacred Practice 17
Ritualizing Your Creative Self-Care 17
Color & Creative Visualization 18

HANDS OF WONDER 22
The Human Hand 23
Beyond The Physical Hand 24
A Way Of Hands: Mudrā Therapy 28
How To Use Mudrās 29
Mudrā Practice, The Human Energy Field & The Human Experience 30

MERAKI 33
Illustrations 34+

ABOUT THE AUTHOR 171
THANK YOU 173

Welcome

Imagine how incredible it would be to dedicate some daily—or weekly—time to your precious self! Some sacred time and space where you can take a deep breath and let yourself be inspired by everything beautiful that surrounds you.

The idea of birthing this creative alchemy and meditation coloring book is deeply rooted in what creative alchemy means: taking a lot of something and creating something new out of it. It is transmutation at its best, and we do not have to attempt to turn lead into gold to achieve it. We can do it in a very subtle and simple place inside of us. It is a multi-level approach that takes advantage of everything and anything you have available to you. It involves letting your heart run wild and unleashing your inner child while cultivating contemplation, meditation, and union with the Divine all at the same time.

Is that even possible? I believe so! From personal experience, I believe there are no rules and no boundaries to what you can co-create in your life. With great delight, I have integrated facets of my daily creative alchemy and contemplative practices into this book, centering on the human hand as the powerful gift of self-expression and self-healing we so often take for granted. It is structured in such a way that it serves as a form of guided meditation, with different elements that prompt for presence, reflection, inspiration, and mindfulness. The goal is to use this tool as a gateway to allow time for the development of mind-body insight and the internalization of new knowledge.

So let yourself be taken through a self-study process that is as creative as it is insightful. Set aside a day or an hour, whatever time you can afford. Create a sacred space for you at home, at the office, at the park, under a tree—you choose. Design your own creative alchemy ritual and give yourself some time to release whatever needs to be let go, to quiet your mind and be open to vast possibility while you delve into the exploration of contemplative practices through guided imagery. Give your body, mind, and spirit some creative alchemy when it so deserves it. A full analysis and presentation of these topics is beyond the scope of this book, however. It is a primer for many concepts and hopefully it will lead you to find your own way through these wonderful techniques. Enjoy!

Irène

THIS BOOK & HOW TO USE IT

Hands of Wonder is my first big offering, and it's my calling in action. It actually started as a self-healing process, a way to commit to making art after having taken so much time off from practicing my craft during grad school. At the time, I was already working on a mudrā series and had started doing custom illustrations that I call "Essence." A Cuban artist and friend, prompted me to put a collection together as a book. My first reaction was that of unbelievingness: *how would I ever do that? Is my art even viable for such an undertaking?* As I started giving thought to that seed, it started germinating in my heart. There was a voice calling me to continue. I asked myself, *what kind of book do I need in my life?*

I always loved coloring books, since childhood. But I knew I wanted something different, something that also aligned with the way I live my life and how I see creative expression and the creative process. I wanted to share some of the basic concepts that I practice as a way of life: *a syncretic collection of theory, thoughts, beliefs, and rituals.* A note on belief systems—They are very personal, I have always kept my mind and heart as open as the sky. Always process all information with your heart, it will guide you and not lead you astray.

Together, my work explores the mythology and science of the biosphere, space cosmology, the contours and fields of the human experience, and my personal ancestral mythos. My calling has led me to merge all my skills into *art medicine*—my personal collage of science, art, and spirituality.

> ***All art intuitively apprehends coming changes in the collective unconsciousness.***
>
> **- Carl Jung -**

37 original illustrations | Since I started illustrating and painting, I have extensively used symbology in my work. *Take it all in, what does it mean to you?* Be curious and if you wish, look for consensus meaning out there. A note on sacred geometry—Elements in my art are naturally occurring patterns as found in nature, and I try to limit inclusion of man-made designs as much as possible. I don't use the term "sacred geometry," instead I opt to use "universal or cosmic strokes." Universal love strokes are everywhere, look for them!

The core of each illustration has been rendered in ink on paper. Each has been made with so much love and devotion, I hope those feelings emanate from these pages and permeate your experience. Each comes with a short story and theme-related narratives. Mudrā illustrations also indicate *how to* do the hand gesture and any *energetic benefits* that have been associated with its practice. Starting at page 50, keep an eye on the cakra (romanized and anglicized to "chakra") symbol at the bottom left corner—All mudrās have been categorized by which of the major cakras they work with best for easy intentional practice.

A note on mudrā names and the use of diacritical marks—One of my most favorite hobbies is the study of languages, learning the how on writing, the rules, the pronunciation. Because I have experienced it with my native language, I believe in respecting the originary form of writing when borrowing the words and belief systems of other cultures. It calls for curiosity and further inquiry into the history, the language(s) and dialect(s), and the stories of those peoples. Through my research, I have made the best effort to find the correct punctuation for non-English words. I make no promise that they are fully correct, but I hope they are.

Journaling prompts | On the back of each illustration there is space to write an intention before you set to work. Use it as part of the ritualization of your creative self-care time. *Thought infusions* are sprinkled throughout to prompt for an inward journey.

Original poems & meditations | Coloring is one of the most accessible tools to experience creativity, even if you don't consider yourself a creative person. But even more so, is writing. Poetry and prose bring you the opportunity to put into words what you may not be able to put into music or imagery. Collaborators have graciously shared their work to adorn the illustrations and pages of this book. *When was the last time you sat down to practice creative writing?*

QR codes & references | Although I advocate disconnecting to connect in our day and age, technology does have its uses. The embedded QR codes can be scanned to access great resources. References that informed my research and narratives are enumerated. Discover, they are inspiring!

The synergistic effect of all these ingredients might just take you to somewhere you haven't been before...

Dive in ↳

SACRED PRACTICE

"What do you seek when you need some space?
Where does your mind wander to,
in those moments within moments of your day?
What is your heart whispering?
You've always held the answer."

- Iréne de Brice -

Many traditions follow sacred practices in the form of cultural or religious ritual and ceremony. However, as the greater world gets caught in the modern to-go lifestyle and the ever-increasing technological infiltration of our daily lives... We are losing sight of things that really matter to us. We have all experienced this feeling at different points of our adult lives; there is also an innate call to rescue and build a sacred practice that helps us stay grounded, focused, energized, and grateful. But above all else, we long for a sacred practice that helps us look inward for the answers we are looking for, and to remember who we are underneath all those layers of social conditioning that have been imposed on us since childhood.

Sacred practice embodies both ritual and ceremony, and it can encompass and adjust to any belief system. Sacred practice is a collective term I use for ***contemplative practices,*** which can include meditation, journaling, visualization, Earthing, and contemplative arts and movement. It seeks the constant serenity and peace of your being, the opening of mind and heart to radiant Divine compassion. It seeks contemplation as a foundation to align yourself to your belief system and life purpose, and the well-being of your physical temple as well, through movement practice. It also seeks soul work through your shadow body—tackling the not-so-pretty aspects of ourselves like vulnerability, unhappiness, jealously, or any past experiences we don't want to deal with or we haven't fully overcome yet. It seeks to deal with aspects of ourselves that no longer serve us, and to aim our life path into the light.

Mapping Your Contemplative Practices

A second term I use to describe my personal daily practice is ***creative alchemy.*** If you are reading this right now, chances are that you are attuned to your creative process needs at a conscious or subconscious level. Creative alchemy is the transmutation of your energy into creative force in order to elaborate the full potential of the human being, a potential that is within all of the elemental particles that make you *you*. For me, it's a process that emerges from contemplation, where creative alchemy turns mundane activities into intentional contemplation through awareness.

The Center for Contemplative Mind and Society (CMind) describes contemplative practices in a way that cannot be rivaled, through a graphical representation called *The Tree of Contemplative Practices.* Depicted in the roots are two foundational intentions: ***awareness*** and ***communion or connection.*** These roots transcend the belief systems from which many of the practices originated. Different practices are grouped by their nature and outcomes, and are symbolized by the tree's branches. This book aims to cultivate ***stillness*** practice through centering and insight meditation, ***generative*** practice through beholding, visualization, and image gazing, ***creative*** practice through contemplative art meditation, the creative process, and music, ***relational*** practice through the many prompts for journaling and inspiration, ***ritual or cyclical*** practice through the establishment of your own sacred space (both physically and in your mind-spirit) and the ***ritualization of your creative self-care time.***

> **Ritual**[1]
>
> *noun*
>
> **a stereotyped sequence of activities involving gestures, words, and objects, performed in a sequestered place.**
>
> *adjective*
>
> **ritual activity, to create a sacred space that rapidly achieves structure.**

Take a moment to study the The Tree of Contemplative Practices illustration in the next page. It has been adapted from CMind, and it's your first encounter with an illustration that you can mark-up or color if the need arises. We'll discuss color therapy shortly, but for now just follow your intuition as to what approach you will take with it, if any at all other than observation.

Start at the roots and gaze at each branch, quietly spending at least sixty seconds on each segment and taking mental note of any thoughts, words or feelings that come to mind. Annotate any observations in the blank spaces provided or in a journal. Highlight or circle any practices that call your attention.

For more information about how to understand the The Tree of Contemplative Practices, more contemplative practice resources, or to support CMind; scan the code below or visit *www.contemplativemind.org.*

CMind

1. Turner VW. The Ritual Process: Structure and Anti-Structure. Ithaca, NY, US: Aldine Publishing (1969)

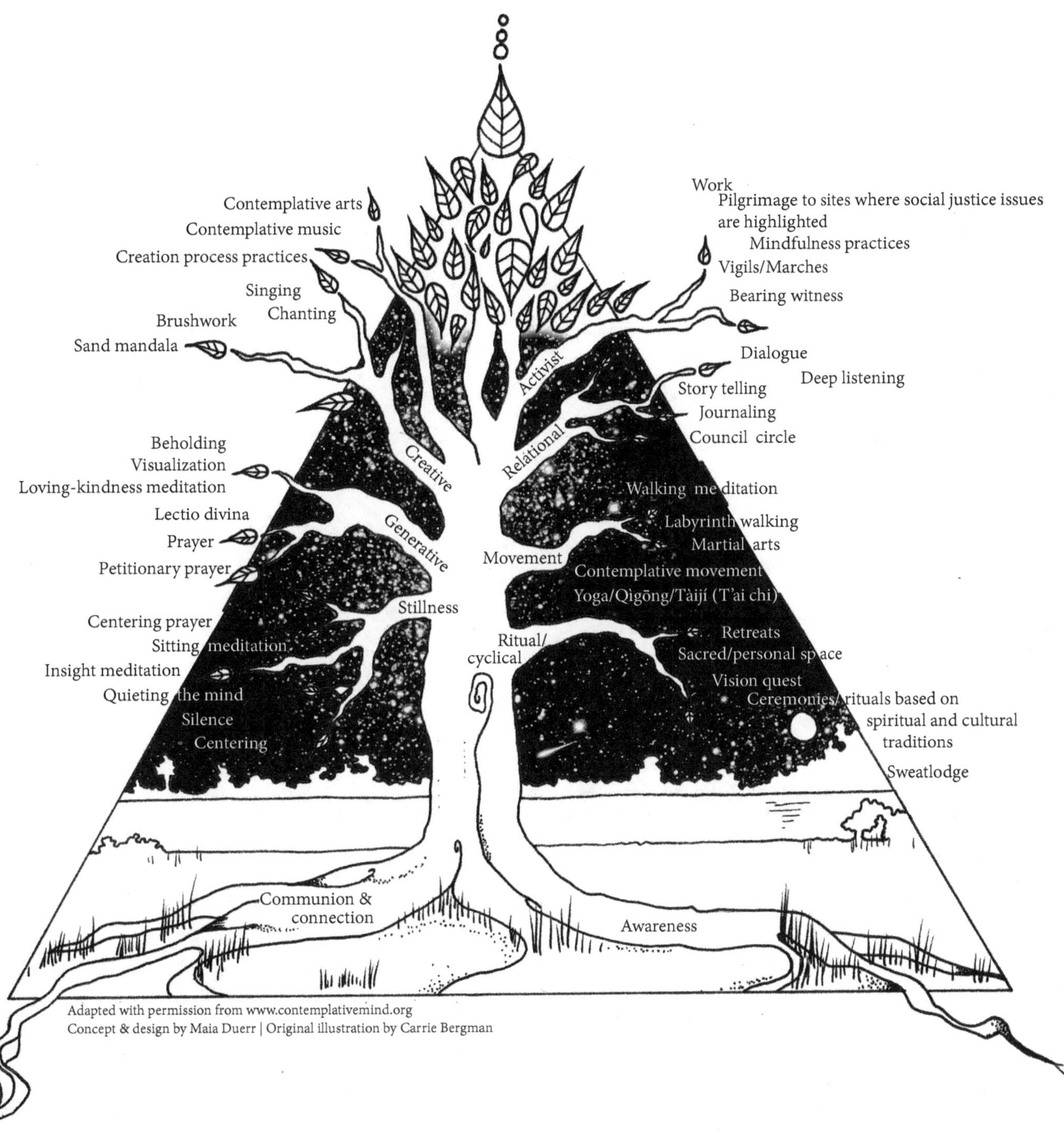

Adapted with permission from www.contemplativemind.org
Concept & design by Maia Duerr | Original illustration by Carrie Bergman

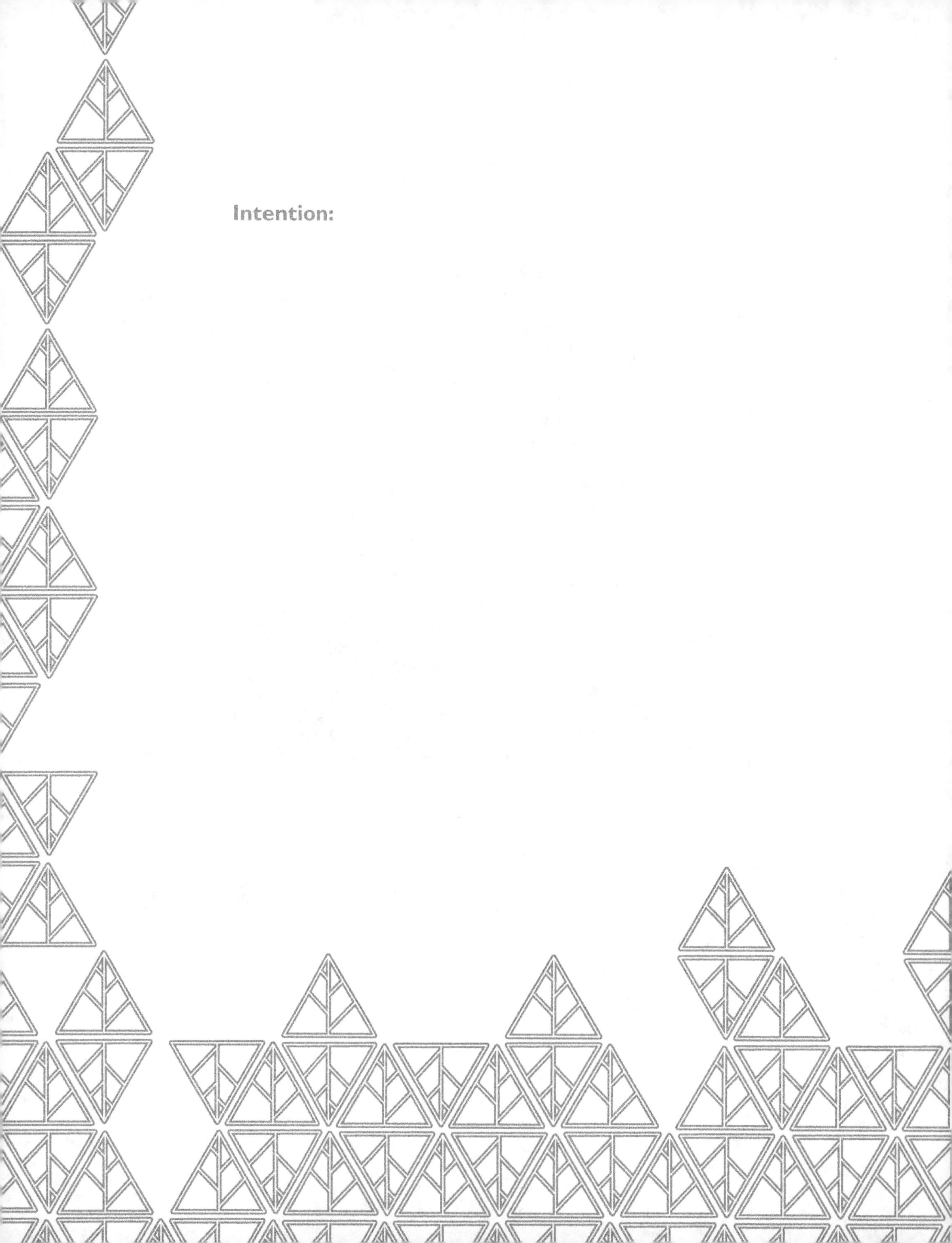

Intention:

Thought Infusions

1. To which part or branch do you feel more attracted to?

2. How do you feel about exploring new ways to connect with yourself through art? What does art mean to you?

3. Not all practices are included in the illustration on page 7. Write down additional activities you already do that are contemplative in nature, or could be contemplative through intention. Is there anything you do that you consider an expression of your inner artist?

4. Note when you do activities that are contemplative or those that can be turned into contemplation through intention. How often do you engage in these activities? What are barriers or enablers?

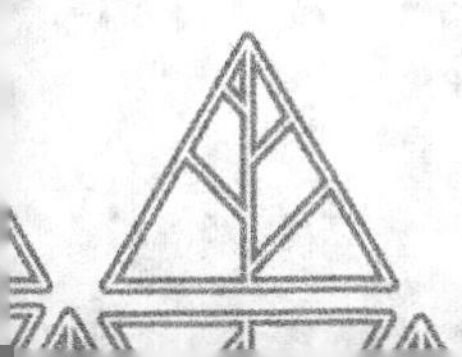

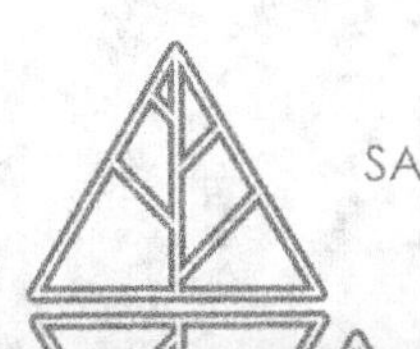

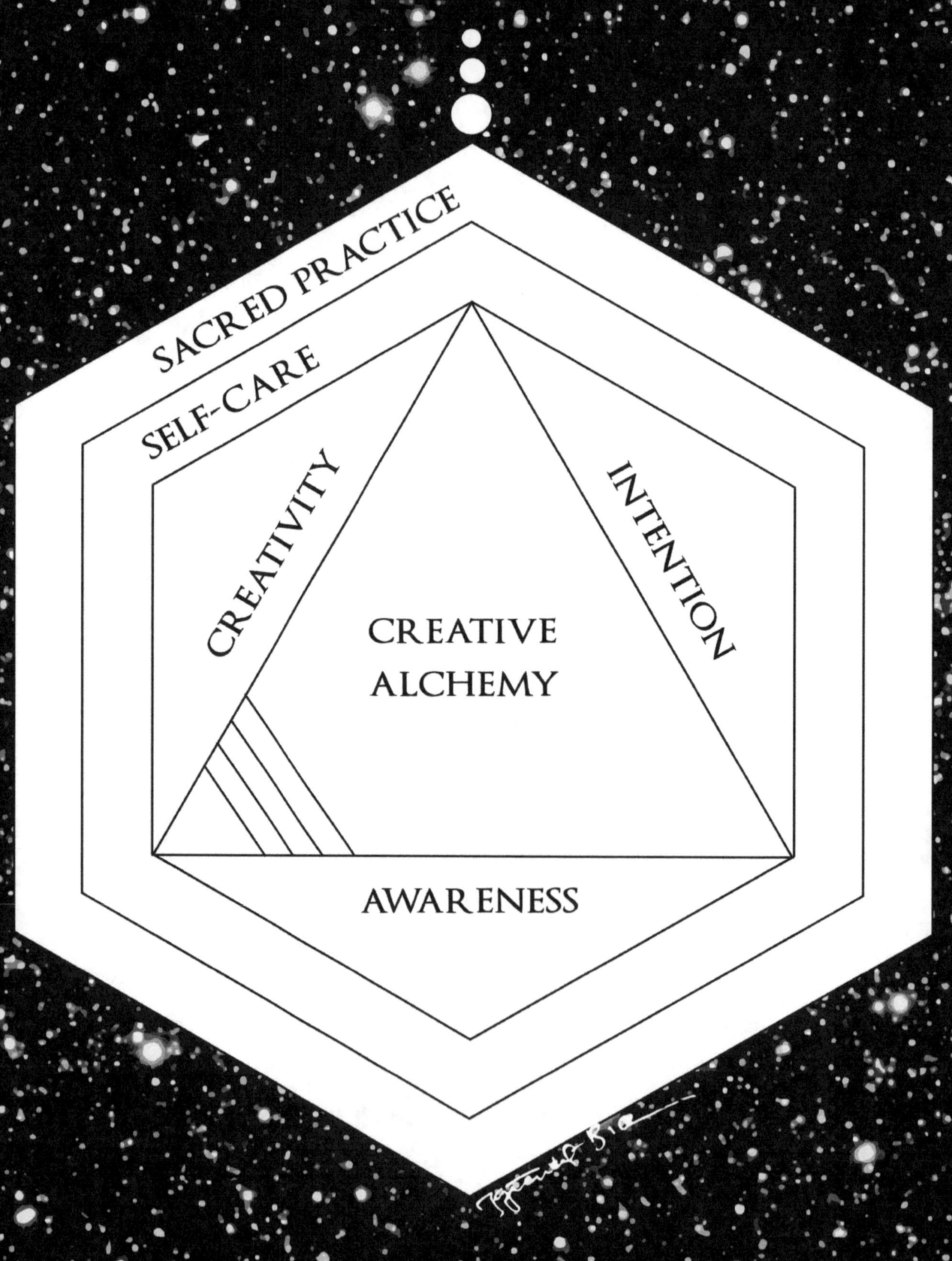
SACRED PRACTICE
SELF-CARE
CREATIVITY
INTENTION
CREATIVE
ALCHEMY
AWARENESS

Contemplative Art & Creative Alchemy As Meditation

The next few pages present an opportunity to color-in and annotate to personalize your process. The illustration on the left is my representation of how creativity, awareness and intention come together to synergistically give life to creative alchemy; and how these elements are a facet within self-care and sacred practice. Work on them at your own pace to unearth self-inquiry about your own potential creative self-care activities.

Learning to apply these three elements, alongside gratitude and simplicity, to everything you do on a day-to-day basis, can really shift your internal energy, and therefore your vibrational level. It may not happen overnight; for me it certainly has been a life-long effort and a practice that was luckily woven with the faith of the belief system I was raised in.

Thought Infusions

Your energy, vibrational frequency, and physical body are interchangeable. If you can raise the vibrational frequency of that energy, then you can enter a state of resonance that oscillates alongside with the high energy frequencies of love, peace, and contentment.

•

You don't have to be an exceptional artist to be creative every day and bring that alchemical element of creativity into your life. Creative alchemy calls for simplicity—***what comes easy?*** Maybe for you is writing, coloring, drawing, making your own herbal medicines, or cooking for your loved ones. For me it's all of the above, but no matter how non-creative my daily tasks may seem to be (e.g., daily scientific duties and procedures), I always make sure that I do it with love and that I add a touch of beauty to whatever it is I happen to be doing (e.g., paperwork, training manuals or presentation slides). ***Remember, you have a unique signature of gifts that were given to you only, to express and share with others. You alone may hold the key to unravel someone else's potential, so please, share!***

Creating Space To Practice

Creating a comfortable space for your sacred practice is an important factor when it comes to carrying out your rituals—those remembered and the new. Looking at a sacred practice from a big picture perspective, we can admit that our ultimate goal is to ***convert our entire***

life into one sacred experience... From the intention we set upon waking, to the way we act and communicate during the day, to the moment we come back home and close our day. ***We want to surround ourselves with simplicity, beauty, and elements we enjoy.*** The following list includes elements that you may want to incorporate into your practice:

Sacred space | Create a dedicated space where you are comfortable and is inviting to the intention of your ritual. This can be anywhere depending on what you are doing... The outdoors, your bathroom sink, your breakfast table.

Natural beauty | Whenever possible, incorporate natural elements in your surroundings to invite the soothing quality of nature into your life. Things to consider include rocks, crystals, plants and greenery, flowers, water fountains, and candles.

Purpose | Separate your rituals and ceremonies by purpose: ***what and why?*** Set an intention for the space as well as for each practice.

When | Timing is important and goes hand in hand with purpose. For example, you may have days or periods of time in your personal belief system that hold special significance.

How | Connect to yourself and flow. Everything you need is already inside of you.

The next three pages provide you with some space to work on your ***thought infusions*** for the writing prompts below. Please try to write your answers as a natural stream of consciousness contrary to really thinking what you want to write. Maybe do a sketch or diagram flow of your daily activities and how you can add a touch of your hidden or very evident creative spark.

If you are like me, you might need a little bit more space than these pages. While working on this book and just for life in general, I recommend having at least one journal or notebook handy. ***Journaling*** is a great contemplative practice to record your thoughts, impressions, feelings, or creative ideas that may arise spontaneously. Carry a little pocket journal with you as you go about your day and especially when traveling. Have it nearby when you meditate to record any transcending moments or visions you experience, and by your bedside in case you want to write memories of a dream that you may not remember later. ***Handwriting things is a more "you" way than just typing them into your smart phone, tablet, or laptop. It's also a very powerful tool for manifesting your intentions.***

Thought Infusions

1. What is your favorite way to nurture your mind-body-spirit that is creative in nature?

2. What feeds your spirit and makes your heart tingle with excitement when you think of creating something?

3. What creative process brings you calm? How can you weave its essence into day-to-day activities?

4. What are your current rituals? What are the things you do on a daily basis? Take a moment to go through your day and identify recurrent activities you enjoy. Take into account when they occur and how they make you feel.

5. How can you ritualize creative self-care into your daily schedule? Even if it's just 10-15-20 minutes? Tip! Think of adding a start and end to your creative self-care time... Light a candle, light some incense or aromatic smoke stick, use evoking chromo-, aroma- and audio-therapy, move your body, brew yourself a cup of tea, drink something vitalizing or that you enjoy.

6. How do you define the sacred? What do you view as sacred in your life and all existence?

7. How can you design sacred space for your creative self-care—mentally, physically, emotionally, and spiritually?

8. How can you turn everyday life into an ongoing ceremony? Imagine the rituals you envision could transform your daily life into a living ceremony and an offering to yourself and what you hold sacred.

Additional thoughts...

CREATIVE SELF-CARE

"I believe in allowing creativity to flow
into self-care time as the ultimate medium for
self-healing, self-expression, and Divine expression."

- Iréne de Brice -

Integrating Personal Creative Self-Care Into Your Sacred Practice

Independent of whether your contemplative practice choices are within this book or not, set aside some time to close your eyes, take in some long deep breaths, and contemplate what thoughts cross your mind when you inquire within. Your goal is to design a daily practice that supports your creative self-care, which under the umbrella of contemplative practices befits a big spectrum of activities.

Why creative self-care? Because human nature contains an intrinsic creative factor and creativity is known to facilitate being present, in the moment, and deliver a sense of well-being. Creative self-care is something that we have forgotten as adults, mostly because the system and the average lifestyle tends to not endorse, highlight, or nurture creative endeavors in our day-to-day life. ***Start with this coloring book, set the intention of making some time to color or just gaze at the illustrations daily until that space-time becomes a constant.*** Experiment holding the mudrā forms for 10-30-60 seconds and see how you feel, increase your time on the weekends or when you have down-time, try new things that you have always wanted to learn or do but you "never had time" or neglected them for being "juvenile" or "not something adults do."

Ritualizing Your Creative Self-Care

The structure of your creative time is like a blank canvas. Whether you have a meditation practice or not, I like to integrate all of the elements we have discussed so far into my creative self-care practice, and beyond that, into my day-to-day life. For designated (and sacred) creative self-care time, I have designed the beginning and end of my ritualized creative time. Since the longer segments of time I dedicate to creative self-care happen at home, I have also sequestered a little space just for me, and I have added essentials into that space that remind me it is sacred. If space is tight and doing so is not an option (recognize that such small things we may take for granted are in fact a luxury), borrow a place in your home that is temporarily yours only (e.g., the kitchen table from 4-6am before everyone else wakes) or seek some space such as in a public library (sometimes you are able to book study rooms for free). Whether you have a traditional job or not, schedule creative time during your assigned breaks: integrate music and listen to something new or a favorite, do some writing, look at your week schedule and make a plan of when you will insert creative time, and download some podcasts that will inspire you for your commute.

Over the years, I have aimed to turn my life into a living ceremony: life itself becomes something I celebrate independently of whether I think that what I am tasked to do, by will or duty, is interesting or enjoyable. For example, incorporate mudrās—these will be covered in the next chapter (page 22). My favorite is añjali mudrā (pages 158-159): take 5-15-30 seconds before you do the task at hand to say thank you and offer that action you are about to do, to what you hold sacred. Take your mind inward, to the inner experience, so that you may explore that magical realm of infinite potential. ***Remember who you are, and use that wisdom to fuel your innate creativity.***

Color & Creative Visualization

After many years of studying and practicing complementary healing techniques as well as practicing science and art as my most beloved kinds of meditation, I believe in the power of the mind-body connection to ease healing. The intention of this book is to provide you with raw imagery derived from my eye of contemplation that, together with color therapy, poems, and music, will bring about a focused creative alchemy experience. A quick search for the key words ***guided imagery*** on PubMed Central (PMC), a free search engine accessing a huge database of peer-reviewed research on life sciences and biomedical topics, reveals more than 2,000 hits! Collectively, these manuscripts address the application and results of mind-body experiments on a varied range of topics. These include the analysis of the subject's psychophysiologic responses to guided imagery and its effects on the psychoemotional state. Outcomes have been documented in multiple conditions such as in the alleviation of chronic pain and headaches, and its benefits to cancer patients.[2-4] I invite you to check out this incredible abundance of information that is available to us in this journey.

Color is part of nature's healing properties, and the influence that both imagery and color have over our minds and therefore, our lives, is fascinating. Different colors of the spectrum have different effects on our mind-body connection (including our energy field)—there is a wealth of information that can be researched on this matter as well. Renowned Russian painter and art theorist, Wassily Kandinsky, remarked that "Color provokes a psychic vibration. Color hides a power still unknown but real, which acts on every part of the human body." To begin, let's color in these lotus flowers and explore some key primary (red-yellow-blue), secondary (green-orange-violet), and tertiary colors (indigo).

2. Watanabe E, *et al. BMC Complement Altern Med.* 5: 21 (2005)
3. Velikoba S, *et al. Front Hum Neurosci.* 11:644 (2018)
4. Velikoba S, *et al. Front Hum Neurosci.* 10:664 (2017)

RED

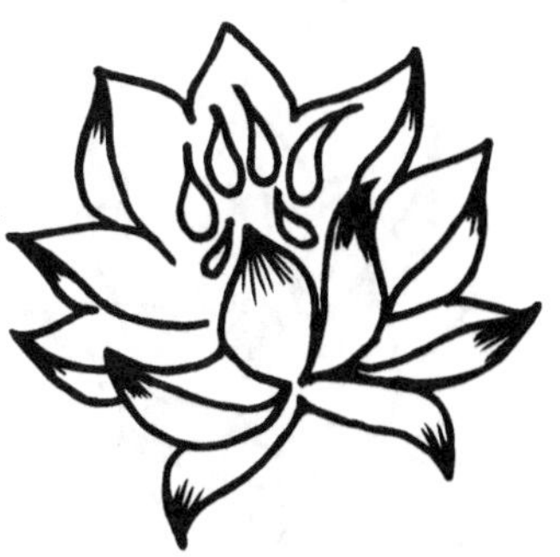

activates | passion and intensity | love | stimulates entire system
releases stagnant energy | linked to reproduction and fertility

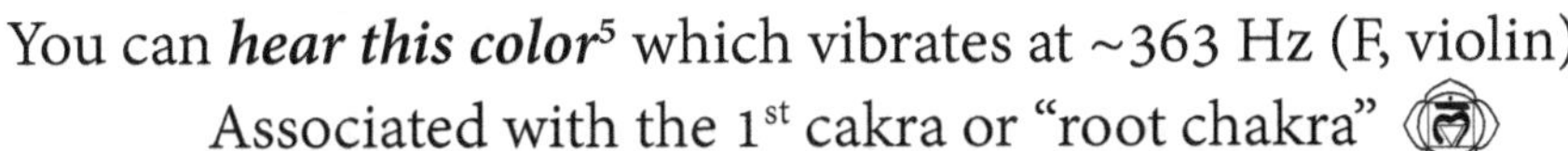

You can ***hear this color***[5] which vibrates at ~363 Hz (F, violin)
Associated with the 1st cakra or "root chakra"

ORANGE

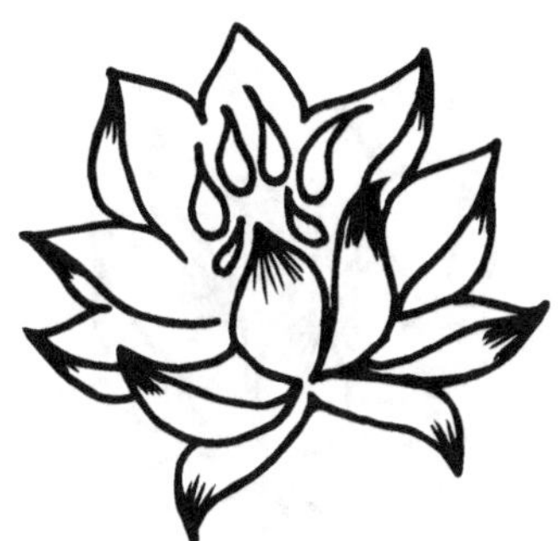

excitement and enthusiasm | gentle energizer | abundance
exotic | inspires | creativity | stimulates immune system

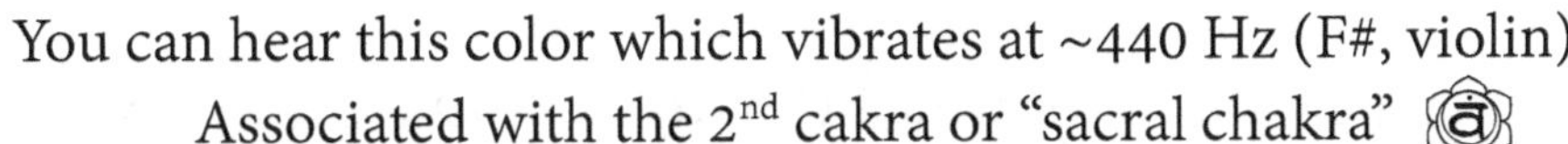

You can hear this color which vibrates at ~440 Hz (F#, violin)
Associated with the 2nd cakra or "sacral chakra"

YELLOW

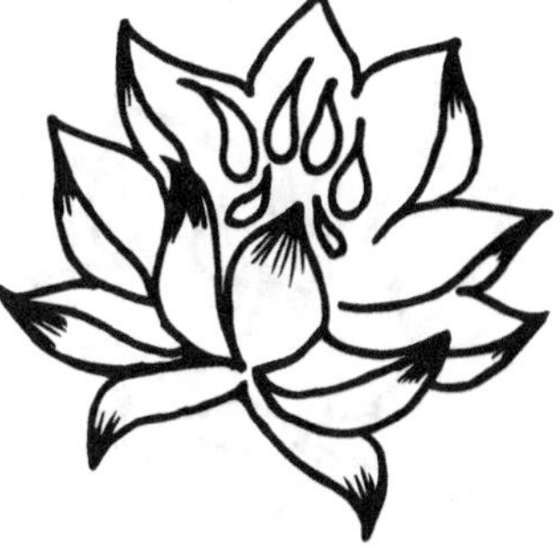

cheerfulness | hope | encouragement | luminous | color of light
openness | stimulates mental process and nervous system

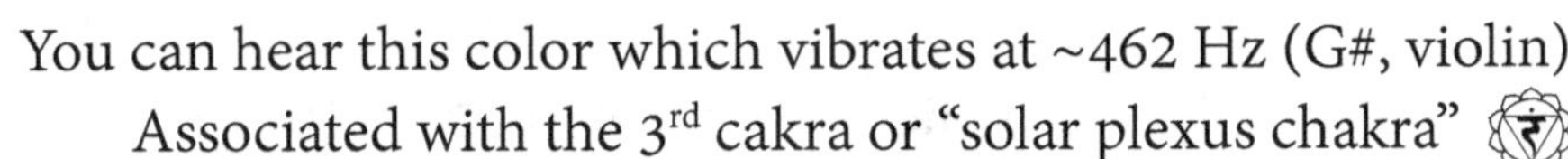

You can hear this color which vibrates at ~462 Hz (G#, violin)
Associated with the 3rd cakra or "solar plexus chakra"

GREEN

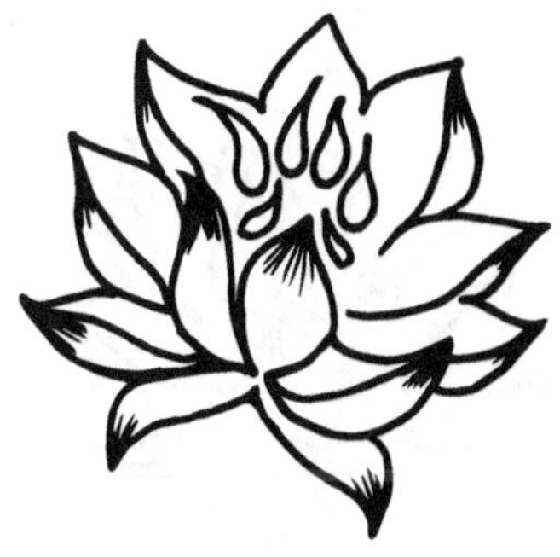

serenity | balances energy | health | tranquility | nature
new growth | alleviates depression | strengthens the heart

You can hear this color which vibrates at ~478Hz (A, violin)
Associated with the 4th cakra or "heart chakra"

5. Gonzalez A, *et al.* Coloresia: An Interactive Colour Perception Device for the Visually Impaired. In: Multimodal Interaction in Image and Video Applications. Springer: Berlin, DE (2013)

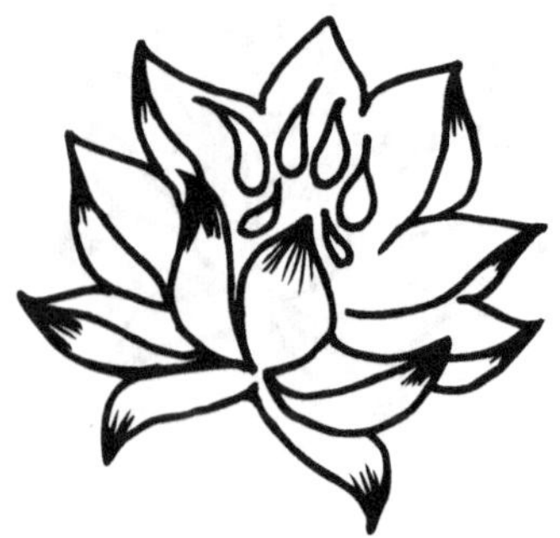

BLUE

soothing | calming | brings focus | protection
perceived as a constant in human life | increases productivity

You can hear this color which vibrates at ~573 Hz (C#, violin)
Associated with the 5th cakra or "throat chakra"

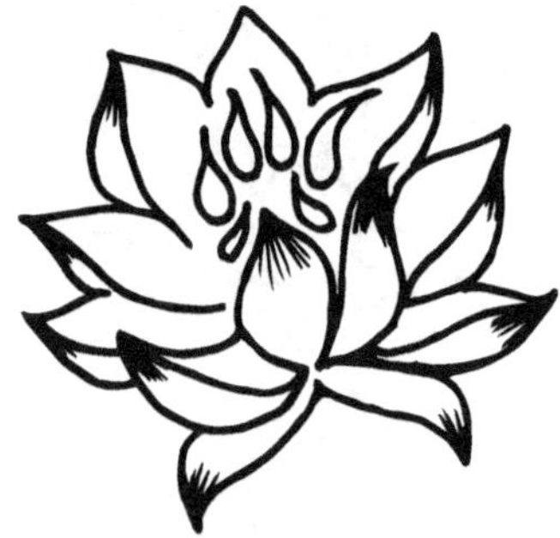

INDIGO

intuition | perception | deep concentration | wisdom
great devotion | common in rituals and ceremonies

You can hear this color which vibrates at ~612 Hz (D#, violin)
Associated with the 6th cakra or "third eye chakra"

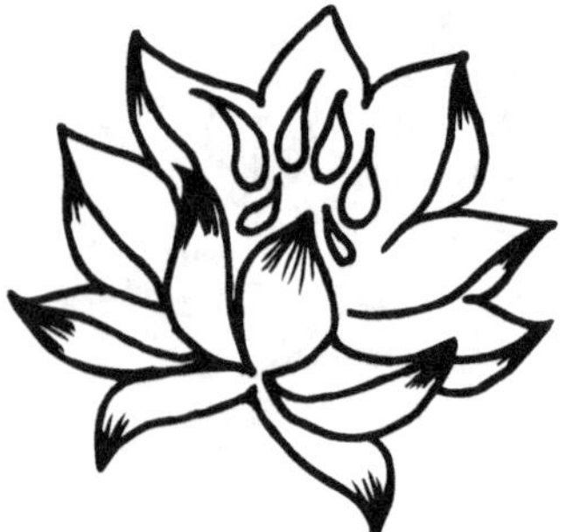

VIOLET

success | wealth | royalty | wisdom | transmutation
benevolence| potent for healing spirit | all-healer

You can hear this color which vibrates at ~607 Hz (D, violin)
Associated with the 7th cakra or "crown chakra"

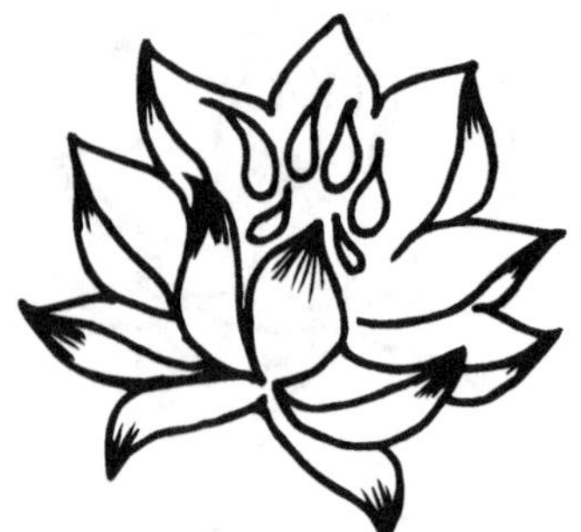

BLACK | WHITE

protection | mystery | silence
power | rebirth
absorbing | darkness

innocence | purity | peace
reflecting | all inclusive | light

Black/white and dark/light are representative of dualism
This is best depicted through the concept of yīnyáng, described on page 154
You can hear black as a C (violoncello), and white as a B (violoncello)

Thought Infusions

1. What are your favorite colors?

2. What colors predominate in your wardrobe?

3. If you had to pick a color as a visual prayer right now, which color would you pick?

4. Close your eyes and connect with your hands through breath and focus. Feel your physical hand, all fingers, your palms. Feel the space in between your hands. Without giving it too much thought [write down the first color(s) that comes to mind], what colors do you see beaming out of your hands in these different scenarios:

- *Right now, when in thought and contemplation?*
- *Consoling your child, family, or friend?*
- *While doing your day-to-day job or profession, whatever that may be?*
- *While doing your house chores?*
- *While relaxing?*
- *While doing a creative activity?*

HANDS OF WONDER

"Draw your attention inward and be inspired
by your story and the gifts you have to share.
Listen to your heart. Use your hands as an extension of your heart,
which like your breath and your existence, are gifts of the Divine."

- Iréne de Brice -

I have always been naturally inclined to the arts and sciences since I can remember, but art and creativity have always reigned supreme over any of my philosophical or scientific pursuits. You must be wondering, why did I pick the human hand as the focus subject of this contemplative art meditation book, or what on Earth do they have to do with creative self-care? It may seem random. So let me explain, as briefly as I possibly can.

My hand obsession started in 1998 when I was watching, for the first time, a children's movie that had just come out called "The Prince of Egypt." Mind you, I was already fascinated with ancient civilizations, including Egyptian culture and lore, way before this but that is a whole other story. In this movie, there is a shot of Yocheved's hands when she parts with the weaved basket containing her infant child. I can remember this like it was yesterday. I was struck with wonder of how you could communicate so much pain by how her hands behaved and were portrayed during that moment in the film.

Up until then, all my drawings and paintings had been mythical in nature, but I had never truly emphasized the hands. From that day on, I had found a new passion... The human hand. I wanted to be able to communicate stories through the hands of my illustrated maidens and muses.

The Human Hand

The hand is one of the most complex structures of the human body, providing you with great mobility, dexterity, and strength. Within what meets the eye, there is bone and muscle structure. There are also fibrous protective tissues, fascia, nerves, and vascular vessels that bring fresh nutrients and oxygen so all of these components can function together.

We have a miracle right at our hands, quite literally, like our very existence. They are one of the greatest gifts we have received. Think about it, they are your number one tool to interact with the world at large, especially in the age of social media... Handling our gadgets, typing and texting. If you are blessed with having them, stop for a few minutes and give thanks for the ability you have in being able to use your hands for they are tools in our Divine journey that allow for self-healing, communication, healing of others, and self-expression.

The bones of the hand are divided into three groups: the carpal bones at the wrist joint, the metacarpal bones, and the phalanges of the finger. Together, your hand is composed of 27 bones and is innervated by three nerves with functional sensory and motor qualities. Specifically, your fingertips have the densest area of sensory receptors in your body averaging ~2,500 receptors per cm^2, and each of these nerve endings are constantly transmitting information to your brain. Recently, new research has suggested that nerve endings in the fingertips perform neural computations that were thought to occur in the brain, building yet another layer of complexity to our hand-brain-mind interactions.[6] In his book, Learning About the World Through Modeling, Arthur Auer brings to light the importance between sensory learning of the fingers during childhood for an individual's all-around development. He argues that, neglecting the comprehensive development of tactile sensitivity and bimanual function at this critical stage, may hinder their ability to understand "the unity in things" and interfere with their creative capacity.[7]

Beyond The Physical Hand

Journeying beyond what meets the eye again, let's explore some syncretic concepts relating to the unseen powers of the human hand. Hand imagery has long been a constant (page 38), with early representations found in Paleolithic caves through to ancient civilizations. Like I mentioned before, for example, the act of handwriting intentions, stories, wishes, and dreams into a journal is powerful. There is power in manually transcribing your thoughts from the ether into this reality. Speaking of ***man***-ually, the Latin word for hand is ***manus,*** and just like ***man***-ualities, there are plenty other words that share the Latin word root. One very special word shares this as well, a word that carries a lot of intrinsic power—***man***-ifest. To me, the fact that ***manifest*** carries this rooted meaning is no coincidence. Instead, it sheds light on my own belief that to manifest one has to create with the hands (and the heart). It makes complete sense! And because of this, I chose the incredibly wonderful, beautiful, and powerful human hand as the focus topic for this first contemplative art book. How could I not? It's from this same wonder that the title stems: ***Hands of Wonder.***

Now that we have discussed this string of thoughts, let's go back at the diagram on page 10. You, as in the intersection of your mind-body-spirit, are holding the objects of sacred practice, self-care, and the three elements that invocate creative alchemy—creativity, awareness, and intention. Your hands, in this case, are an extension of that intention, an intention that is born out of your heart center. ***Your hands are connected to your heart, and just like the heart they give and receive love, they give and receive light, they give and receive creation.***

6. Pruszynski JA, Johansson RS. ***Nature Neurosci.*** (10):1404-9 (2014)
7. Auer A. Learning About the World Through Modeling: Sculptural Ideas for School and Home. Catham, NY, US: Waldorf Publications (2014)

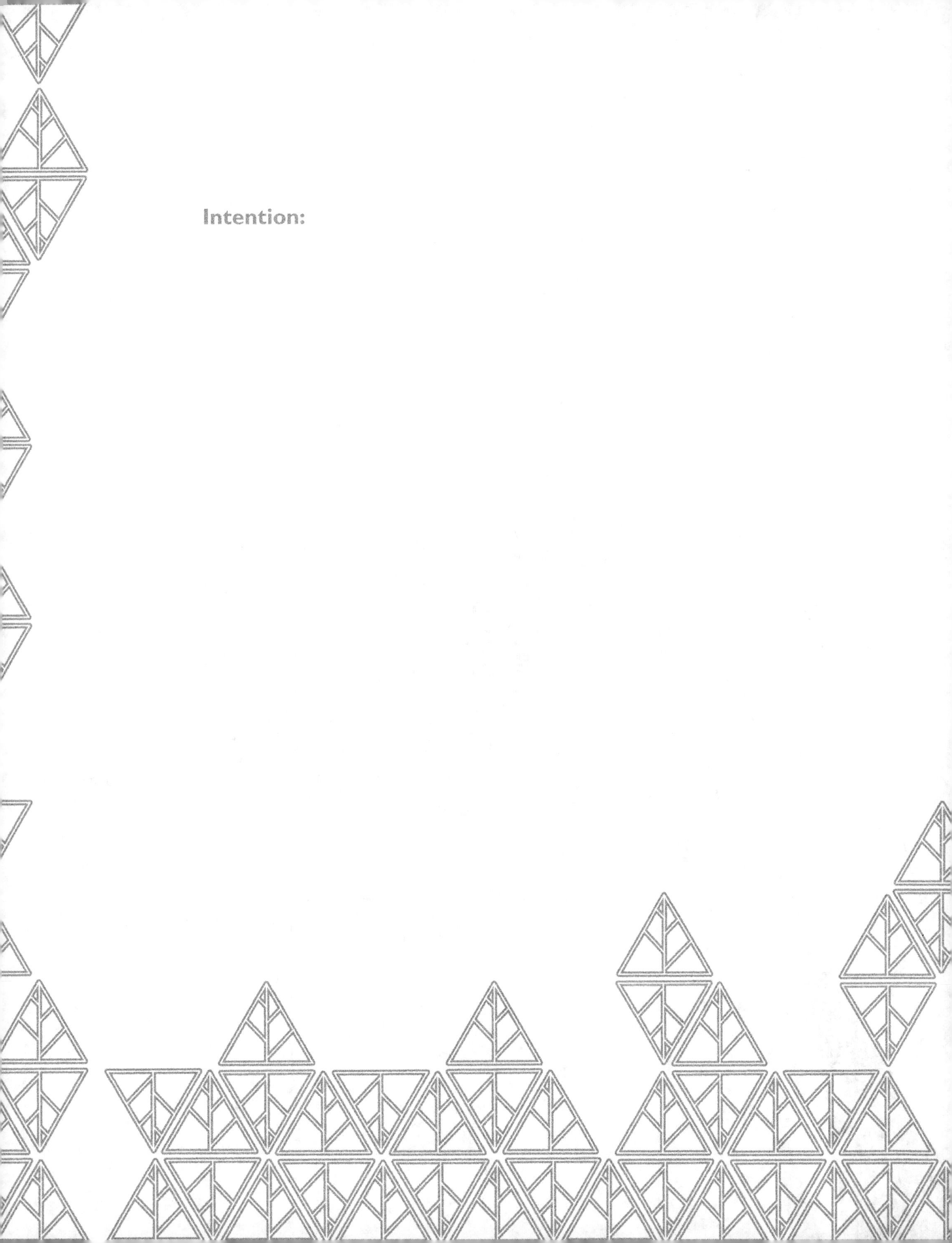

Intention:

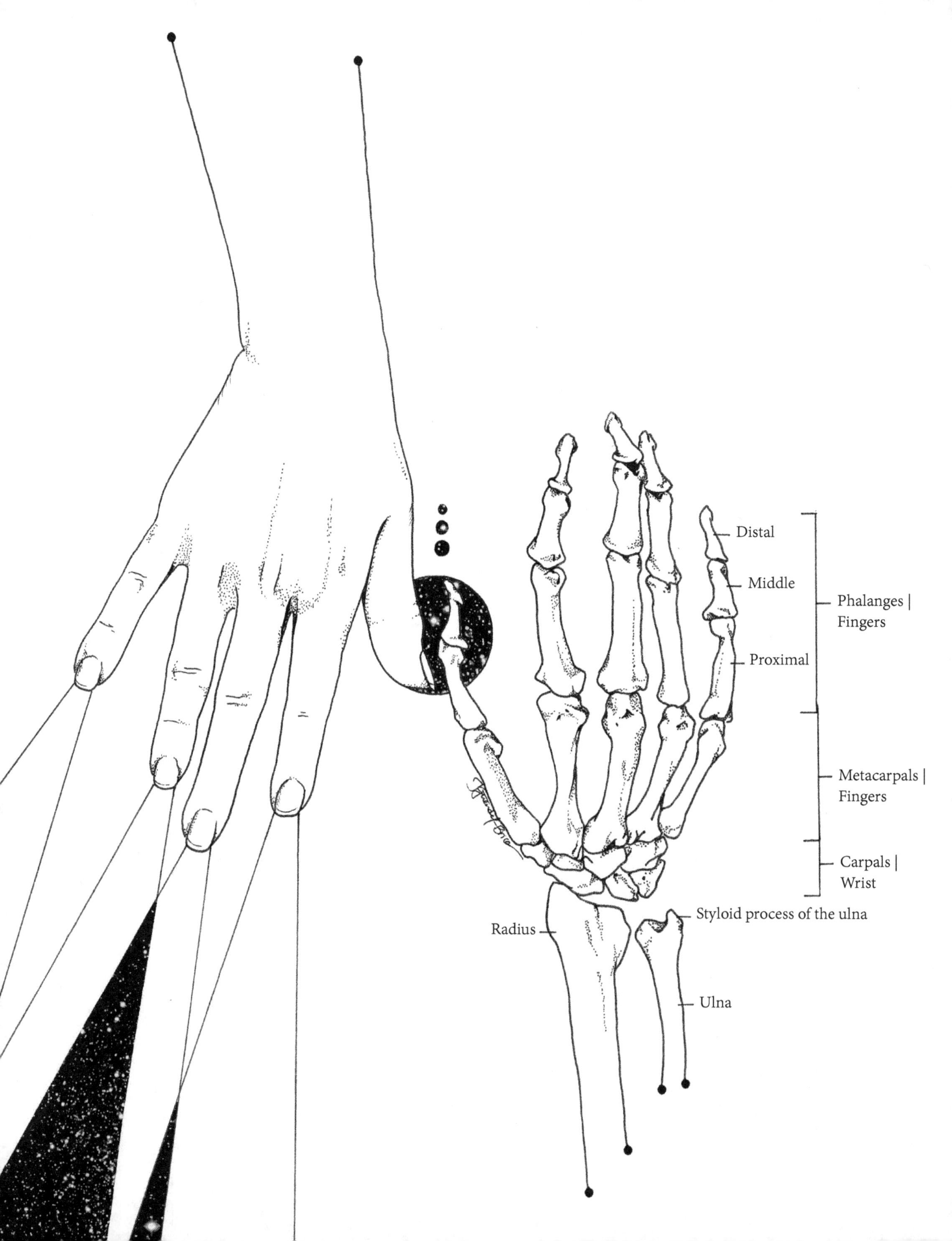
Distal
Middle
Phalanges | Fingers
Proximal
Metacarpals | Fingers
Carpals | Wrist
Styloid process of the ulna
Radius
Ulna

Thought Infusions

1. When you look at your hands, what is your first thought?

- *Do you like them?*
- *Do you take them for granted?*

2. How do you take care of your hands? How do you nurture them? How do you say thank you?

3. What wonders do you create with your hands that you may not rightfully acknowledge?

4. One of my favorite things to do when I was a child, was to play with a flashlight at night and press it against my palms and fingers... And wonder. Have you ever tried it? I certainly still do sometimes. Think about your hands, explore them. Look at your visible veins, at every nook and cranny. At that beautiful crimson shade. They are beautiful.

A Way Of Hands: Mudrā Therapy

One of the many techniques I have picked up along the way is the practice of what is commonly known as ***hasta (hand) yoga or mudrā therapy.*** There is so much history and theory to convey that I can't do it service within the pages of this book. Nonetheless, it's such a subtle and simple practice, that it can be included not only into your sacred practice but also as a regular throughout your daily life as each different symbolic finger and hand gesture has a specific meaning that can be applied with purpose to multiple situations.

> "Mudrā[8]
> 1. Seal, mark, or gesture.
> 2. A mudrā is a spiritual gesture and an energetic seal of authenticity used in the iconography and spiritual practice of various belief systems, including Hindu, Buddhist and Christian traditions and imagery.
> 3. A mudrā is a hand gesture that balances energy in the body and mind.

Mudrās are most predominant in Eastern spiritual traditions and have been used for thousands of years; they are an essential component of yogic science. They can be seen in religious iconography such as Buddha and Hindu deity representations, including Christian paintings, statues, rituals and ceremonies. An iconic example is the joining of both hands at heart level (añjali mudrā) used for salutation, greeting and gratitude gesture, or as a symbol of prayer (page 158). Additionally, their use encompasses a variety of contemplative practices like meditation, yoga, Tàijí (T'ai chi), and oriental or Indian classical dances.

In fact, even though I had noticed them before, the very first time I truly became aware of the position of the hands in each of the statues and paintings in my church was after that moment of realization given to me by watching that movie scene. I know it sounds silly: how can a children's movie scene have such a profound effect on someone's life? Regardless, I'm happy it did. Once I noted these hand positions in religious imagery around me, I found a new extracurricular subject to study. It took another five years before I found yoga in 2003, and with it, the immense amount of information regarding mudrās. I had found some answers.

8. Iyengar KR. The Science of Yoga Mudras: Physical and Mental Health, Philosophical and Psychological Mudras. Bangalore, IN: Sapna Book House (2013)

How To Use Mudrās

In yogic science, mudrās are integrated alongside breath work (prāṇāyāma), physical body postures (āsana), and energy-based sounds (mantra). Basic gestures can be used in a ***passive or active form,*** as illustrated below through gyān mudrā:

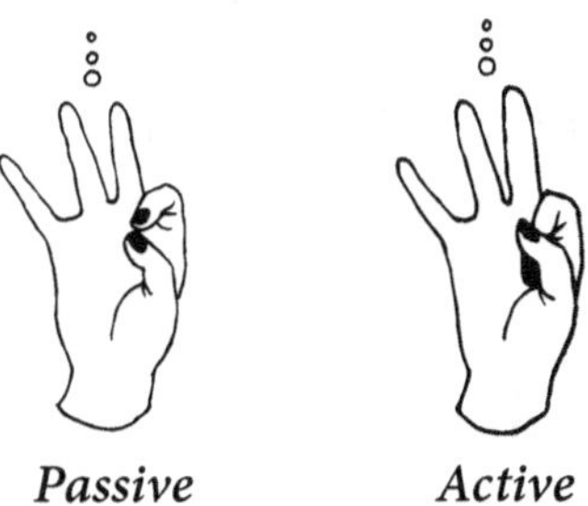

Passive ***Active***

The passive form is achieved by bringing fingertip-to-fingertip, and it's the common mudrā seal practiced unless otherwise indicated. It is best applied when making use of stillness energy, such as in silent meditation (e.g., calming and receptive energy). The active form is practiced by placing the thumb pad against the fingernail. This allows for more active and intense energy to flow when engaged in practices such as prāṇāyāma, āsana, or mantra recitations (e.g., projecting energy).

Because of their nature, mudrās can be practiced anytime and anywhere during your day, bridging the gap to accessibility for those people who are physically impaired and can't practice other forms of physical yoga. I don't like to recommend any particular regimen, but more so, I like to suggest that you always follow your heart and practice what resonates within—they can be tailored to your specific needs and, with a little use of your imagination and research, it's easy to set up your own personal sequence.

You can start your practice by holding a mudrā for a few breaths and build your hold to minutes at a time. Once again, feel what works and seek guidance from a teacher since some gestures do have contraindications.

When ***mindfully*** practiced, mudrās will create expression of sacred practice qualities or virtues in you, as the practitioner, that may include feelings of fearlessness, love, gratitude, peace, and the ability to direct attention inwards and focus more easily.

Thought Infusions

"Hand mudrās can access the subconscious and cellular memory
as well as enhance your somatic awareness.
You can sustain relaxation
while mapping out the pathways of energy within the framework of your body."

- Vivia Astraia -

If it is in your spirit, take notes as you color and progress through the book: What mudrās would you like to try out for needs you have right now?

•

Mudrā, The Human Energy Field & The Human Experience

While mudrās are mainly seen as mere symbolic hand postures, they have a profound effect in the human energy system. They are believed to exert an effect over moods, thoughts, and emotions through pressure and posture manipulation of the hands and fingers. Like we discussed earlier, the density of nerve endings in our fingers is immense and comparable to the discriminatory capacity of our sight,[7] however, it doesn't end there if we embrace the concept of the human energy field (HEF). For healing art therapies such as reflexology; hands, feet and ears are like maps of the human body. They contain zones and reflexes that correspond to every part, gland, and organ of the body. Like a perfect microcosm, they contain the information of our whole body. By activating these reflexes, you are bringing changes to your body that will convey balance and wellness to your mind-body-spirit.

Yogic philosophy believes that there are energetic channels called nāḍīs (similar to the meridian system in Chinese medicine, romanized to jīngluò) by which prāṇa (life force) travels to the brain, sense organs and other physical body destinations. According to the first Upaniṣads, there are 72,000 nāḍīs in the human body, sometimes even more are cited depending on the yogic lineage.[9] In Āyurvedic texts (Āyurveda is the ~5,000 year-old Vedic science of life, page 49), nāḍīs are classified into three kinds: dhamani-nāḍī (carries body fluids and air), nāḍī (carries prāṇa), and śira-nāḍī (carries sensory and subtle perceptions to the heart center and inward consciousness).[10] Mudrās help to awaken the kuṇḍalinī (primal force that lies "coiled" at the base of the spine), as they move prāṇa through the central suṣumṇā-nāḍī, which flows through our spinal column.

9. Dale C. The Subtle Body: An Encyclopedia of Your Energetic Anatomy. Boulder, CO, US: Sounds True (2009)
10. Jois SKP. Yoga Mala: The Seminal Treatise and Guide from the Living Master of Ashtanga Yoga. New York, NY, US: Farrar, Straus and Giroux (2010)

There are multiple descriptions of the HEF with variations dependent on lineage or belief system. According to Barbara Brennan for example, the HEF is composed of seven layers in the auric body system that exist within three planes.[11] The etheric, emotional, and mental bodies represent the physical plane. The astral body represents the astral plane and is a bridge or mediator between the physical and spiritual planes. Lastly, the etheric template (physical aspect), celestial body (emotional aspect), and ketheric body (mental aspect) represent the spiritual plane. By the same token, Diane Stein describes multiple templates, cakras, and grids, including seven energy bodies: the physical, etheric, emotional/astral, mental, spiritual, essence self/causal, and core soul/causal body.[12] In the Kuṇḍalinī lineage, there are ten bodies: the soul, the negative mind, the positive mind, the neutral mind, the physical, the arcline, the aura, the pranic, the subtle, and the radiant.[13] Together, independent of belief system or lineage, these subtle bodies are several layers of interpenetrating energy fields that conform not only the HEF, but the human existence, as they control the prāṇa or Divine vital energy. This vital energy is dynamic and flows through our subtle bodies, cakras and aura depending on our vibration.

As you take your attention to a certain part of the body, like you do when you consciously use your hands and fingers to make a mudrā, you are influencing the energy that flows through that part of the body. In yoga,[14] mudrās are seen as influencers of the energy at the vyāna vāyu. The vyāna vāyu is one of the subdivisions of prāṇa in the body, it moves prāṇa throughout the body and across the nāḍīs, and controls the movement of the fingers and toes. Now you can understand that by doing a mudrā, you're not only connecting with the symbolic meaning of the mudrā, but also moving energy to your hands and fingers and sealing the prāṇa in the body. As mudrās are experienced as part of a spiritual practice, like when using the mudrās and chanting mantras, they help the seeker to achieve higher levels of consciousness faster.

Mudrās are also seen as ritual, since they are used as manual ritualistic gestures to pleasure the devas, deities, or the Divine in general. For example, in the āvāhana mudrā (illustrated), which can be transliterated as a "call to action," the devotee makes the mudrā as a welcoming gesture to invite the deity to worship. It can also be used as a symbol of offering or pūjā.

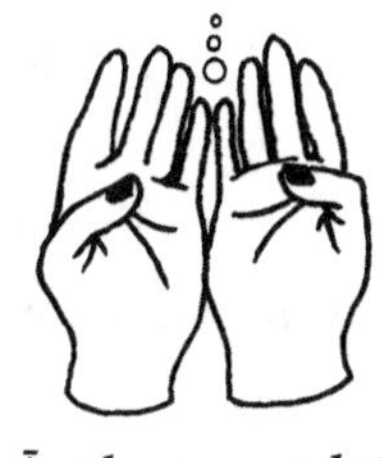

Āvāhana mudrā

11. Brennan BA. Hands of Light: A Guide to Healing Through the Human Energy Field. New York, NY, US: Bantan Books (1988)
12. Stein D. The Women's Book of Healing: Auras, Chakras, Laying On of Hands, Crystals, Gemstones, and Colors. New York, NY, US: Crossing Press (2004)
13. Bhajan Y. The Aquarian Teacher: KRI International Teacher Training in Kundalini Yoga, Level 1. Santa Cruz, NM, US: Kundalini Research Institute (2010)
14. Desikachar K, *et al.* ***Int J Yoga Therap.*** Vol. 15, No. 1, pp. 17-39 (2005)

As you will learn when you work through the illustrations, the particular gestures and hand or finger positions are able to move or channel the constitutional elements in our bodies (page 46), which results in positive wellness outcomes at the mental, physical, and spiritual levels. I've curated, among the many, a selection of specific mudrās with various benefits, yet there are many more beyond those here enclosed.

Before continuing to the main body of work, take a moment to sit with the following healing decree. We invite you to use it as often as needed throughout your life to give yourself a chance to release any negative imprint your hands may be carrying. In fact, I have integrated it as part of the ritualization of my personal creative time, as a prayer so that I wield my hands as an intentional tool of love for myself and all. If you choose to use it as part of your creative self-care ritual, you may want to adapt "from now on" to "in this moment or today."

Healing Decree

"*I release* all harmful, destructive and negative energies
I might be carrying in my hands.
I forgive myself
from any times I have used my hands
to express anger, to harm another being, or to harm myself.
I release all low energies
that are not connected to the higher frequencies of light and love.
I heal myself
from any less than perfect energies held within my hands and myself.
I lay my hands
in front of my heart as an offering to the Divine,
so I can co-create a world of harmony, light and love.
I place the intention that...
From now on, I will use my hands only to express kindness.
From now on, I will use my hands as an extension of my own heart to share my love.
I have now hands of wonder
to create and manifest the highest and best good for myself and for all beings."

-Maricel Flores Díaz -

MERAKI

This chapter contains the main body of illustrations. It's titled with the Greek word ***meraki*** (μεράκι), a word that perfectly embodies the qualities of the creative process: to do something with intention, soul, creativity, and love—so much so, that it results in a perceivable essence of yourself in that work.

Tapping into creativity can be challenging for some because of many reasons such as believing that we're not good at what we intend or want to do, or the simple fact that we often box-in creativity with activities that involve drawing, painting, and other visual arts.

Like mentioned earlier, use these illustrations as a gateway to slowing down, breathing, and contemplating art. Take a moment to gaze at the illustration you choose to work on. Seep in the visual component and process the message that it's bringing to you. My T'ai chi teacher believes that you don't even need to color to get something out of these illustrations. However, coloring is one of the most accessible and easiest forms to kick start your creativity for the one purpose of sparking, initiating, and igniting that creative flare in your day. So pour a little bit of yourself into them! See what comes up, explore and connect to your visionary self.

Discover. Inspire. Create.

IN THE BEGINNING

The Hopi Tribe is a sovereign nation in northeastern Arizona, on the continental United States of America, and is organized in a matrilineal clan structure. The designation of Hopi is a shortened form of their autonym, *Hopituh Shi-nu-mu* which translates into *The Peaceful People.*[15] The Hopi Way unfolds in the maintenance of the balance between nature and people across the entire livelihood of the individual and community. To learn more about the Hopi Tribe and reservation, visit *www.hopi-nsn.gov* or scan the QR Code below.

The Hopi hand symbol is a hand imprint with a central spiral that represents life, creativity, and healing. Spirals are a symbol that characterize the infinite consciousness and as believed by the First Peoples, it's the movement of the life force and cosmos. As united with the hand as symbol, it parallels the essential journey of the human life cycle and their life path.

"Let me walk in beauty, and make my eyes
ever behold the red and purple sunset.
Make my hands respect the things you have made
and my ears sharp to hear your voice.
Make me wise so that I may understand the things
you have taught my people.
Let me learn the lessons you have hidden in every leaf and rock.
I seek strength, not to be greater than my brother,
but to fight my greatest enemy—myself—
Make me always ready
to come to you with clean hands and straight eyes.

- Hopi Prayer to The Great Spirit, Asquali, Kawquai -

Hopi Tribe

15. Joseph F. Advanced Civilizations of Prehistoric America. Rochester, VM, US: Bear & Company (2009)

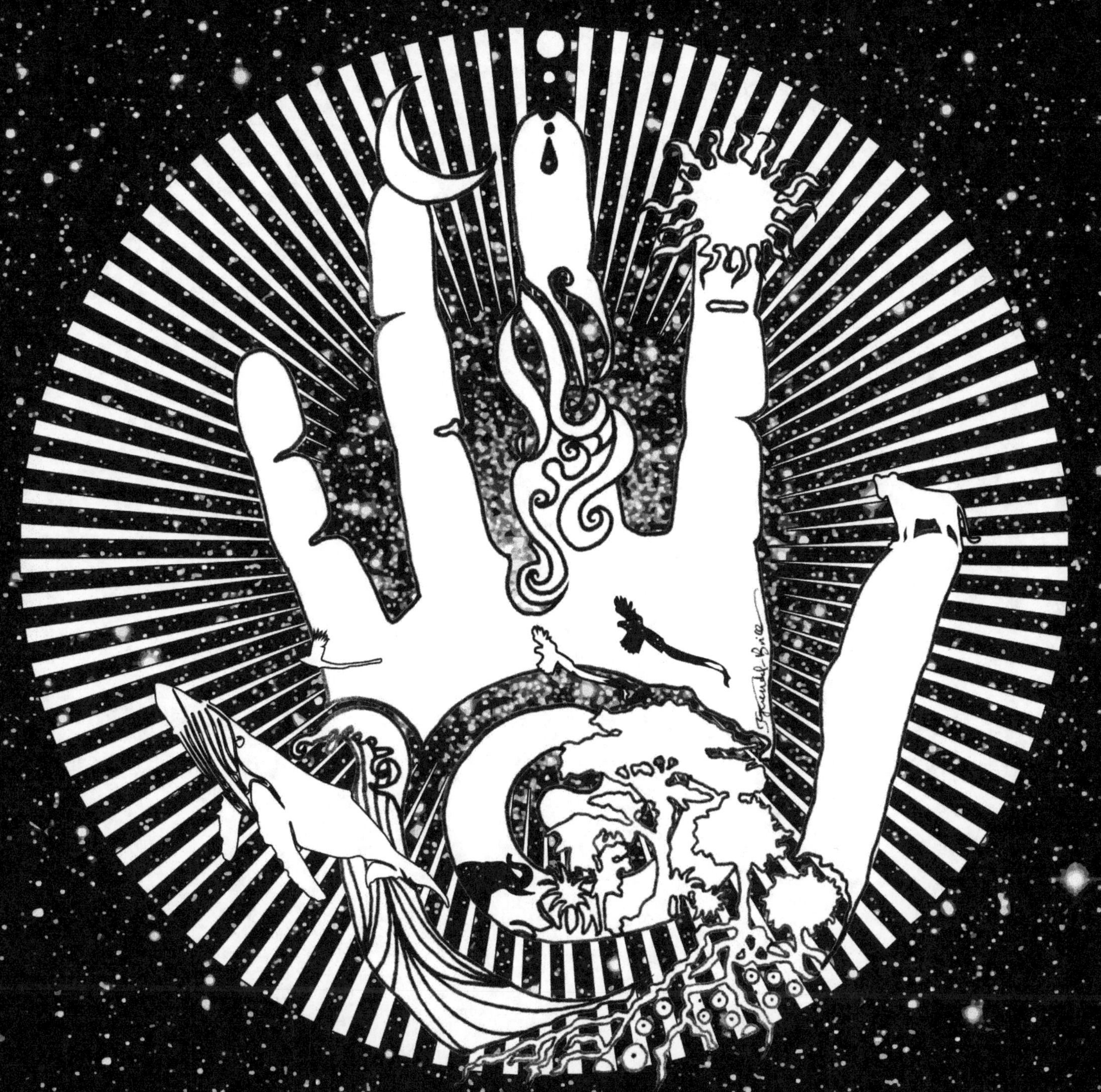

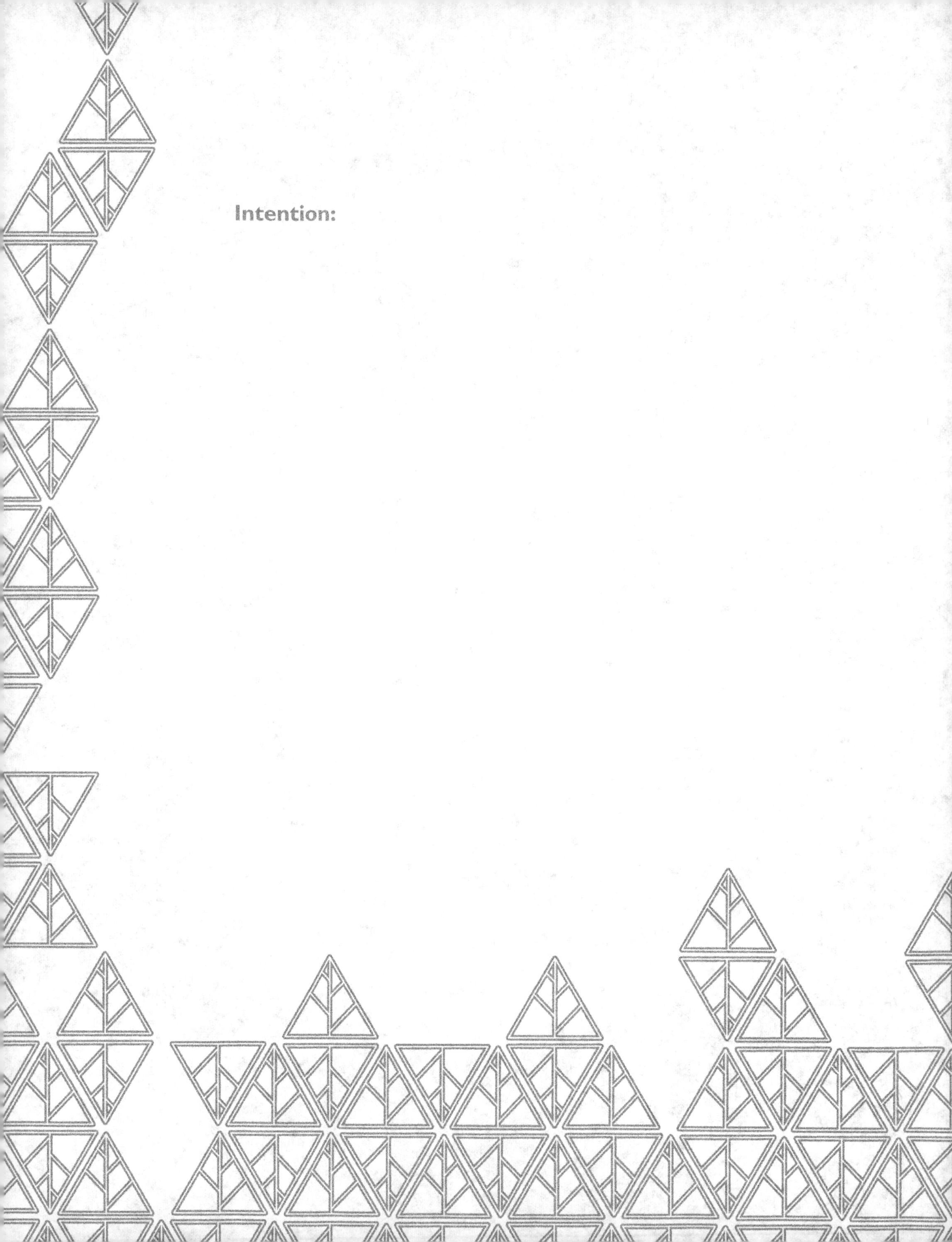

Intention:

Thought Infusions

1. In your mind, what represents life and creative healing?

2. How do you bring love and healing to others?

3. What steps/actions can you take to increase internal and external peace in your life?

4. Contemplate your colored illustration. How does color change your initial perception of the image? What colors did you use? Look up #anewkindofcoloringbook and #puraprana, share your work. Explore other being's colors and see what new messages come to mind through observation.

5. In your day-to-day life, have you noticed any naturally occurring spirals or spiral-like patterns?

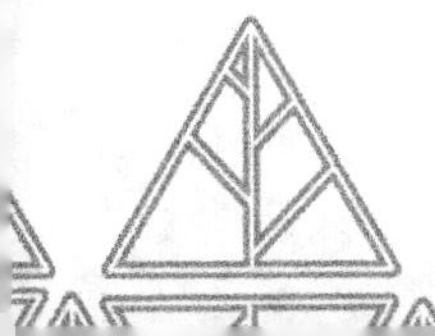

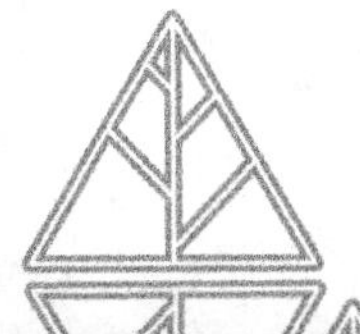

THE HAND[16-17]

The apotropaic use of a palm-shaped amulet (open right hand) for good fortune and Divine protection against evil, specifically the "evil eye," is a commonality throughout cultures, particularly in the Middle East and Africa. Known as "The Hamsa or Khamsa," depictions include a bilaterally symmetrical, two-thumb representation, and a more realistic one-thumb interpretation. The Hand represents the feminine and therefore, regarded as the woman's holy hand. It means not only protection, but hope, blessings, peace, power, and strength. The hamsa hand sometimes includes a medial evil eye symbol (illustrated). The human eye is an unique and powerful symbol that continues to be deemed as a projector of energy and light. This is a great example of how different cultures and different peoples, at different points in time, can generate similar belief systems and symbology. Adaptations include:

• Hand of Miriam—Jewish adaptation, "hamesh or שמח (five in Hebrew)." Miriam was the sister of Moses and Aaron according to Biblical records.
• Hand of Fatima—Islamic adaptation, "khamsa (hamsa) or ةسمخ" (five in Arabic)." Fatima was prophet Mohammed's daughter, Fatima Zahra.
• Hand of Mary—Catholic, Christian adaptation.
• Hand of the Goddess—Innana (Sumerian), Ishtar (Mesopotamian), Venus (Roman), Aphrodite (Greek), and Tara (Buddhist).
• Ahiṃsā or Jain Hand—Jainism adaptation. Ahiṃsā transliterates from Sanskrit (Saṃskṛta) to "non-violence." Ahiṃsā is one of the five yamas listed by Patañjali in Yogasūtra II.30.

My hands, activated prayers.
My hands, activated offerings.
My hands, recipients of love.
My hands, givers of love.
My hands, vessels of radiance, Divine.
My hands, healing touch.
My hands, bridges of co-creation.
My hands, sacred gifts.
My hands, channels of love, Divine.

-Iréne de Brice -

16. Elliot JH. Beware the Evil Eye Volume 3: The Evil Eye in the Bible and the Ancient World. Eugene, OR, US: Wipf and Stock Publishers (2016)
17. Fisher MP. Living Religions: An Encyclopaedia of the World's Faiths. London, UK: I.B.Tauris (1997)

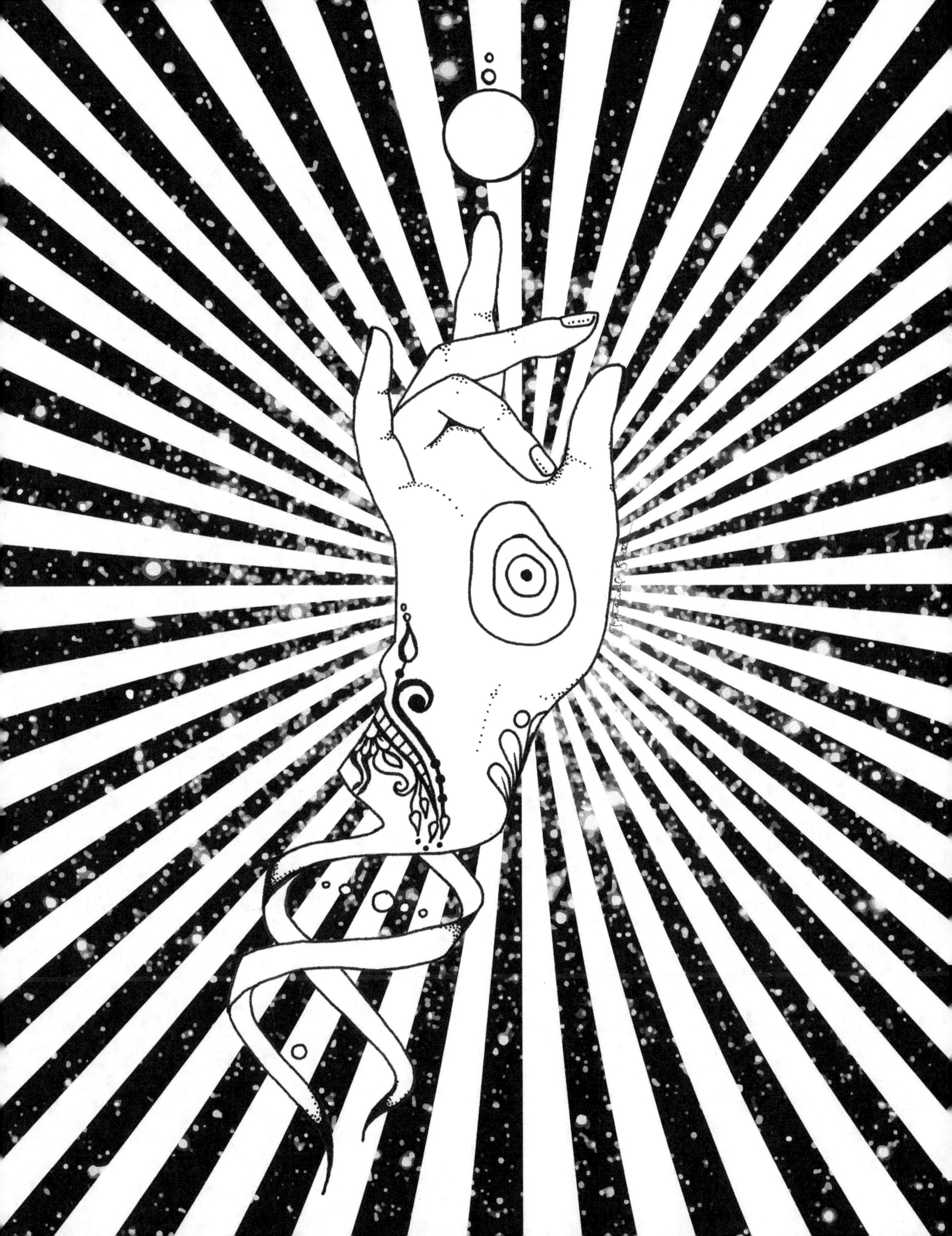

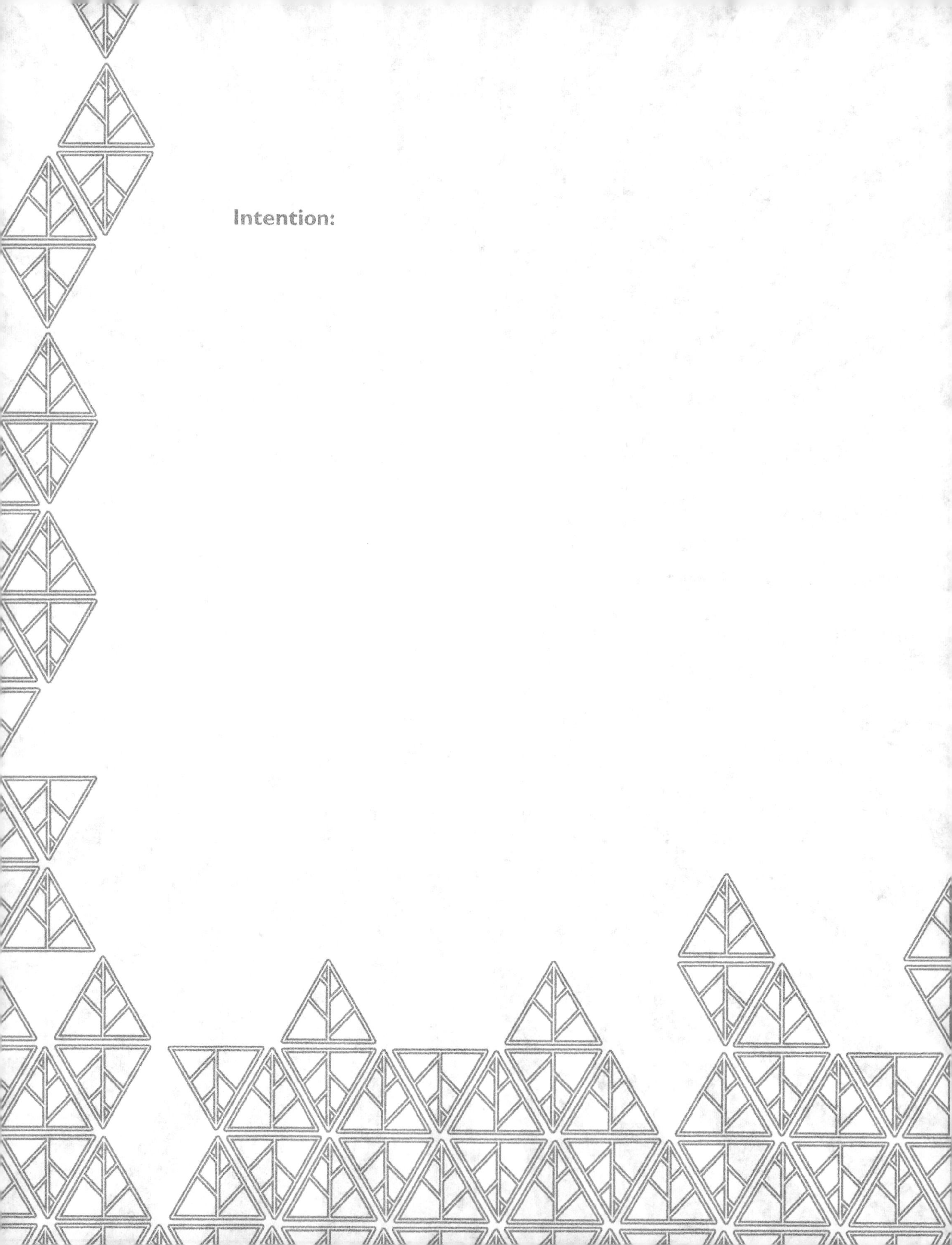

Intention:

Thought Infusions

1. Hands are so much... So much more than what we normally think. Think for a moment, how many times have you used your hands for actions that were not seeded in love?

2. How do you think your hands are an expression of your whole self? All of creation or existence?

3. There is a mighty power of a hand in action. What do you want to use it for? How do you want to use it? What do you want to build? Are you using your hands (in the imaginal realm or in reality) to create the reality you desire?

4. Contemplate your colored illustration. How does color change your initial perception of the image? What colors did you use? Look up #anewkindofcoloringbook and #puraprana, share your work. Explore other being's colors and see what new messages come to mind through observation.

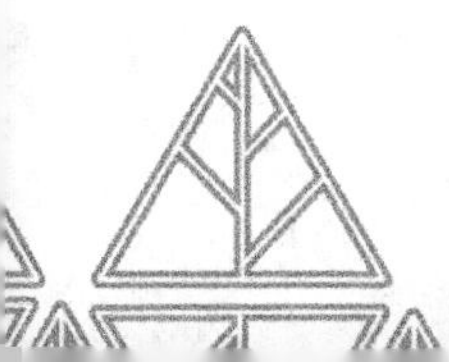

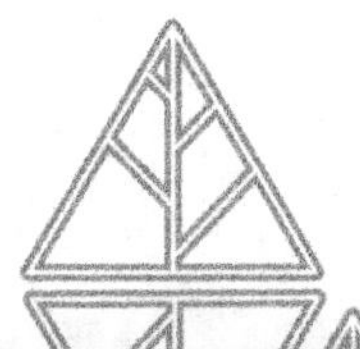

ŚAUCA

Śauca is one of the five niyamas of yogic science, and represents "purity." Very much in line with other religious and spiritual belief systems, purity goes hand-in-hand with cleanliness, order, and clearness. In this case, purity applies to your mind (thoughts), how you communicate and talk to yourself and others (speech), and your physical reality (your body and other spaces you dwell in). In the Yogasūtra II.41, Patañjali explains that "Through cleanliness and purity of body and mind comes a purification of the essence, a goodness and gladness of feeling, a sense of focus with intentness, the mastery and union of the senses, and a fitness, preparation and capability for self-realization."[18]

Śauca as applied to intentional living is thinking of yourself as an instrument for the greatest and most unlimited good. As co-creators of our realities, practicing śauca not only serves to uplift ourselves but also those we encounter on our daily journey. Seeking to live in purity, untarnished by the ego, aligns us with the ambrosial flow of inspiration and allows our body and mind to open for creativity to flow freely through us. Creativity and the creative process, as I see it, enable our capability for self-realization.

The light captures the moment the day is born.
The rising sun, the moon is ghost.
A subtle transition births a glorious gift.
Given the opportunity, gentle steps carry you
to your future path...
Pureness dressed in hope.
It's said that magic dances from an open heart.
Descending into your own truth...
You peacefully accept this life as it unfolds in front of you.

- Louisa Wargo (Lotus Rising) -

18. Woods JH. The yoga-system of Patañjali; or the ancient Hindu doctrine of concentration of mind. Cambridge, MA, US: The Harvard University Press (2003)

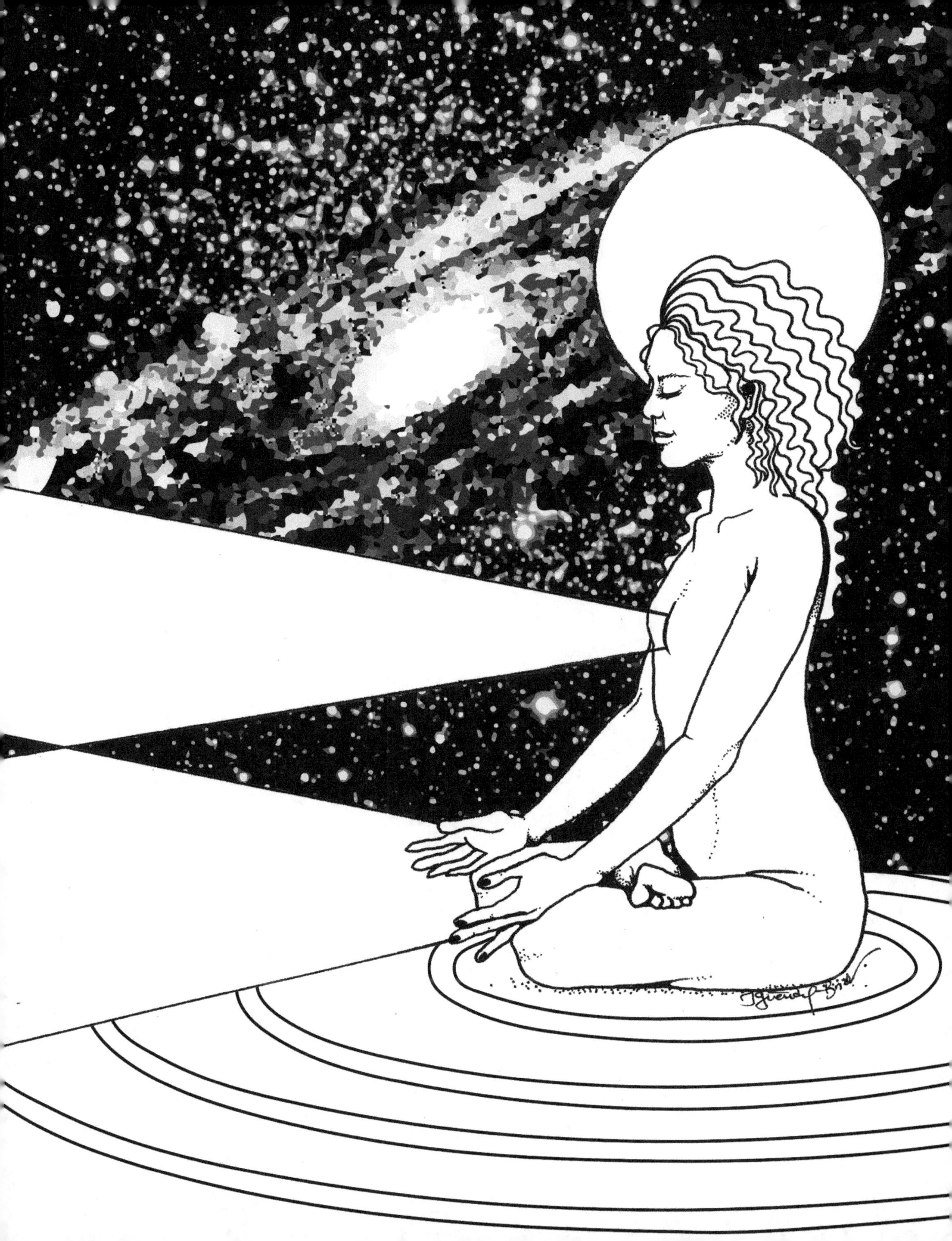

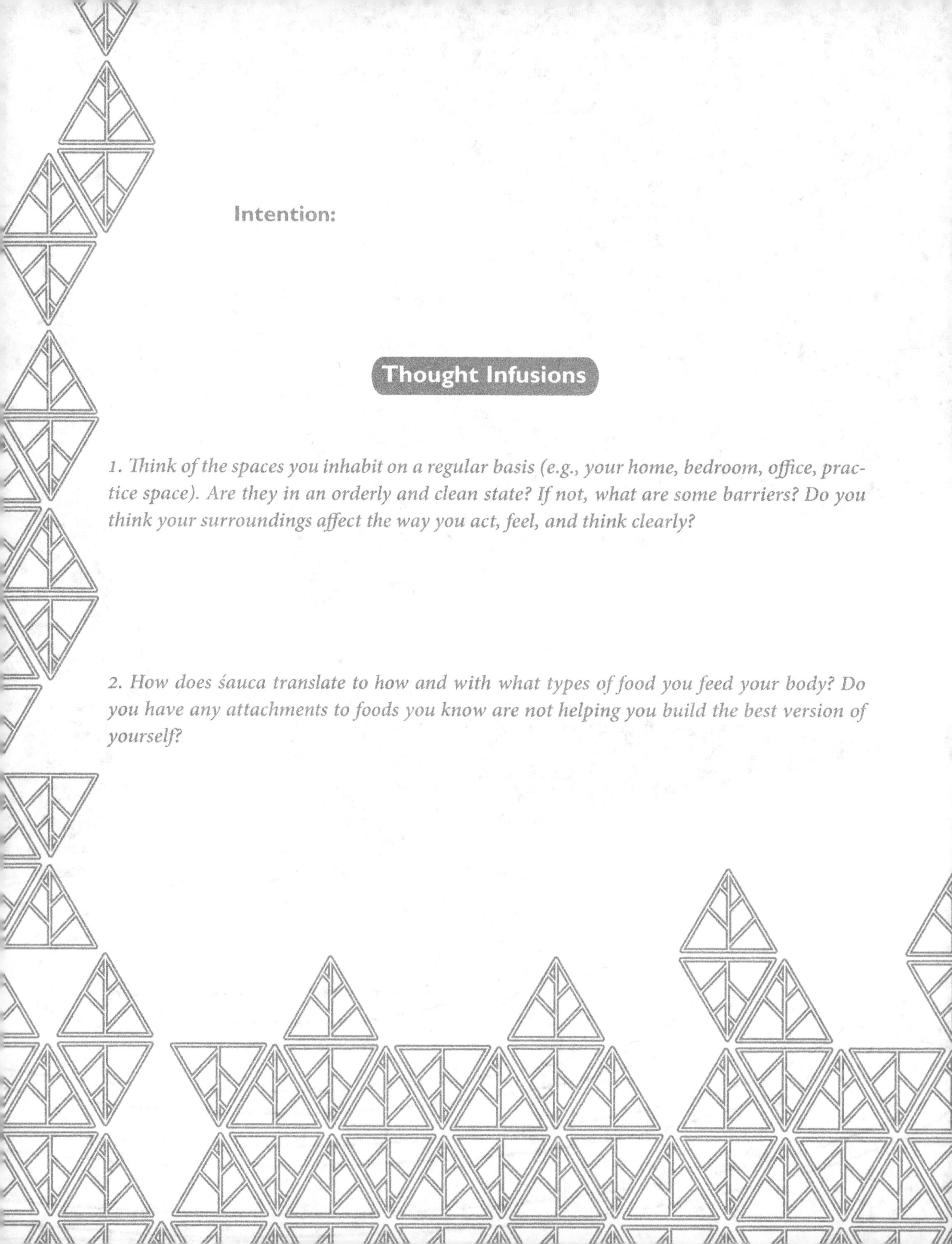

Intention:

Thought Infusions

1. Think of the spaces you inhabit on a regular basis (e.g., your home, bedroom, office, practice space). Are they in an orderly and clean state? If not, what are some barriers? Do you think your surroundings affect the way you act, feel, and think clearly?

2. How does śauca translate to how and with what types of food you feed your body? Do you have any attachments to foods you know are not helping you build the best version of yourself?

3. Matthew 15:18 reads "But the words you speak come from the heart—that's what defiles you." How does śauca translate to the way you speak and the words you say?

4. How does śauca translate to the way you live your life? How can purity in practice help you align with intentional living and how you wish to interact with everyone and everything?

5. How can śauca align your mind and body with your creative nature and potential? Think for a moment how much good we can co-create in the world if at every moment we would connect our hands (also our actions, movements) with the power of our heart's love (page 24)?

6. Contemplate your colored illustration. How does color change your initial perception of the image? What colors did you use? Look up #anewkindofcoloringbook and #purapraṇa, share your work. Explore other being's colors and see what new messages come to mind through observation.

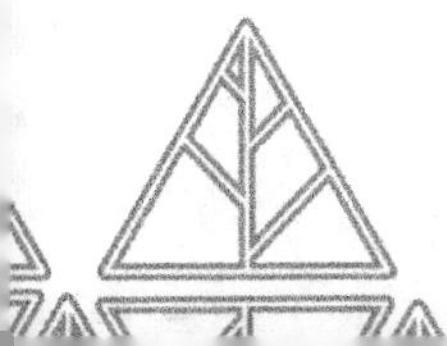

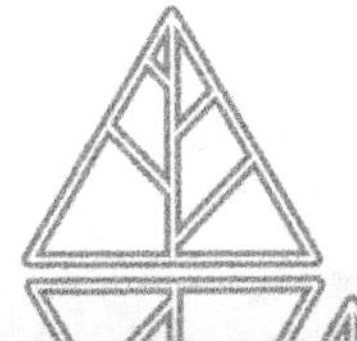

THE ELEMENTS[19]

Many Eastern philosophies take into account four-plus elements, dependent on belief system—fire, air, ether (space), water, metal, wood, consciousness... In yogic science, the human body and all physical creation, are constituted by the five great elements or mahābhūta that originate from tanmātras (the vibratory subtle essence that creates the elements). The five tanmātras or subtle physical essences are: sound, touch, vision, taste, and smell; in themselves related to the sense organs.

In Āyurveda, each finger has an element associated with it. Ether supports fire, air, earth and water, allowing their existence and function.

• *Thumb: agni or fire element | Tanmātra: vision* •
• *Index: vāyu or air element | Tanmātra: touch* •
• *Middle: ākāśa or ether element | Tanmātra: sound* •
• *Ring: pṛthivī or earth element | Tanmātra: smell* •
• *Little: varuṇa or water element | Tanmātra: taste* •

When practiced together with other element-based and holistic systems such as Āyurveda and yoga, they can be utilized to bring mind, body, and spirit into equilibrium. Element-specific mudrās are illustrated below.

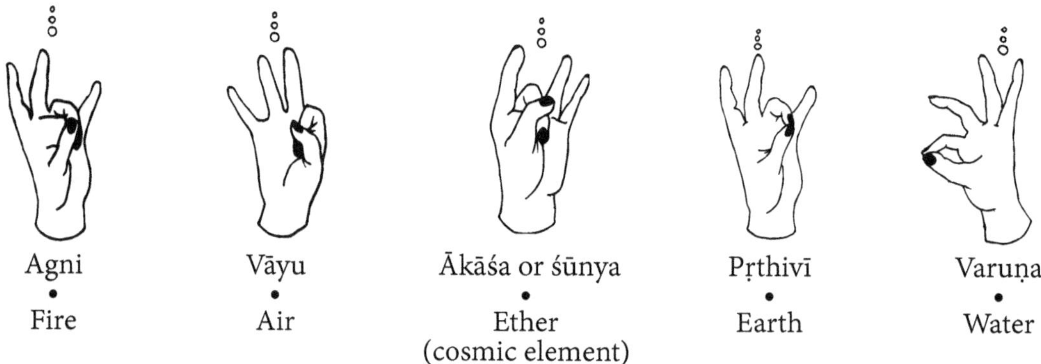

Mudrās are able to redirect the energy flow, linking the individual pranic energy with the universal life force. Through the use of pressure, direction, and hand or finger position, we can stimulate sensory pathways that run from our hands to the brain.

19. Billington R. Understanding Eastern Philosophy. London, UK: Routledge (1997)

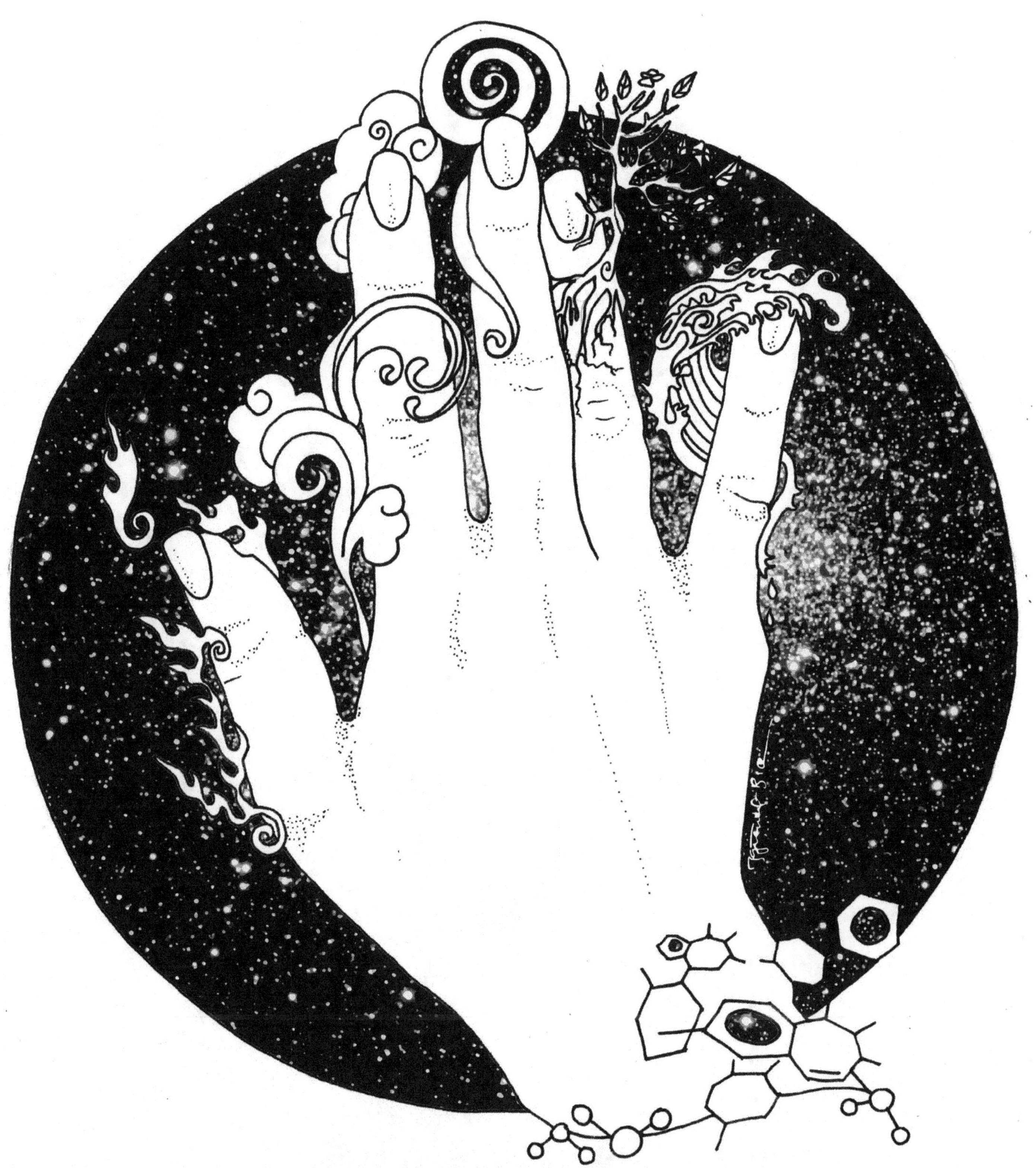

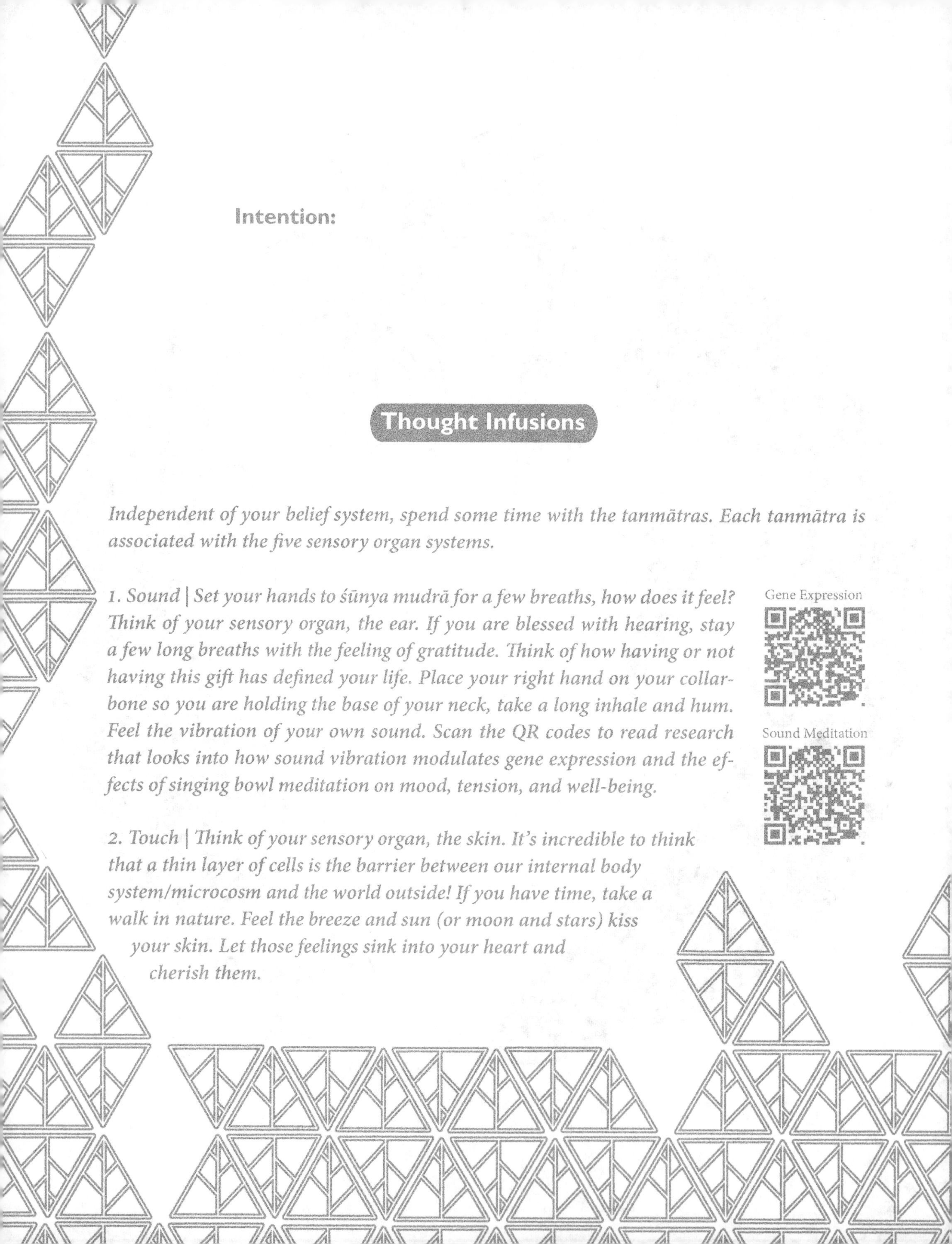

Intention:

Thought Infusions

Independent of your belief system, spend some time with the tanmātras. Each tanmātra is associated with the five sensory organ systems.

1. Sound | Set your hands to śūnya mudrā for a few breaths, how does it feel? Think of your sensory organ, the ear. If you are blessed with hearing, stay a few long breaths with the feeling of gratitude. Think of how having or not having this gift has defined your life. Place your right hand on your collarbone so you are holding the base of your neck, take a long inhale and hum. Feel the vibration of your own sound. Scan the QR codes to read research that looks into how sound vibration modulates gene expression and the effects of singing bowl meditation on mood, tension, and well-being.

2. Touch | Think of your sensory organ, the skin. It's incredible to think that a thin layer of cells is the barrier between our internal body system/microcosm and the world outside! If you have time, take a walk in nature. Feel the breeze and sun (or moon and stars) kiss your skin. Let those feelings sink into your heart and cherish them.

The skin is our largest organ, and it has millions of sensory receptor cells that make it possible for you to sense the surrounding environment. These cells are activated by a stimulus, which then the brain and/or muscles interpret as a sensation.

3. Vision | Think of your sensory organ, your eyes. Like many other things, we may take our sight for granted. If you are blessed with the gift of sight, take a moment to say thank you. Rub your hands together and place them, cupped, over each eye. Sit in gratitude for a few long breaths. What are the favorite things you see everyday? How do your eyes shape your human experience?

4. Taste | Think of your sensory organ, your tongue. Our tongues are wondrous as well, and I certainly often forget to give thanks for this organ. It allows us to experience life through flavor, but it is so much more. It allows us to give form to words. In Āyurveda, it serves as a great indicator of your digestive system—take a look first thing in the morning, if it's pink, great! If it's coated with a white film you may have "ama," the result of poor digestion and nutrition habits. We recommend trying a tongue scraper tool and coconut oil pulling first thing in the morning as well. To explore Āyurvedic knowledge on food and health in contemporary healthcare, scan this code!

Āyurveda

5. Smell | Think of your sensory organ, your nose. Have you ever smelled something that evoked a memory? Sometimes it can even be so powerful that it stirs up your emotions to the point where you may cry with longing for that person or place. Behavioral studies have linked the sense of smell to be more potent at triggering vivid emotional memories, even more so than through visual inputs. Olfactory-triggered memories activate the limbic system (which includes the hippocampus and amygdala). The first QR code will take you to a scientific review of the role of odor-evoked memory in psychological and physiological health. We are firm believers in the power of this sense, specially when it comes to the therapeutic use of aromatherapy. Have you heard or researched about therapeutic uses of smell? Scan the second code to explore a recent research article that looks at the use of lavender essential oil (LEO) in anxiety disorders.

Odor Memory

Anxiety and LEO

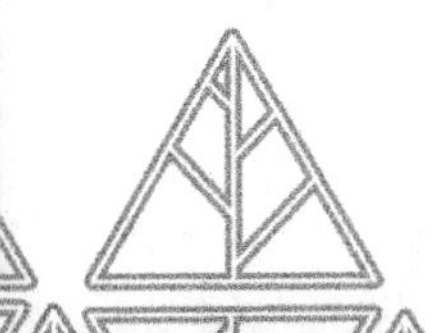

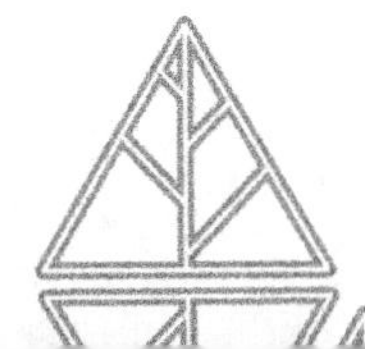

THE HUMAN ENERGY FIELD
"ROOT CAKRA"

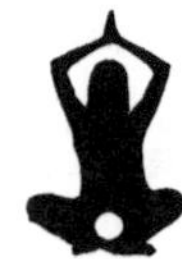

Sanskrit name | Mūlādhāra (original foundation, ground, source)

Honors the Earth | Heal with nature, meditate outdoors, forest bathe (page 86)

Located at | Base of spine, coccyx

Color, element, endocrine gland, finger | Red, earth, adrenals, ring

Mantra | Laṃ, bīja-mantra or "seed-mantra" for pṛthivī or "earth" (page 46)

Affirmation | I am safe, I am grounded, I am where I need to be

Herbs | Dandelion (illustrated), nettle, ashwagandha, reishi and chaga mushrooms

Essential oils | Patchouli, vetiver, rosewood, clove

Crystals | Bloodstone, garnet, ruby, smoky quartz

Foods to find balance | Berries, pomegranate, beets, radish, watermelon

Lesson | Survival, the right to exist

Mudrā | Gyān (illustrated, page 142)

"I feel a thousand capacities spring up in me. I am rooted, but I flow."

- Virginia Woolf -

Symbol:
4 petal lotus

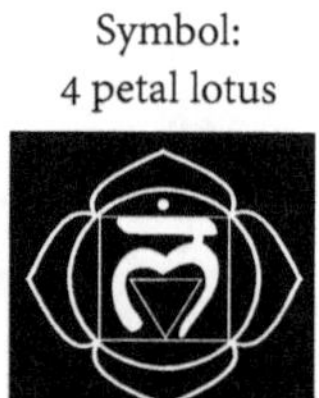

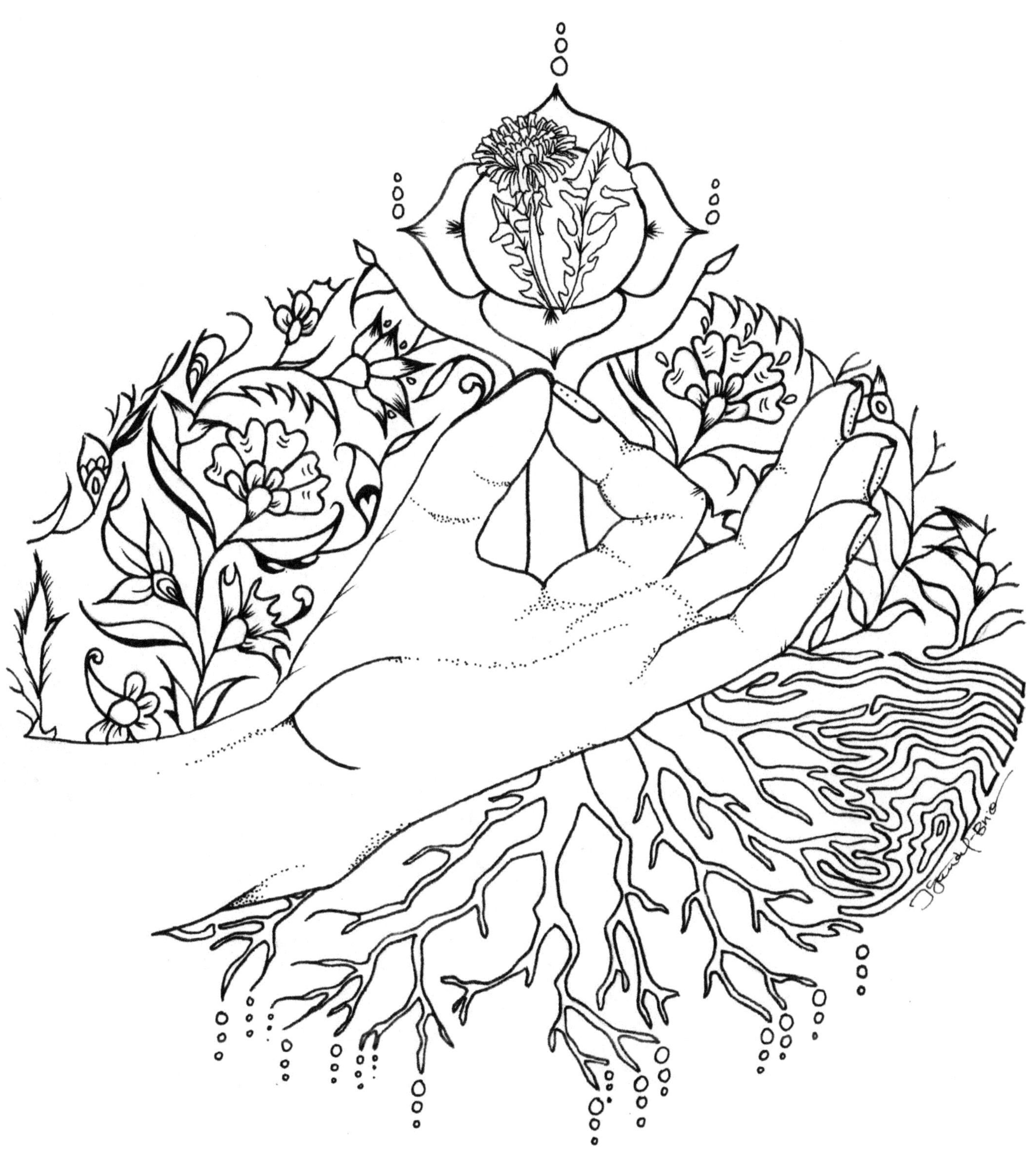

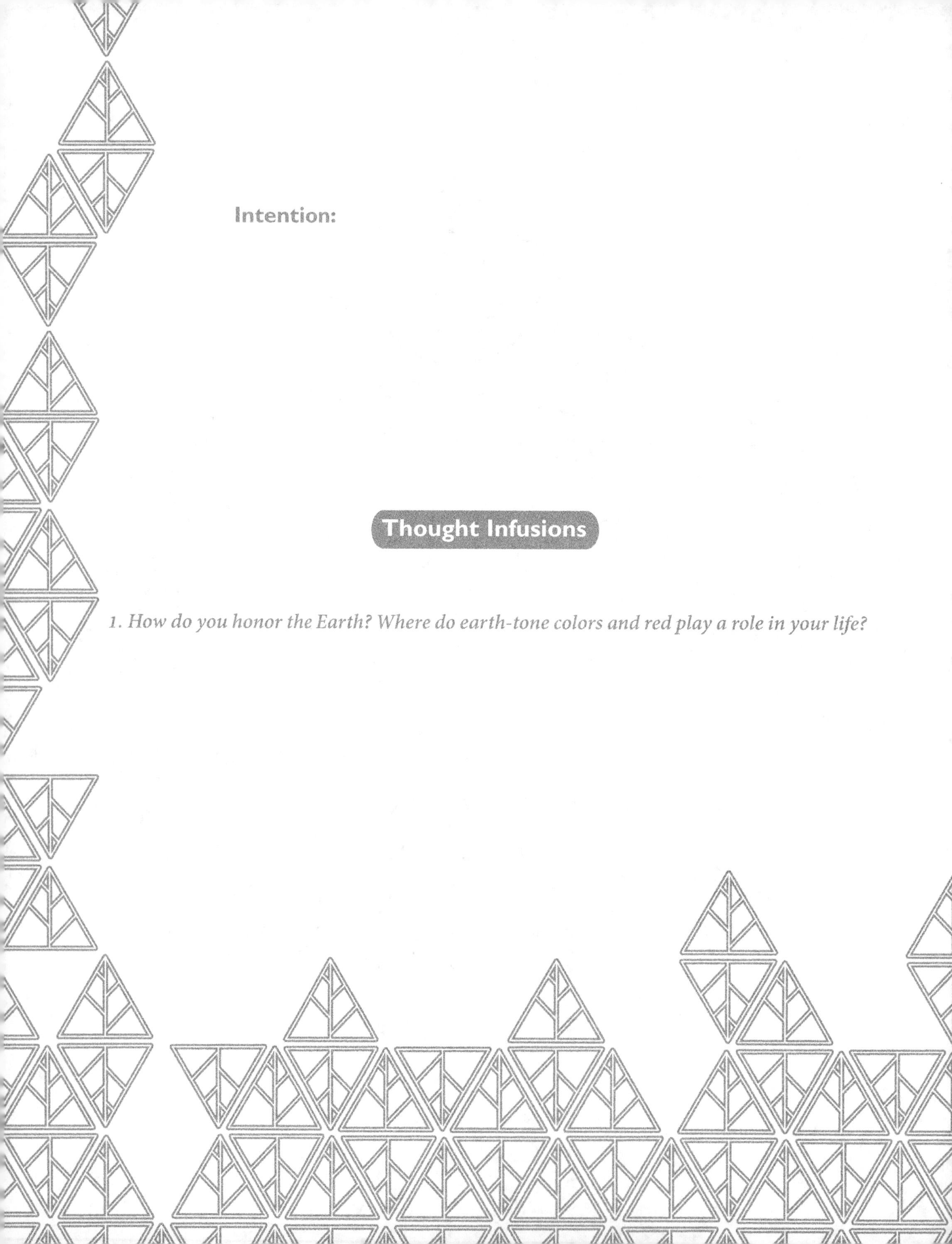

Intention:

Thought Infusions

1. How do you honor the Earth? Where do earth-tone colors and red play a role in your life?

2. How frequently do you have the focused, conscious intention, to use your hands to connect with your physical experience? Feel your existence, feel the textures. Explore.

3. What affirmation best fits your needs right now? Think of the qualities of Mūlādhāra—Rooted: groundedness, security, stability, and support.

4. How do you acknowledge and nurture your right to exist and be present? Can you think of any barriers?

5. Contemplate your colored illustration. How does color change your initial perception of the image? What colors did you use? Look up #anewkindofcoloringbook and #puraprana, share your work. Explore other being's colors and see what new messages come to mind through observation.

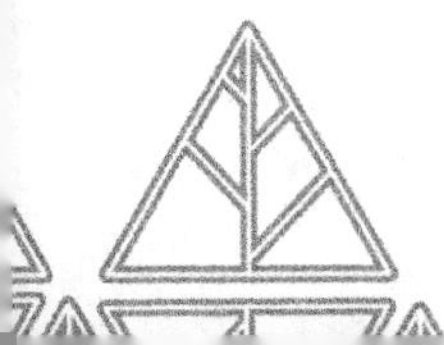

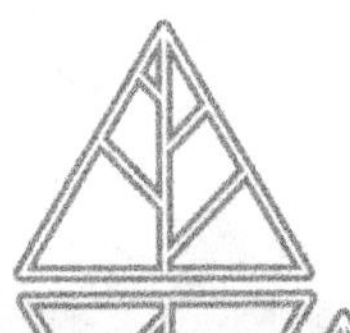

THE HUMAN ENERGY FIELD
"SACRAL CAKRA"

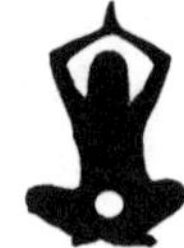

Sanskrit name | Svādhiṣṭhāna (abode of self)

Honors the creative | Heal with creative alchemy

Located at | Below navel, lower abdomen

Color, element, endocrine gland, finger | Orange, water, gonads, little

Mantra | Vaṃ, bīja-mantra or "seed-mantra" for varuṇa or "water" (page 46)

Affirmation | I am unique and radiant, I am sensual and creative, I embrace my life with joy

Herbs | Calendula (illustrated), chamomile, mint, jasmine, damiana, coriander, orange peel

Essential oils | Jasmine, neroli, orange or grapefruit, bergamot, geranium, clary sage

Crystals | Carnelian, garnet, aventurine in red and orange tones

Foods to find balance | Mango, papaya, passion fruit, pumpkin, sweet potato

Lesson | Feelings, the right to feel

Mudrā | Dhyāna (illustrated)

"Make your creative time—no matter what it is you are creating, a personal self-care ritual or ceremony. Make it your prayer, your offering. Offer the experience and lesson in honor of your belief system and whatever it is you hold sacred. Find and nurture your creative talents."

- Iréne de Brice -

Symbol:
6 petal lotus

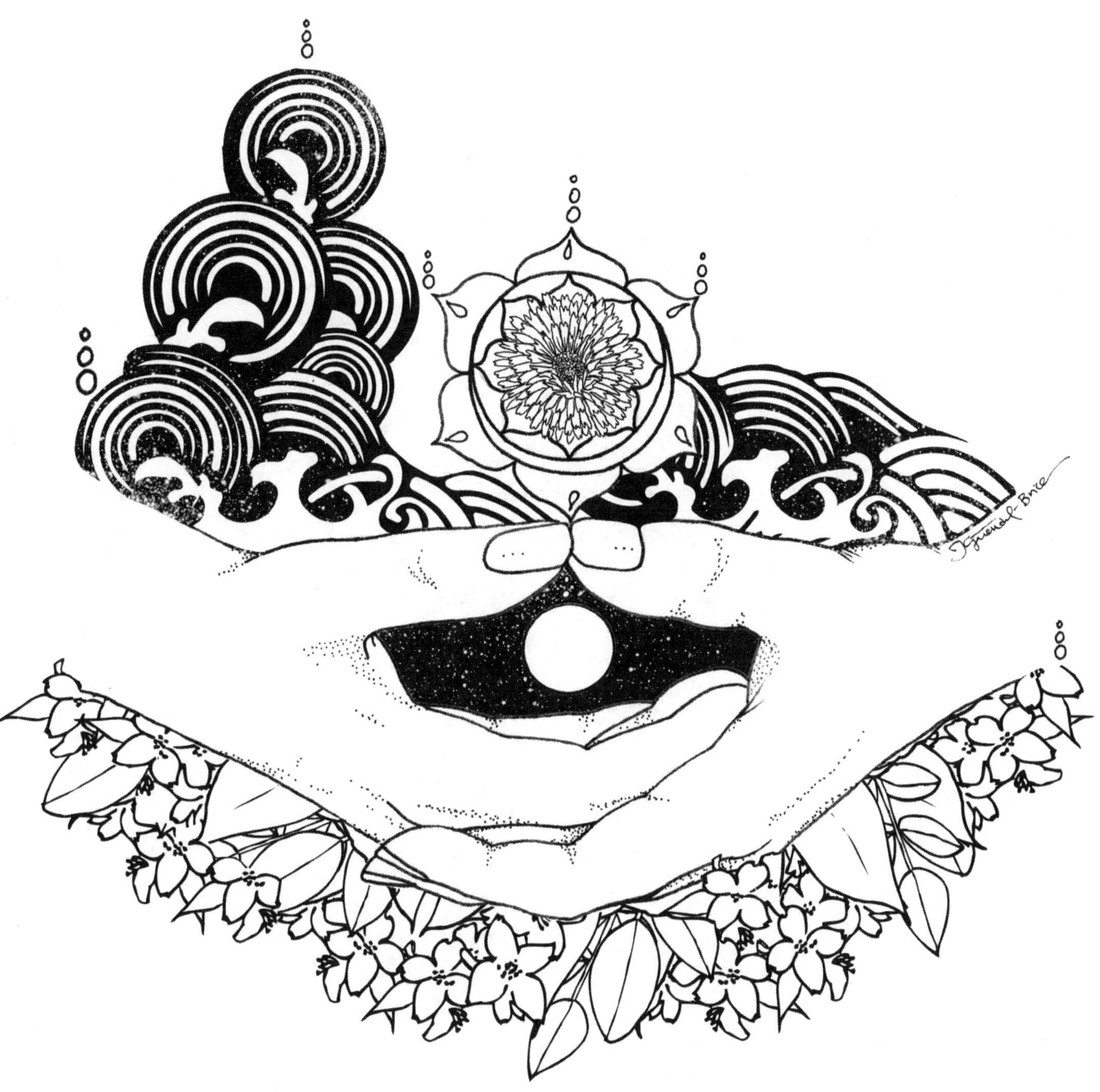

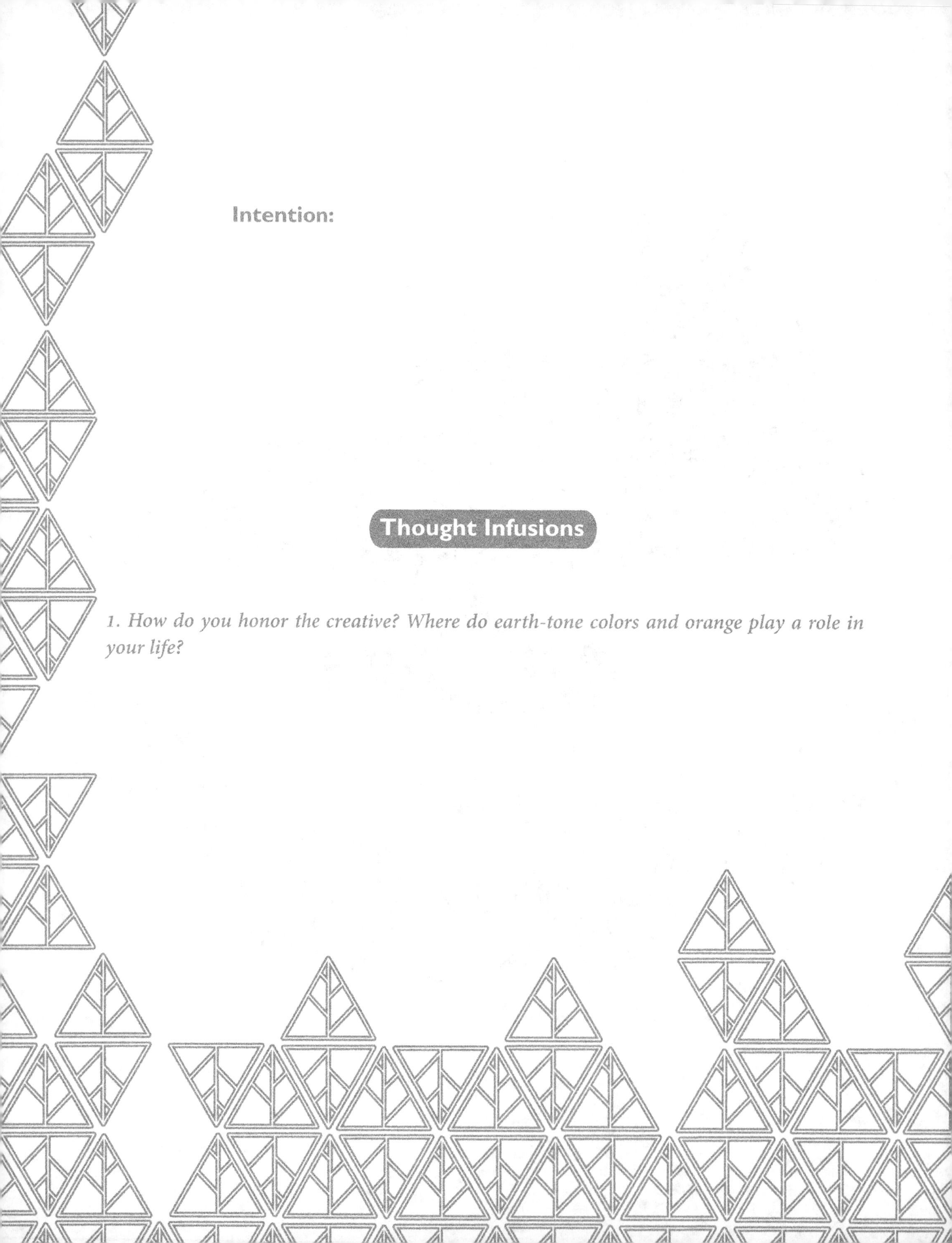

Intention:

Thought Infusions

1. *How do you honor the creative? Where do earth-tone colors and orange play a role in your life?*

2. Have you ever opened your empty hands and trusted that life will bring and provide for you exactly what you need? How open are you to receive abundance?

3. What affirmation best fits your needs right now? Think of the qualities of Svādhiṣṭhāna—Fluidity: flexibility, creativity, sensuality and pleasure, receptivity.

4. How do you acknowledge and nurture your feelings and right to feel? Can you think of any barriers?

5. Contemplate your colored illustration. How does color change your initial perception of the image? What colors did you use? Look up #anewkindofcoloringbook and #puraprana, share your work. Explore other being's colors and see what new messages come to mind through observation.

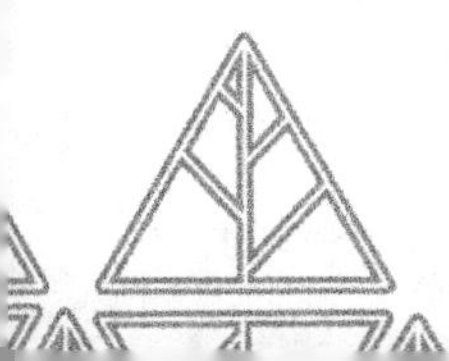

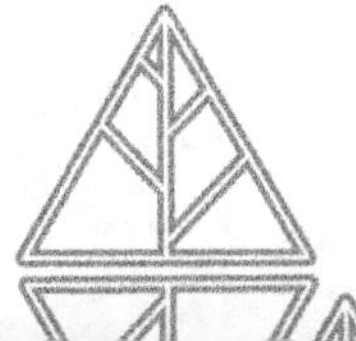

THE HUMAN ENERGY FIELD
"SOLAR PLEXUS CAKRA"

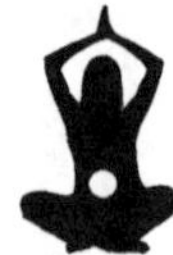

Sanskrit name | Maṇipūra (city of jewels)

Honors the life force | Heal with breathing

Located at | Above navel, stomach area

Color, element, endocrine gland, finger | Yellow, fire, pancreas, thumb

Mantra | Raṃ, bīja-mantra or "seed-mantra" for agni or "fire" (page 46)

Affirmation | I am enough, I accept myself, I live confidently in harmony and with integrity

Herbs | Ginger, lemon balm, and lemon (illustrated); turmeric, mint, fennel, marshmallow

Essential oils | Myrrh, frankincense, lemongrass, lime, coriander

Crystals | Citrine, amber, Tiger's eye

Foods to find balance | Pineapple, banana, squash, quinoa, oats, ginger and turmeric

Lesson | Personal power, the right to think

Mudrā | Variation of añjali (illustrated, page 158)

"Recharging in the moment, cultivating present flow.
Mudrās with momentum, generate an internal glow."

- Vivia Astraia -

Symbol:
10 petal lotus

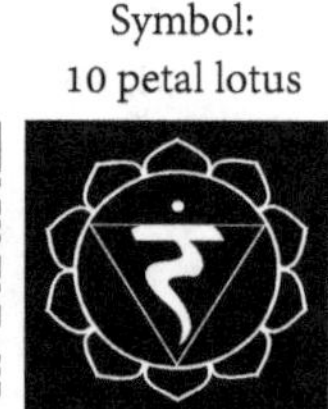

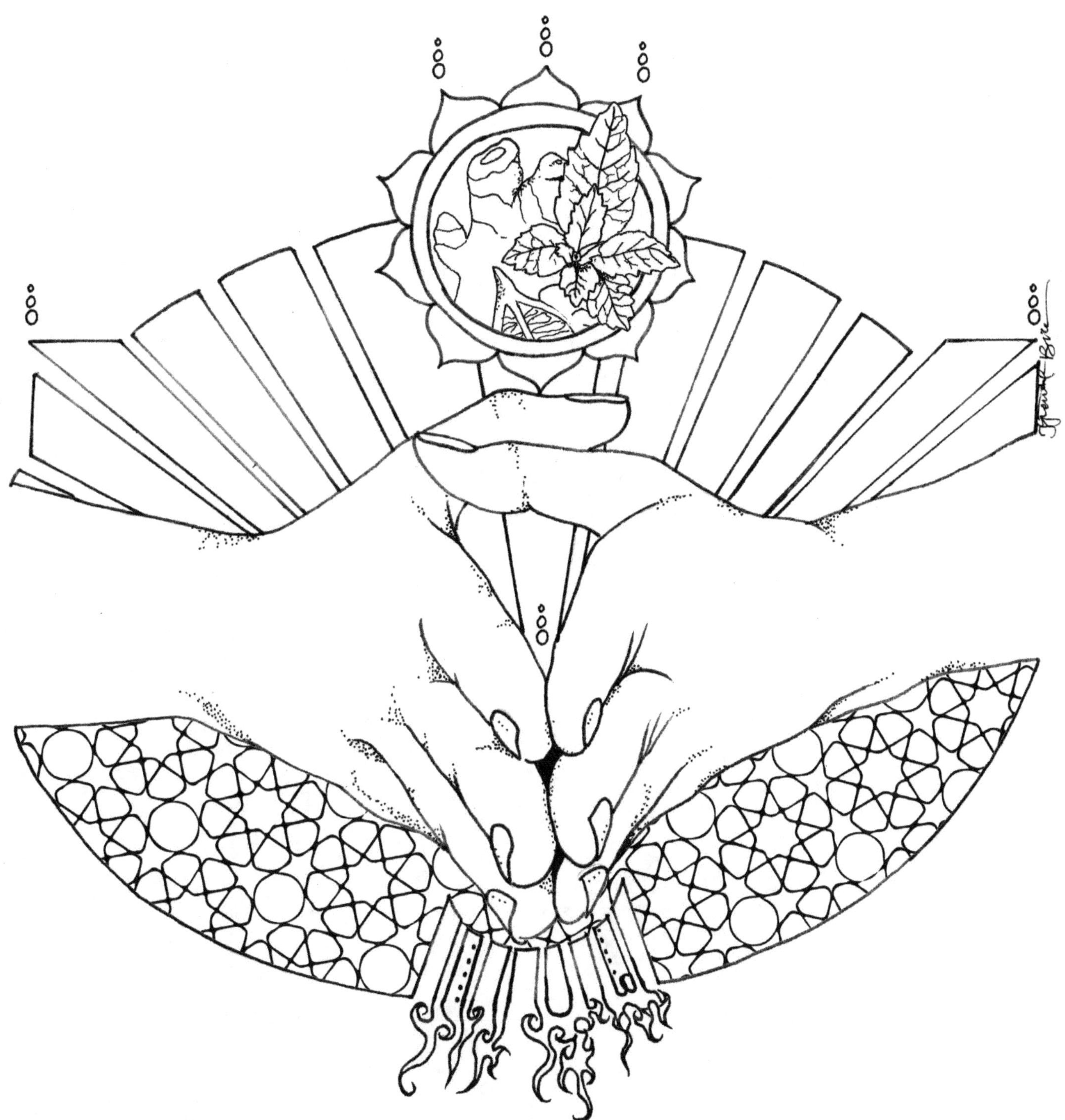

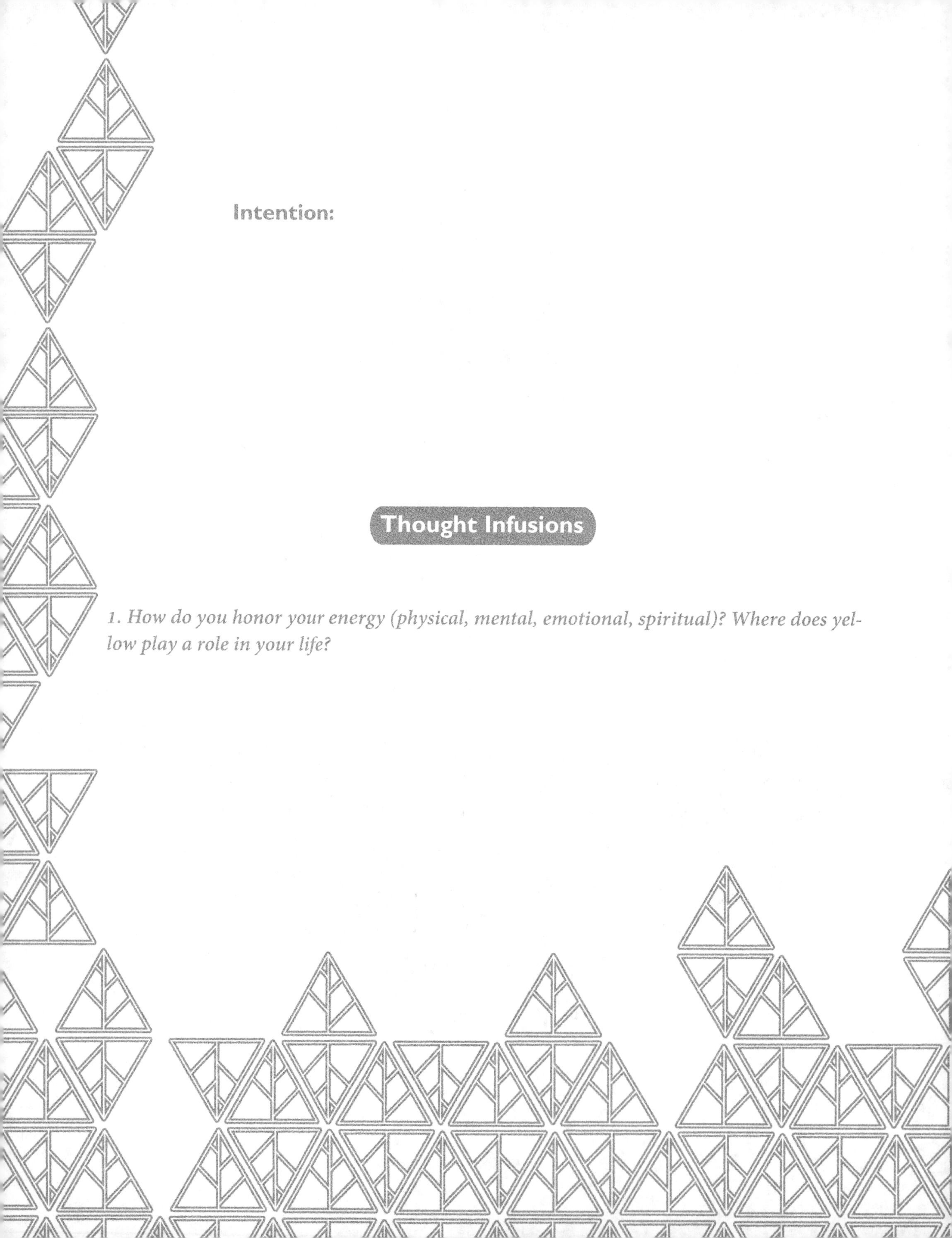

Intention:

Thought Infusions

1. How do you honor your energy (physical, mental, emotional, spiritual)? Where does yellow play a role in your life?

2. What affirmation best fits your needs right now? Think of the qualities of Maṇipūra—Life force: vitality, intentional and determined action, will power, self-esteem and confidence.

3. Just as our physical bodies are exposed to and accumulate contaminants and man-made exogenous compounds from our daily living and lifestyle habits, our energetic bodies accumulate negative energies. How frequently do you clean this key energy center? How can you establish a practice or ritual to let go of anything that affects its qualities (question 2)?

4. How do you acknowledge and nurture your personal power? Your will to act? Can you think of any barriers?

5. Contemplate your colored illustration. How does color change your initial perception of the image? What colors did you use? Look up #anewkindofcoloringbook and #puraprana, share your work. Explore other being's colors and see what new messages come to mind through observation.

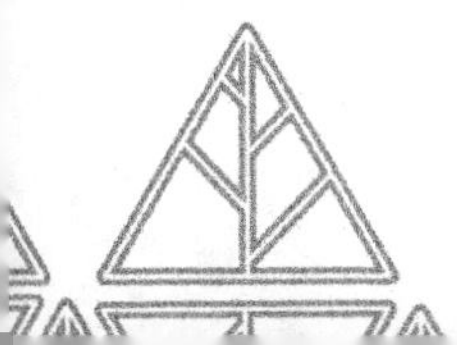

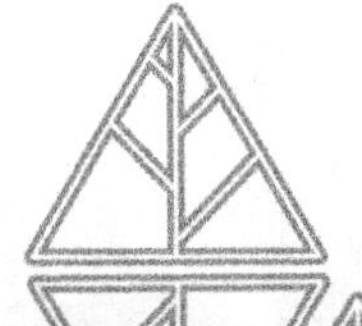

THE HUMAN ENERGY FIELD
"HEART CAKRA"

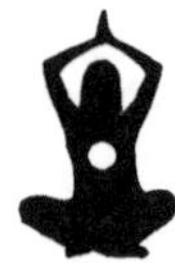

Sanskrit name | Anāhata (unstruck, unwounded, unbeaten)

Honors the heart | Heal with practicing gratitude, forgiveness and sincerity

Located at | Center of chest

Color, element, endocrine gland, finger | Green, air, thymus, index

Mantra | Yaṃ, bīja-mantra or "seed-mantra" for vāyu or "air" (page 46)

Affirmation | I love all, I am a being of compassion, I forgive, I release all fear, I am one

Herbs | Hawthorn and rose (illustrated), motherwort, nettle, lavender, hibiscus/sorrel, tulsi

Essential oils | Jasmine, vetiver, rose, Ylang Ylang, pine, coriander

Crystals | Emerald, pounamu, green garnet, serpentine, amazonite, rose quartz

Foods to find balance | So many to pick from! Avocado, kiwi, cabbage, leafy greens

Lesson | Relationships, the right to love

Mudrā | Abhaya hṛdaya (illustrated)

"Take time to feel the subtle frequencies in the fabric of the space time continuum."

- Vivia Astraia -

Symbol:
12 petal lotus

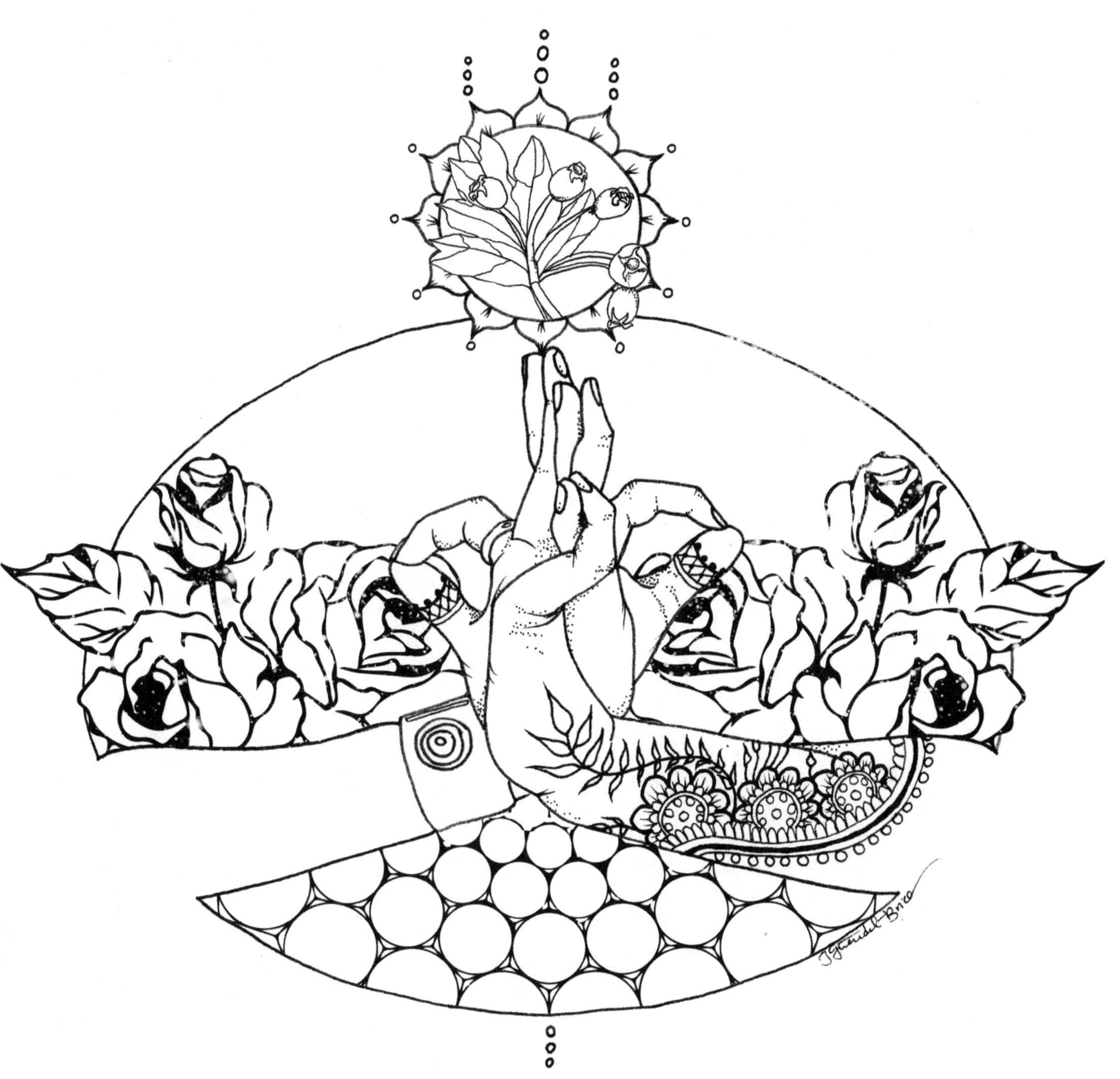

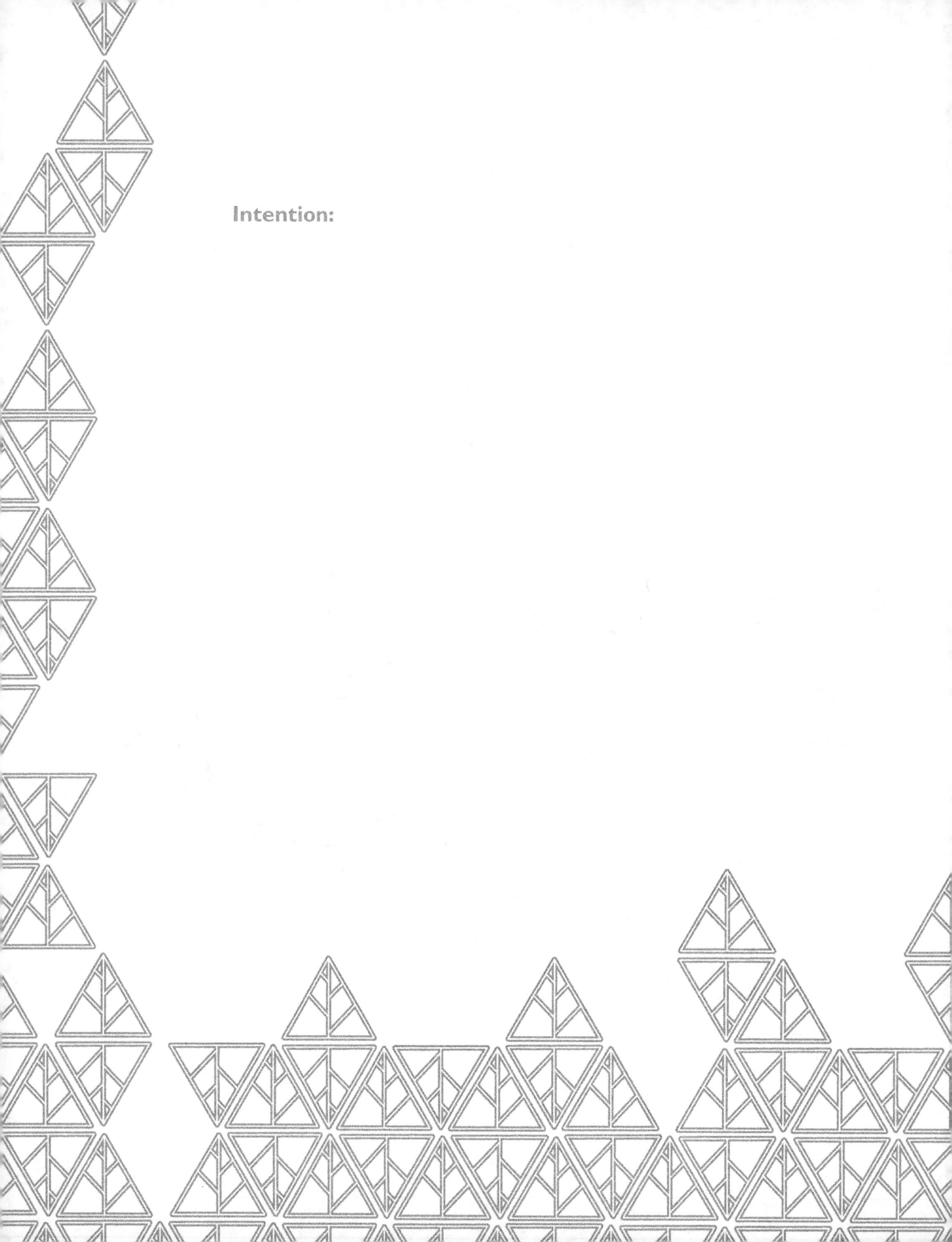

Intention:

Thought Infusions

1. How do you honor the heart? Where does green color play a role in your life?

2. What affirmation best fits your needs right now? Think of the qualities of Anāhata—Love: compassion, forgiveness, empathy, self-love (also intertwined with self-esteem and confidence).

3. How do you acknowledge and nurture your relationships and right to love/be loved? Can you think of any barriers?

4. Contemplate your colored illustration. How does color change your initial perception of the image? What colors did you use? Look up #anewkindofcoloringbook and #puraprana, share your work. Explore other being's colors and see what new messages come to mind through observation.

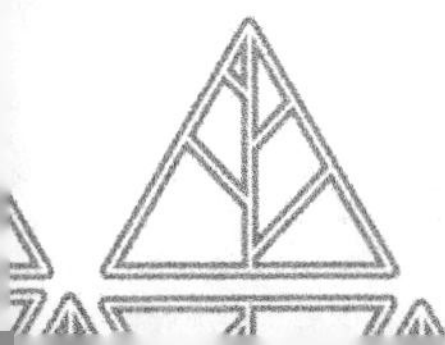

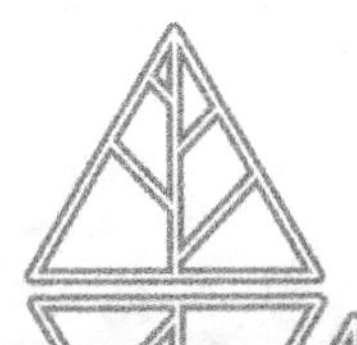

THE HUMAN ENERGY FIELD
"THROAT CAKRA"

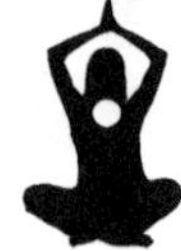

Sanskrit name | Viśuddha (complete purification)

Honors communication | Heal with affirmative vocal expression

Located at | Throat region

Color, element, endocrine gland, finger | Blue, ether, thyroid, middle

Mantra | Haṃ, bīja-mantra or "seed-mantra" for ākāśa or "ether, space" (page 46)

Affirmation | I am aligned with my highest truth and purpose,
I express and communicate with love and certainty

Herbs | Rosemary (illustrated), marshmallow, slippery elm, red clover, skullcap, sage

Essential oils | Nag Champa blend, Indian sandalwood, sage, rosemary, cedarwood

Crystals | Lapis lazuli, turquoise, blue lace agate, aquamarine, chrysocolla

Foods to find balance | Blueberries, kelp and kombu, mushrooms, wheatgrass

Lesson | Expression, the right to speak

Mudrā | Maṇḍala (illustrated)

"Understand the power of your spoken and unspoken words, they shape your daily reality. Live in mindfulness of your sound current and how you wield it."

- Iréne de Brice -

Symbol:
16 petal lotus

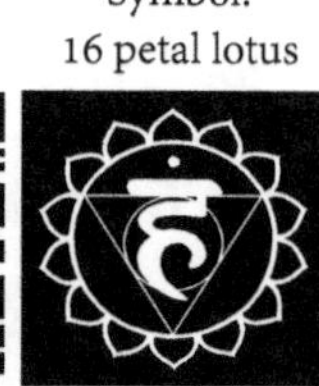

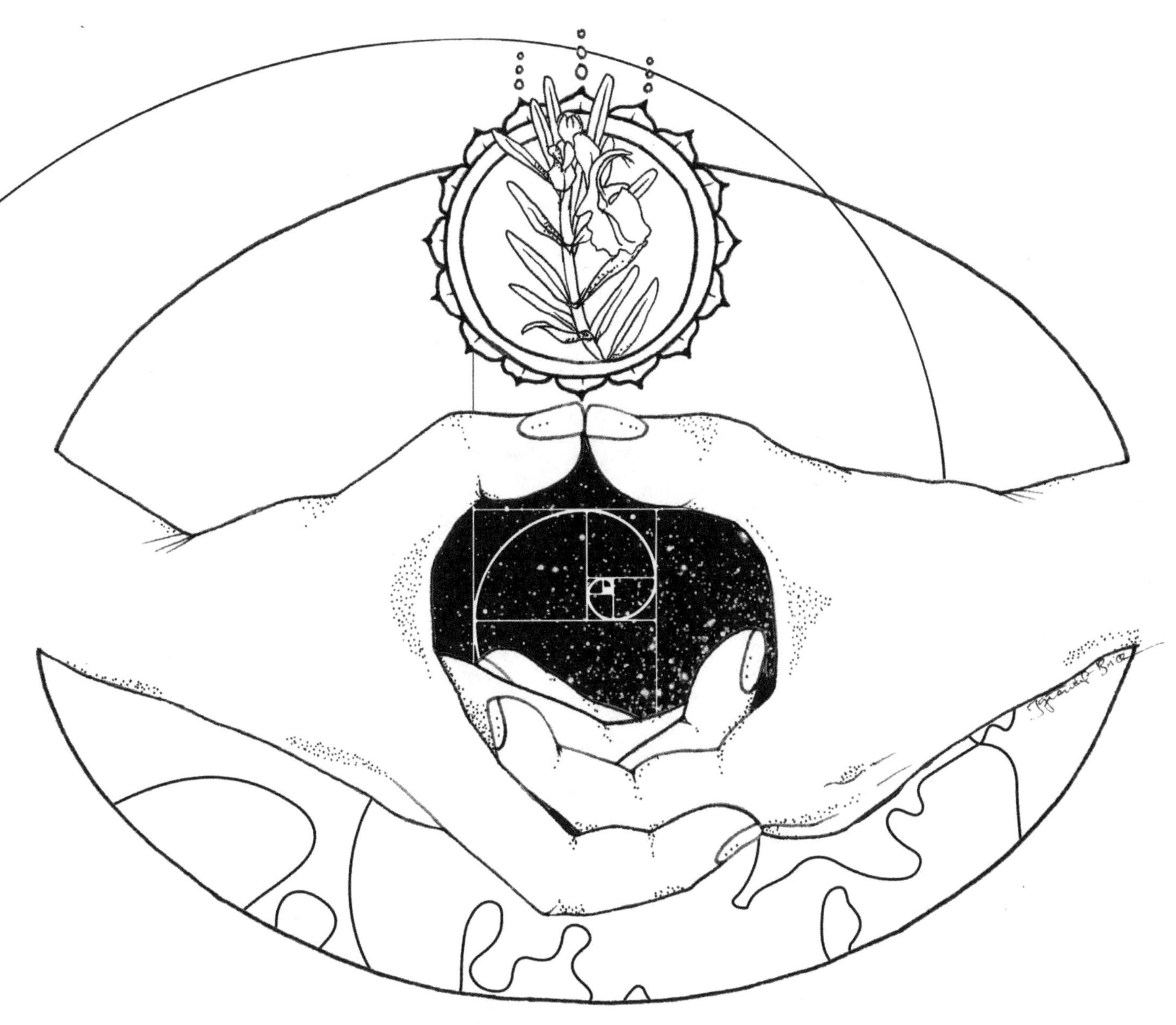

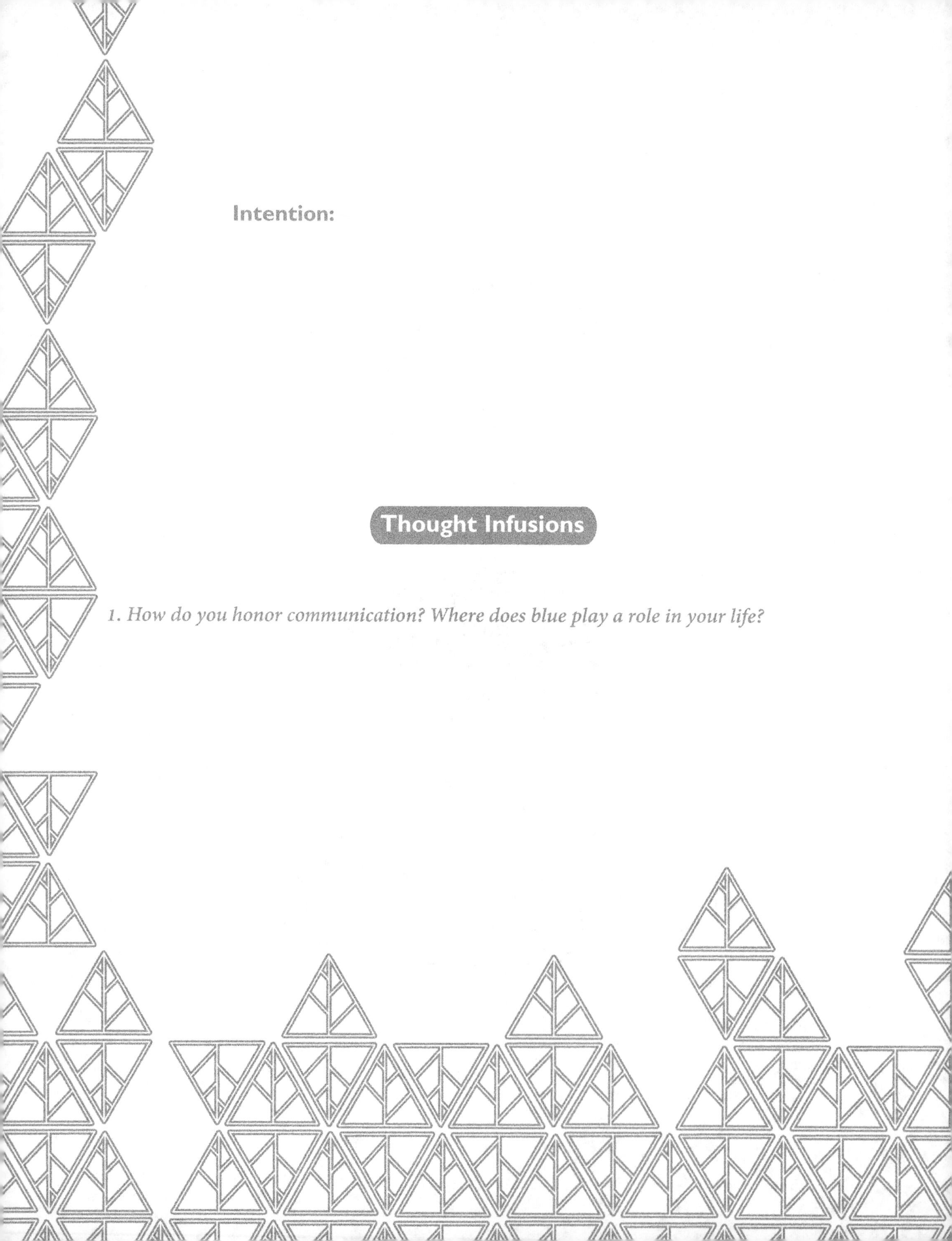

Intention:

Thought Infusions

1. *How do you honor communication? Where does blue play a role in your life?*

2. What affirmation best fits your needs right now? Think of the qualities of Viśuddha—Expression: connection, communication, expansion, projection of creativity, purification.

3. How do you acknowledge and nurture your expression and right to speak/be heard? Can you think of any barriers?

4. How do you use your hands when you communicate? How do your hands communicate your unique offerings and gifts to the world?

5. Contemplate your colored illustration. How does color change your initial perception of the image? What colors did you use? Look up #anewkindofcoloringbook and #puraprana, share your work. Explore other being's colors and see what new messages come to mind through observation.

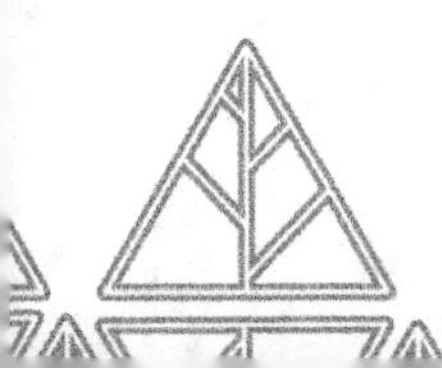

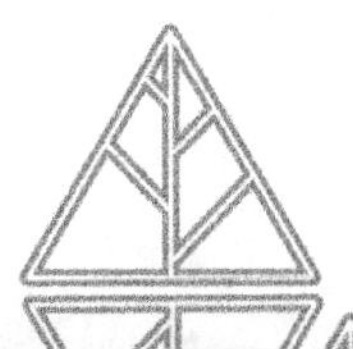

THE HUMAN ENERGY FIELD
"THIRD EYE CAKRA"

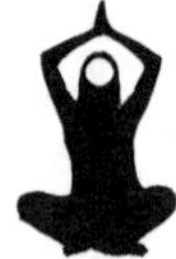

Sanskrit name | Ājñā (command, eye of intuition)

Honors the psychic | Connect with intuition, heal with meditation

Located at | Forehead, in between the eyes

Color, element, endocrine gland | Indigo, light, pituitary

Mantra | Auṃ, the most sacred mantra in Hinduism and Buddhism, "supreme sound"

Affirmation | I am healing, my life is Divinely guided,
I trust my intuition and inner wisdom, I see

Herbs | Jasmine (illustrated), mugwort, eyebright, rosemary, valerian, poppy seed, gingko

Essential oils | Jasmine, lavender, rosemary, geranium, basil, frankincense

Crystals | Kyanite, amethyst, iolite, azurite, lapis lazuli, stichtite

Foods to find balance | Blackberries, figs, eggplant, purple cabbage and kale, grapes

Lesson | Intuition, the right to see

Mudrā | Nāga (illustrated)

According to Carl Jung, active imagination is a tool for visualizing unconscious issues by letting them act themselves out.[19] Cultivate your eye of contemplation and create, as a meditation, to access the imaginal spaces for healing.

Symbol:
2 petal lotus

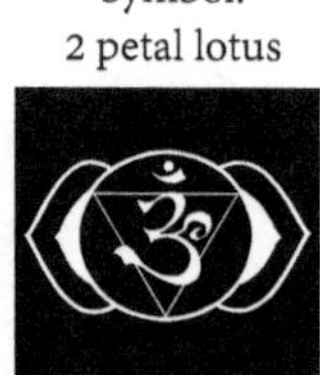

20. Anthony S. Jung: A Very Short Introduction. London, UK: Oxford University Press (2001)

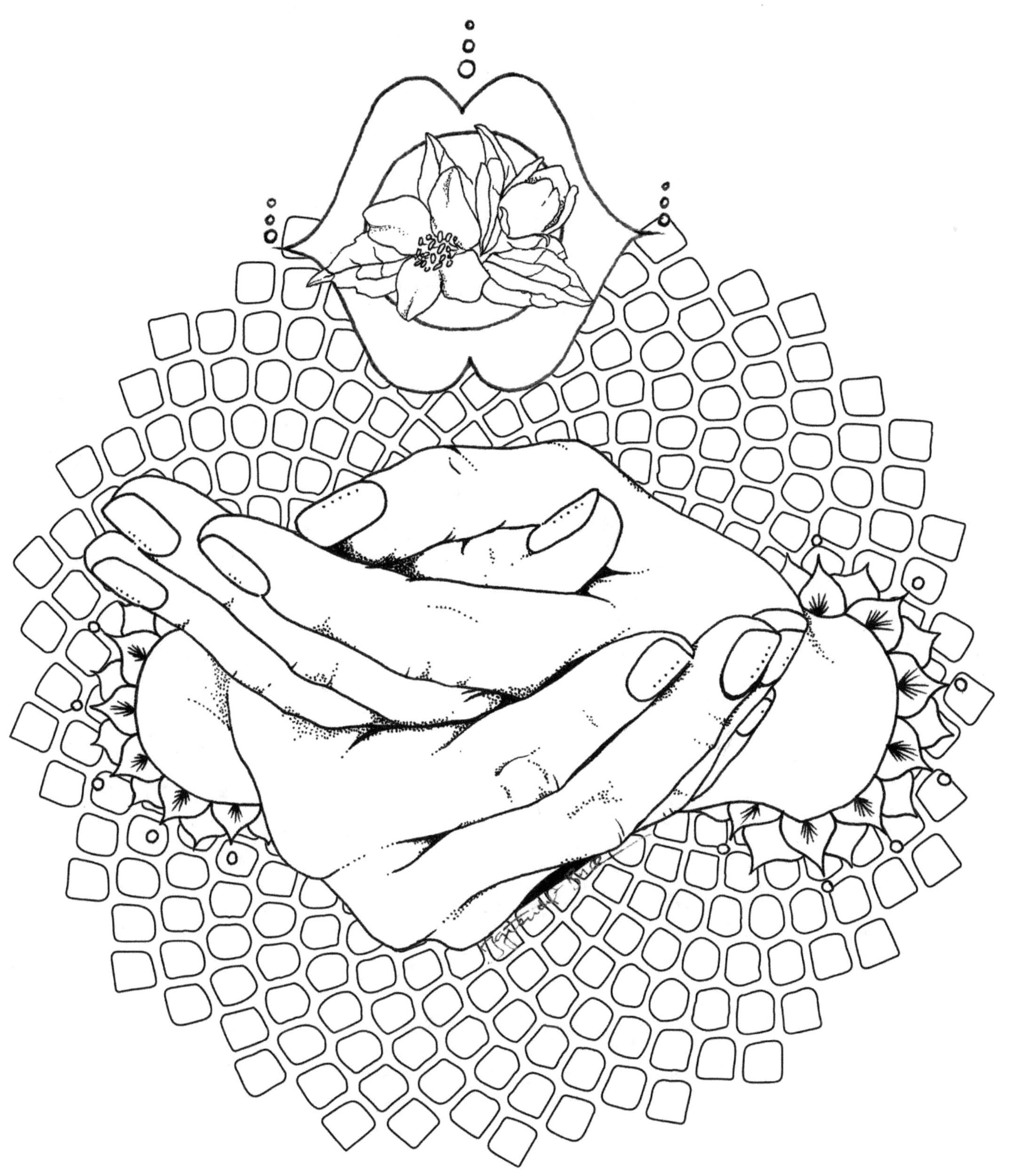

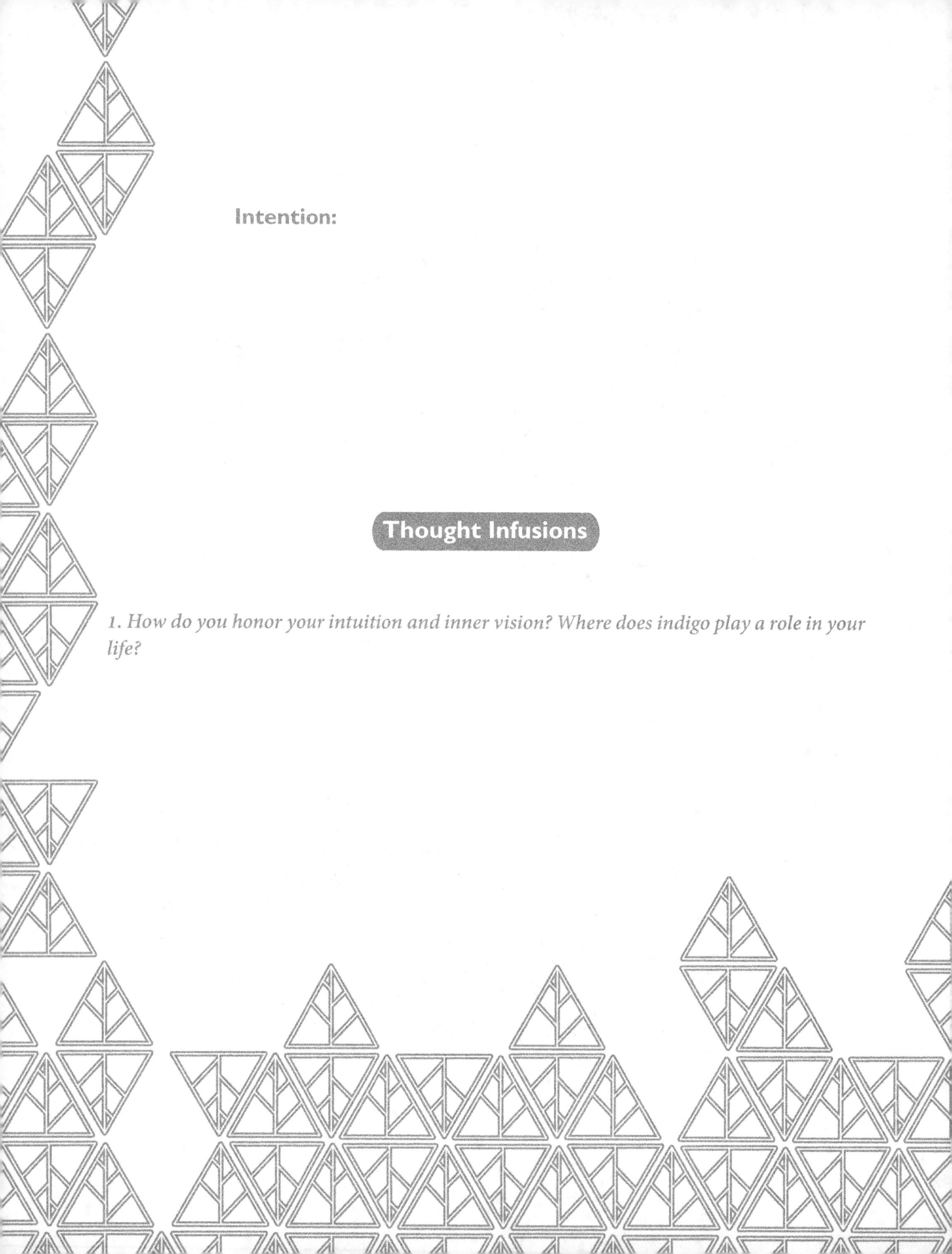

Intention:

Thought Infusions

1. How do you honor your intuition and inner vision? Where does indigo play a role in your life?

2. What affirmation best fits your needs right now? Think of the qualities of Ājñā—Vision: wisdom, intuition, clarity, discernment.

3. How do you acknowledge and nurture your right to travel inward? Can you think of any barriers?

4. Are your hands an open channel for you to experience and see the world?

5. Contemplate your colored illustration. How does color change your initial perception of the image? What colors did you use? Look up #anewkindofcoloringbook and #puraprana, share your work. Explore other being's colors and see what new messages come to mind through observation.

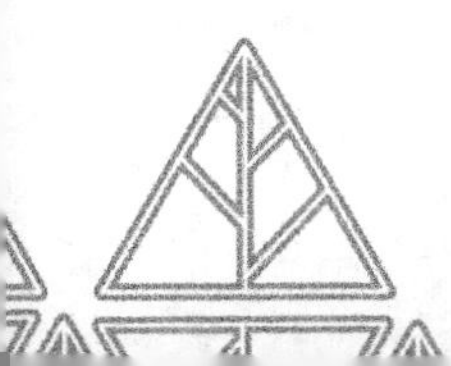

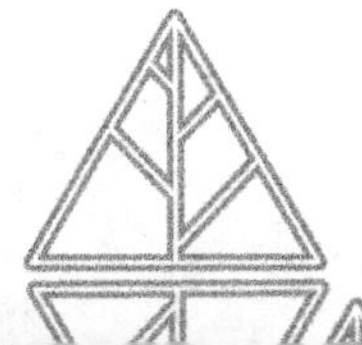

THE HUMAN ENERGY FIELD
"CROWN CAKRA"

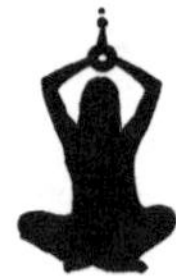

Sanskrit name | Sahasrāra (thousand, infinite, detachment from illusion)

Honors spiritual connectedness | Heal with your spiritual and sacred practices

Located at | Top of head

Color, element, endocrine gland | Violet and white (pure light), all elements, pineal

Mantra | Oṃ, the most sacred mantra in Hinduism and Buddhism, "primordial mantra"

Affirmation | I honor the spirit within me and all things, I invite unity and transformation, I am complete and one with the Great Spirit

Herbs | Gotu kola (illustrated), tulsi, lavender, jasmine, gingko, ginseng

Essential oils | Rose, myrrh, jasmine, sandalwood, frankincense, lavender

Crystals | Amethyst, obsidian, selenite, sugilite, clear quartz

Foods to find balance | Prayer, meditation, and fasting

Lesson | Knowingness and awareness, the right to know and aspire

Mudrā | Bhumisparsha (illustrated)

"Ascend. Vibe. Connect, with future manifest."

- Vivia Astraia -

Symbol:
1,000 petal lotus

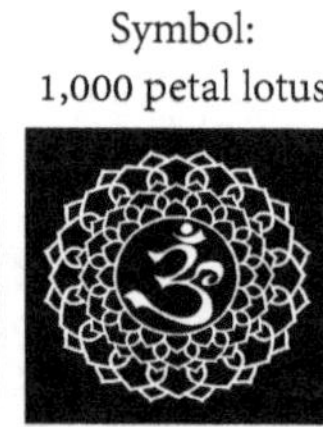

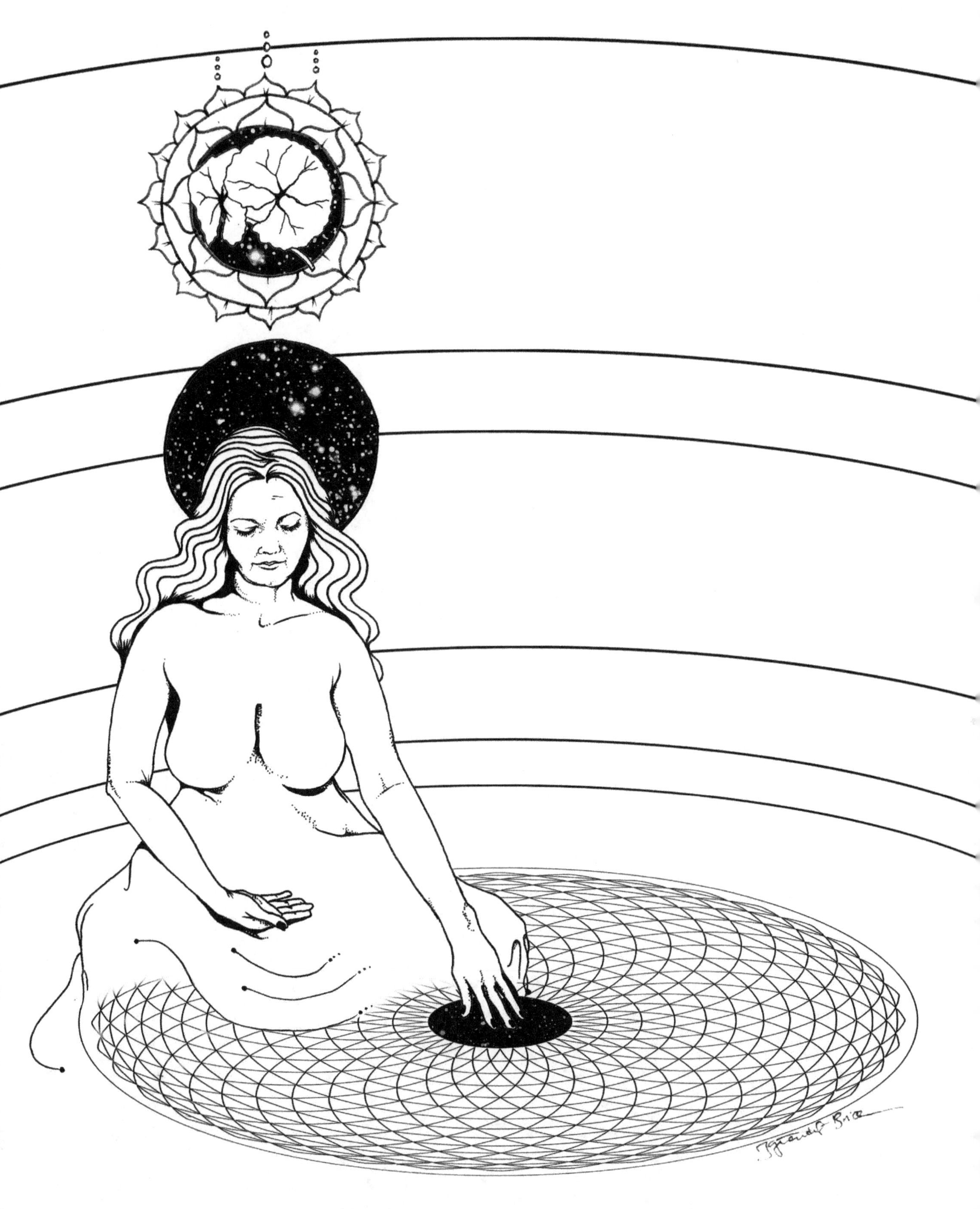

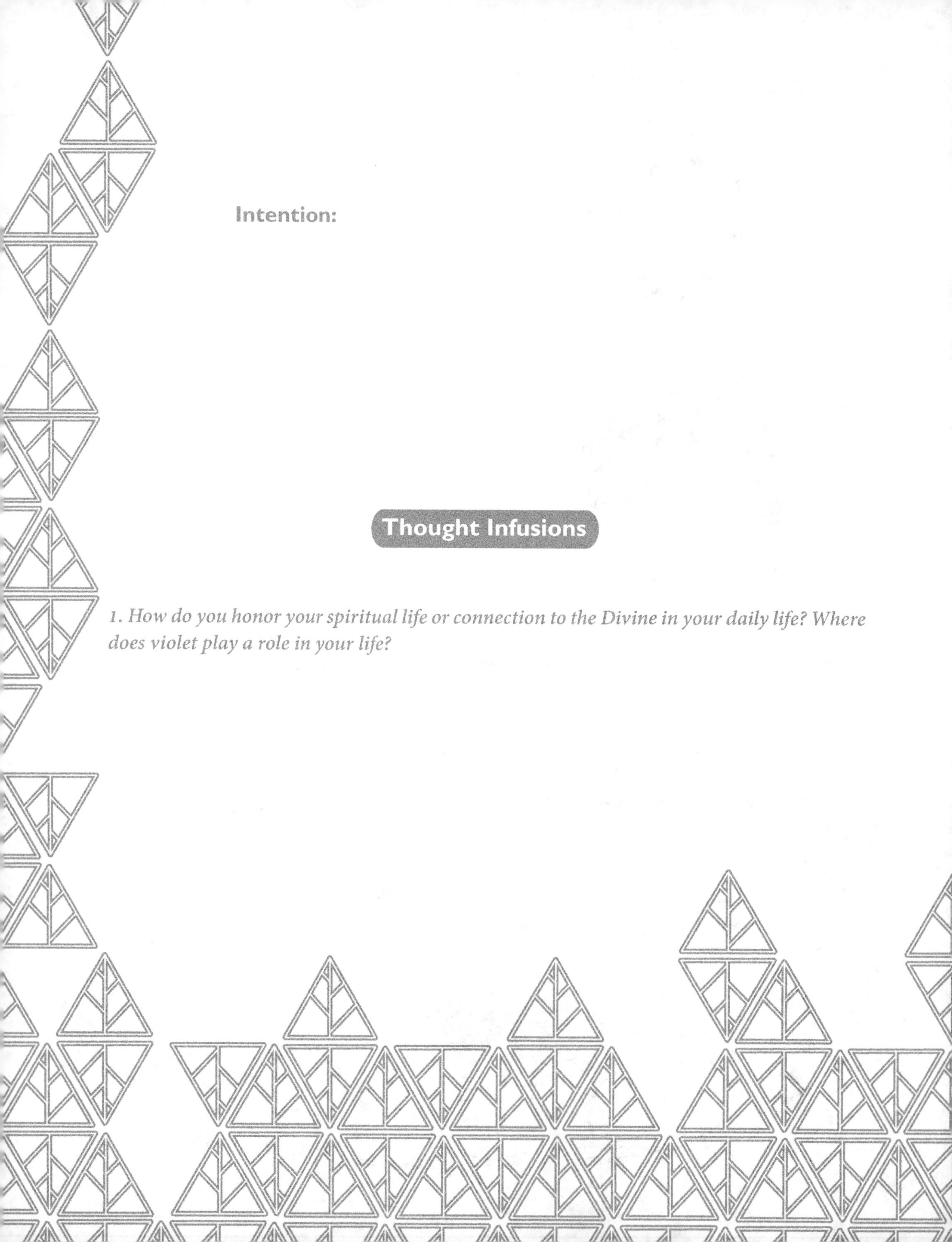

Intention:

Thought Infusions

1. How do you honor your spiritual life or connection to the Divine in your daily life? Where does violet play a role in your life?

2. What affirmation best fits your needs right now? Think of the qualities of Sahasrāra—Universal and transcendental awareness: wisdom and illumination, self-knowledge, unity, devotion, happiness.

3. How do you acknowledge and nurture your awareness, knowingness, and aspirations? What about your right to know? Can you think of any barriers?

4. Do you feel your connection to the Web of Life? What steps can you take to improve that primal connection of awareness?

5. Contemplate your colored illustration. How does color change your initial perception of the image? What colors did you use? Look up #anewkindofcoloringbook and #puraprana, share your work. Explore other being's colors and see what new messages come to mind through observation.

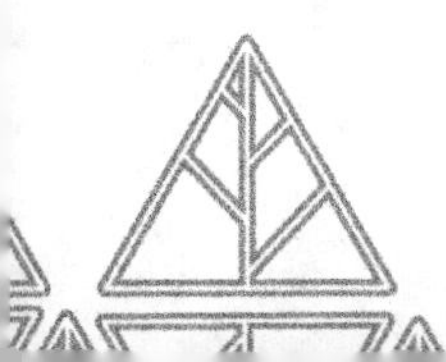

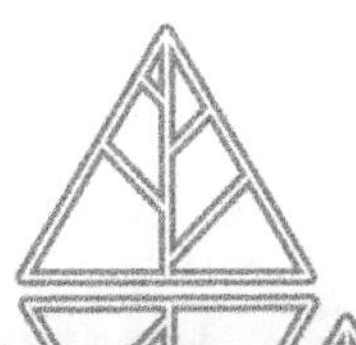

DISPEL ALL FEAR

Abhaya transliterates from Sanskrit to "fearlessness." The abhaya mudrā is one of the earliest mudrās found represented in spiritual imagery of deities, sages, and saints. As the "seal of fearlessness," it is a symbol for benevolence, protection, blessings, and the dispelling of fear.[8,21-22]

Abhaya mudrā is also depicted in *The Elements* illustration (page 47), as it represents the five elements "(...) resting in their natural relationship, with the center of the palm as the *bindu*, or central point of focus."[21]

How | There are several iterations of this mudrā. As illustrated, raise your right hand to chest level with the palm facing outward and fingers toward the sky. Join the right hand with left hand, palm facing inward and fingers facing to the earth.

Benefits | Helps to reduce anxiety and overcome inner conflict, overcome fear, attain inner equilibrium and calmness. It is also grounding and supports the qualities of the first energy center (root cakra), including improved elimination.

Time and space,
sacred place.
Sanctuary is in the heart.

- Vivia Astraia -

21. Carroll C, Carroll R. Mudras of India: A Comprehensive Guide to the Hand Gestures of Yoga and Indian Dance. London, UK: Singing Dragon (2012)
22. Hirschi G. Mudras: Yoga in Your Hands. Newburyport, MA, US: Weiser Books (2016)

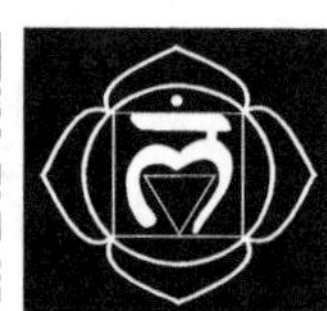

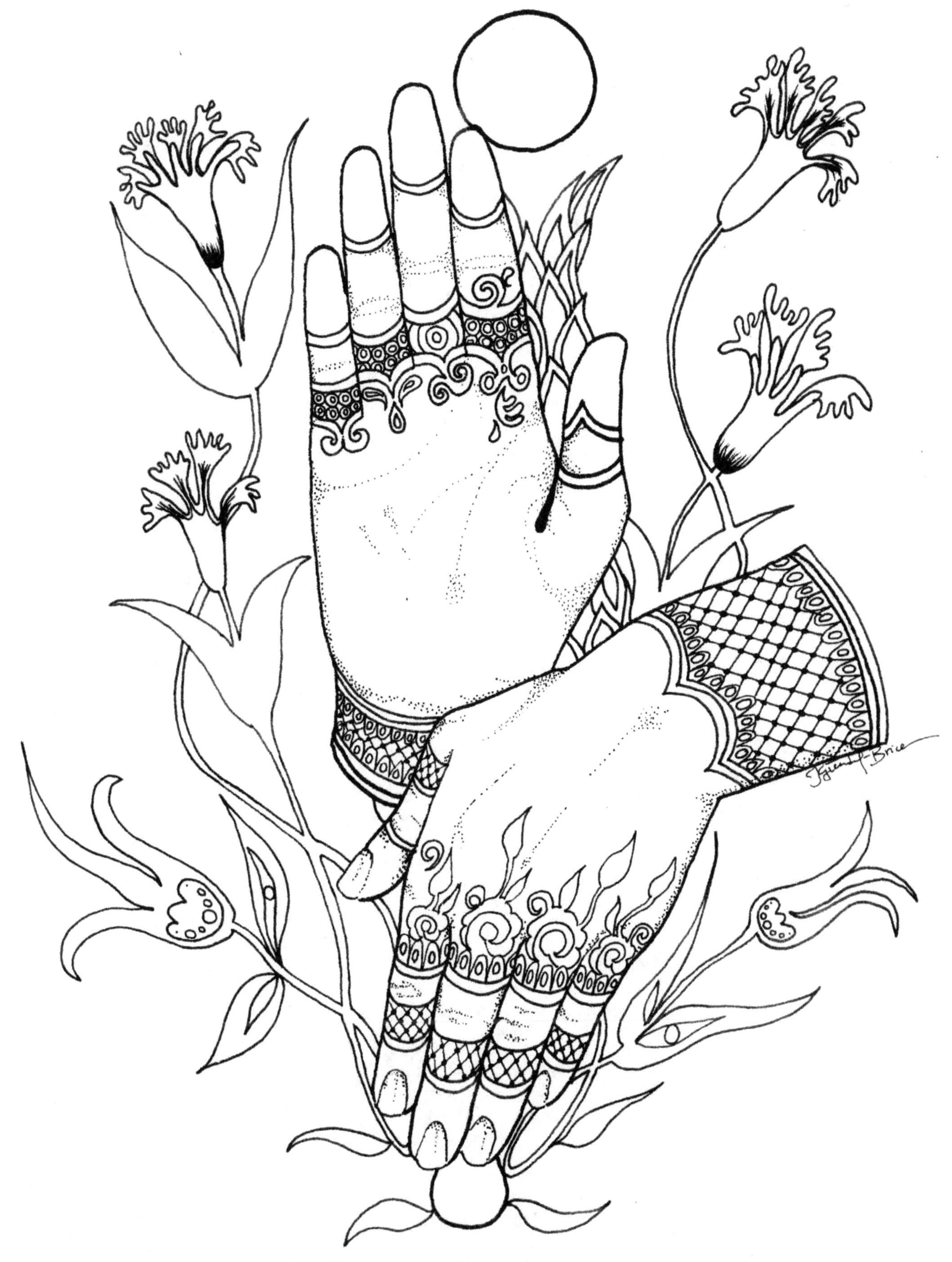

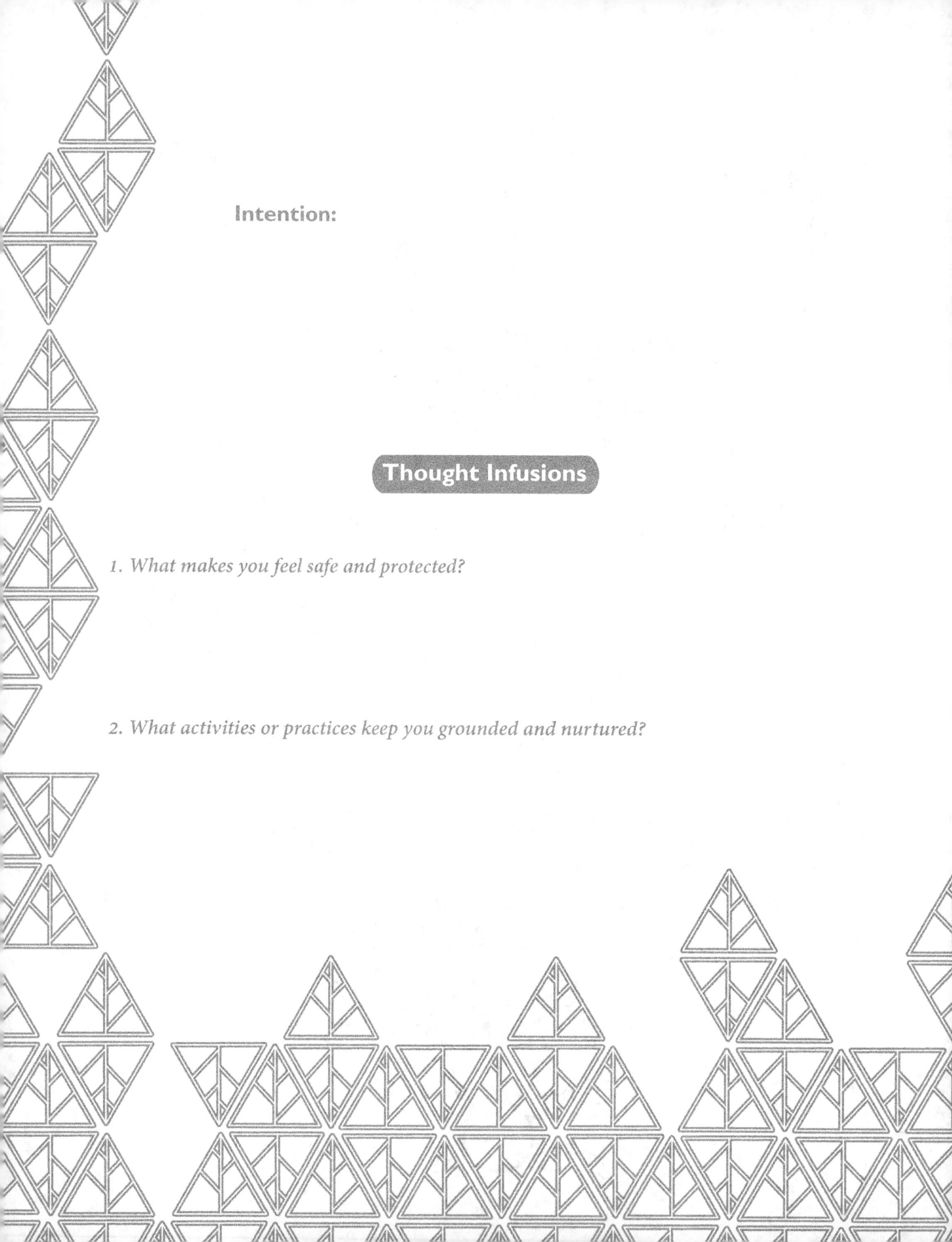

Intention:

Thought Infusions

1. *What makes you feel safe and protected?*

2. *What activities or practices keep you grounded and nurtured?*

3. What triggers your anxiety or inner conflict, if any at all? How can you better react to those triggers?

4. How do you acknowledge your many blessings? How can you start focusing on talking less about what is going wrong, and more about all the good things in your life?

5. If you choose to practice this mudrā see how you feel regarding your fears before, during, and after practice. Can you imagine how it would feel if you could dispel all your fears by just the power of your intention?

6. Contemplate your colored illustration. How does color change your initial perception of the image? What colors did you use? Look up #anewkindofcoloringbook and #puraprana, share your work. Explore other being's colors and see what new messages come to mind through observation.

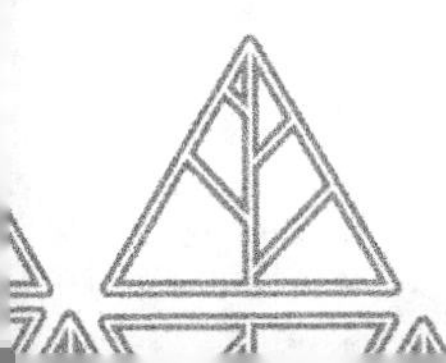

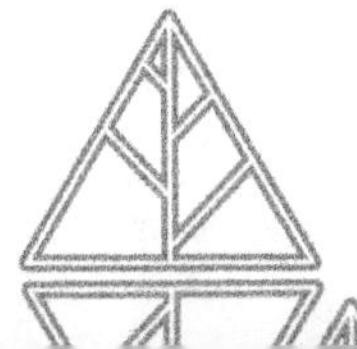

TRUST AND SURRENDER

Praṇidhāna transliterates from Sanskrit as "surrender." Trusting and surrendering is an act of faith, for any belief system. Praṇidhāna mudrā deals with surrendering attachments and limiting beliefs that function as an obstacle to leading a life of ease and flow.

Hummingbirds exist as the *Trochilidae* family, with more than 330 species.[23] They are mainly found within ten degrees latitude north and south of the Equator, and only in the Western Hemisphere. Hummingbirds were and remain sacred to many indigenous peoples of the pre-Columbian and current Americas, and include for example, the 300-foot (~91 meters) long hummingbird drawing of the Nazca civilization in Perú.[24] Spiritual symbolism includes love, joy, happiness, lightness, agility and adaptability, and balance. Likewise, the geometric pattern included can be observed in nature in flower petals (e.g., sunflower) and pine cones. Geometry itself is considered sacred in many cultures, and it is now understood that everything from protein surface roughness to geophysics, physics, leaves, and water; is fractal in nature.[25]

How | Index and little finger pads touch lightly. Touch the ring and middle finger pads to the thumbs. Once in position, stretch and spread the index and little fingers. Feel the expansion. Actively hold this gesture below your navel, or rest the wrists on your thighs.

Benefits[26] | When paired with breath work, it helps to move energy into the pelvis, grounding and sustaining the qualities of the root cakra, including improved elimination and reproductive system support. It reduces tension and stress, while cultivating deep relaxation, inner peace, and acceptance.

Let go,
and
let God.

- Albert E. Cliffe -

23. Bleiweiss R. ***Biol J Linn Soc Lond.*** 65(1): 63–76 (1998)
24. Larson J, Yorinks A. Hummingbirds: Facts and Folklore from the Americas. Watertown, MA, US: Charlesbridge (2011)
25. Simeonov PL. ***Prog Biophys Mol Biol.*** 119(3):271-87 (2015).
26. Le Page J, Le Page L. Mudras for Healing and Transformation. Sebastopol, CA, US: Integrative Yoga Therapy (2014)

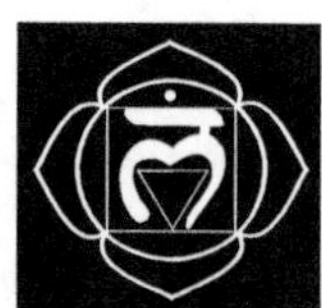

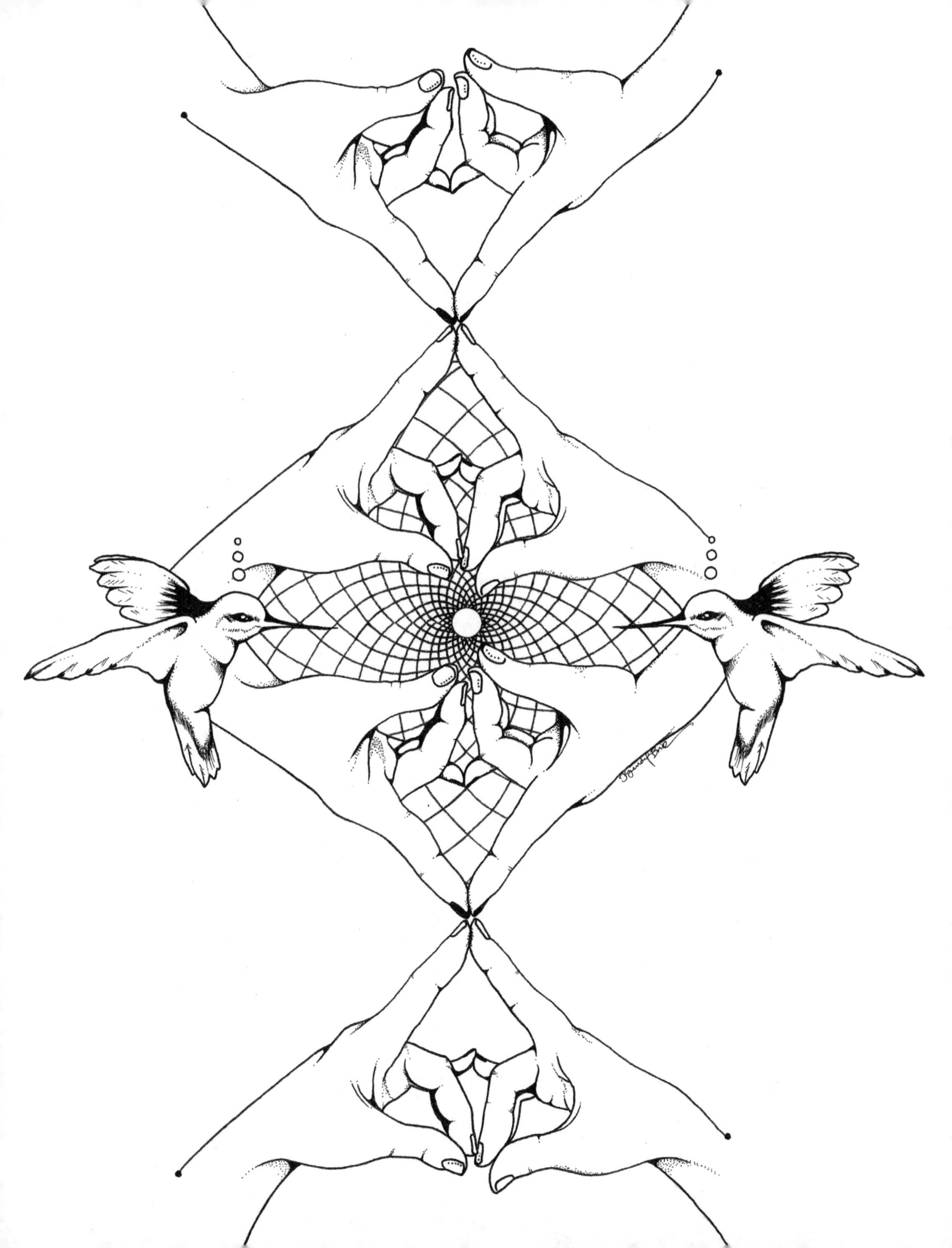

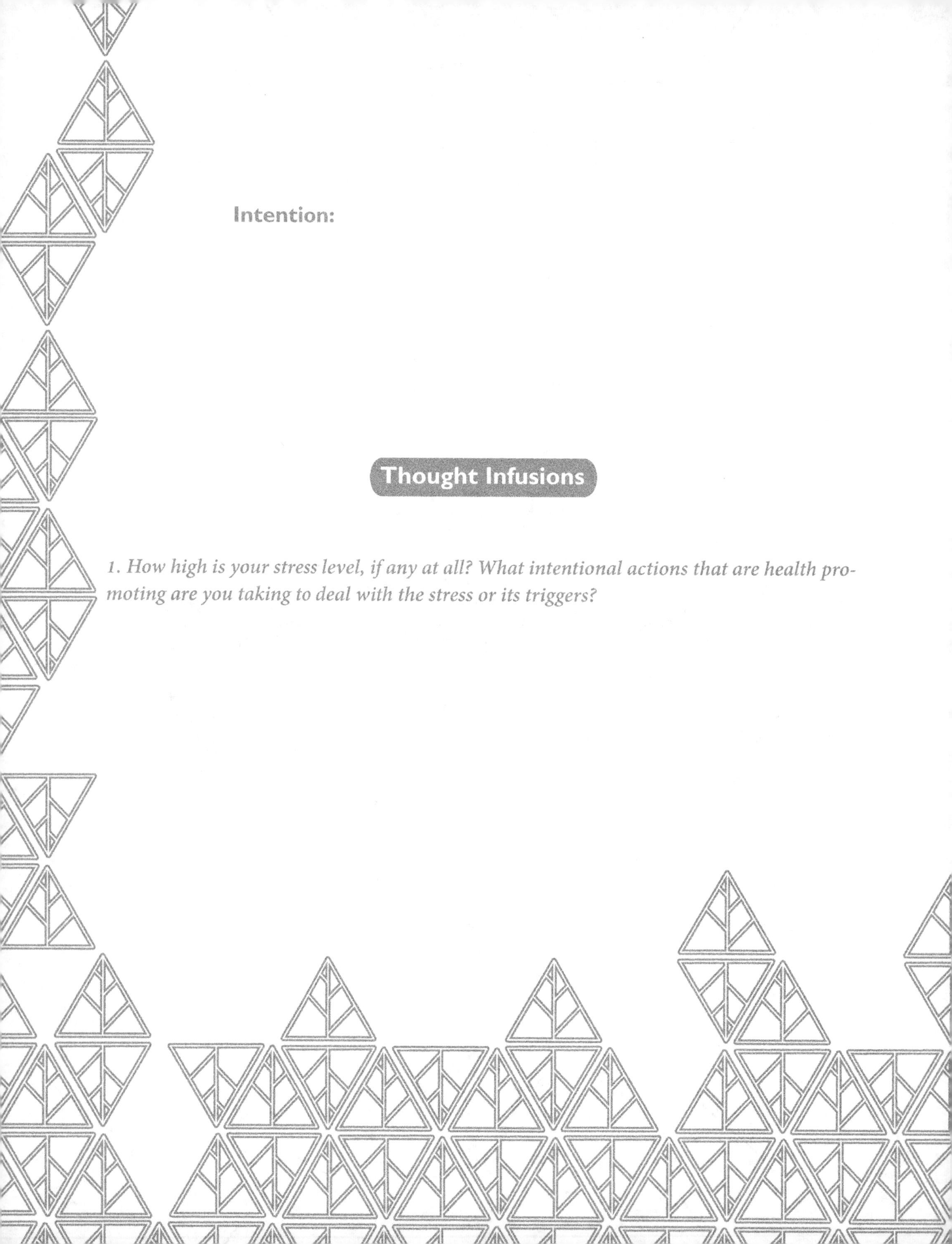

Intention:

Thought Infusions

1. How high is your stress level, if any at all? What intentional actions that are health promoting are you taking to deal with the stress or its triggers?

2. How do you cultivate deep relaxation?

3. What things do you need to surrender to let go and let God?

4. How does surrendering, trust, and acceptance translate into your belief system?

5. When you trust and surrender from your heart, can you see how a path is created for your highest good?

6. Contemplate your colored illustration. How does color change your initial perception of the image? What colors did you use? Look up #anewkindofcoloringbook and #puraprana, share your work. Explore other being's colors and see what new messages come to mind through observation.

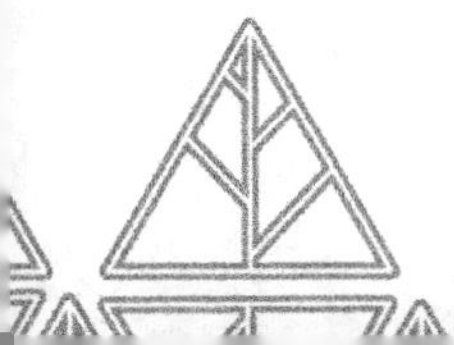

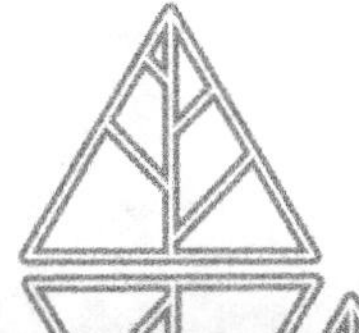

EARTHING

Apāna transliterates from Sanskrit as "downward moving force." Apāna mudrā is used in yogic science to direct the downward flow of energy to the root cakra which rules elimination and purification. It helps to balance the elements of space (middle finger) and earth (ring finger) within the body.[8, 22] *Earthing* occurs when we unplug and reconnect with nature and the cosmos, it's generally practiced by having direct skin contact with the earth, grass, trees, and fresh and salt water. In this illustration, a woman lays on a tree while meditating and holding apāna mudrā. She uses this time to establish a connection with nature, absorbing all the vibrancy from the rainforest surrounding her. Forest bathing or *shinrin-yoku* (森林浴 in Japanese),[27] is one way of Earthing. A significant number of peer-reviewed studies* have shown positive psychological, physiological, immunological, and neurological effects on the human body. A collection of variables may contribute to the health-promoting effects of this practice including humidity, temperature, oxygen concentration, and *phytoncides*, among others. Phytoncides are variable and forest-specific chemical compounds produced by plants that are primarily olfaction-related elements of the forest environment.[27-28] Nature experiences and their impact on human health and well-being include sensory and non-sensory factors, and modern science is taking a closer look at the dynamics at play.[28]

How | Join the tips of the thumb, middle finger, and ring finger. Extend remaining fingers.

Benefits | Has balancing effect on the mind, brings sense of serenity, supports purification and detoxification, supports vision development for new beginnings. Grounds the spirit.

My father explained this to me.
All things in this world, he said, have souls or spirits.
The sky has a spirit;
the clouds have spirits;
the sun and the moon have spirits;
the trees, grass, water, stones, *everything*.

- Edward Goodbird (Hidatsa, from autonym *Hiraacá* or *People of the Willow*) -

27. Tsunetsugu Y, *et al.* ***Environ Health Prev Med.*** 15:27–37 (2010)
28. Franco LS, *et al.* ***Int J Environ Res Public Health.*** 14(8). pii: E864 (2017)
* Refer to page 18 to read more about using PMC as a source of peer-reviewed publications, do a "forest bathing" search to access topic-related articles.

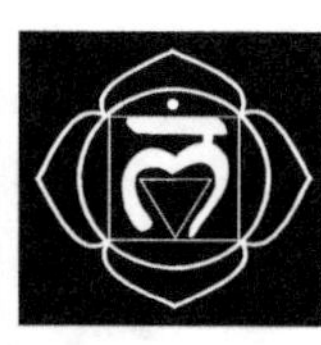

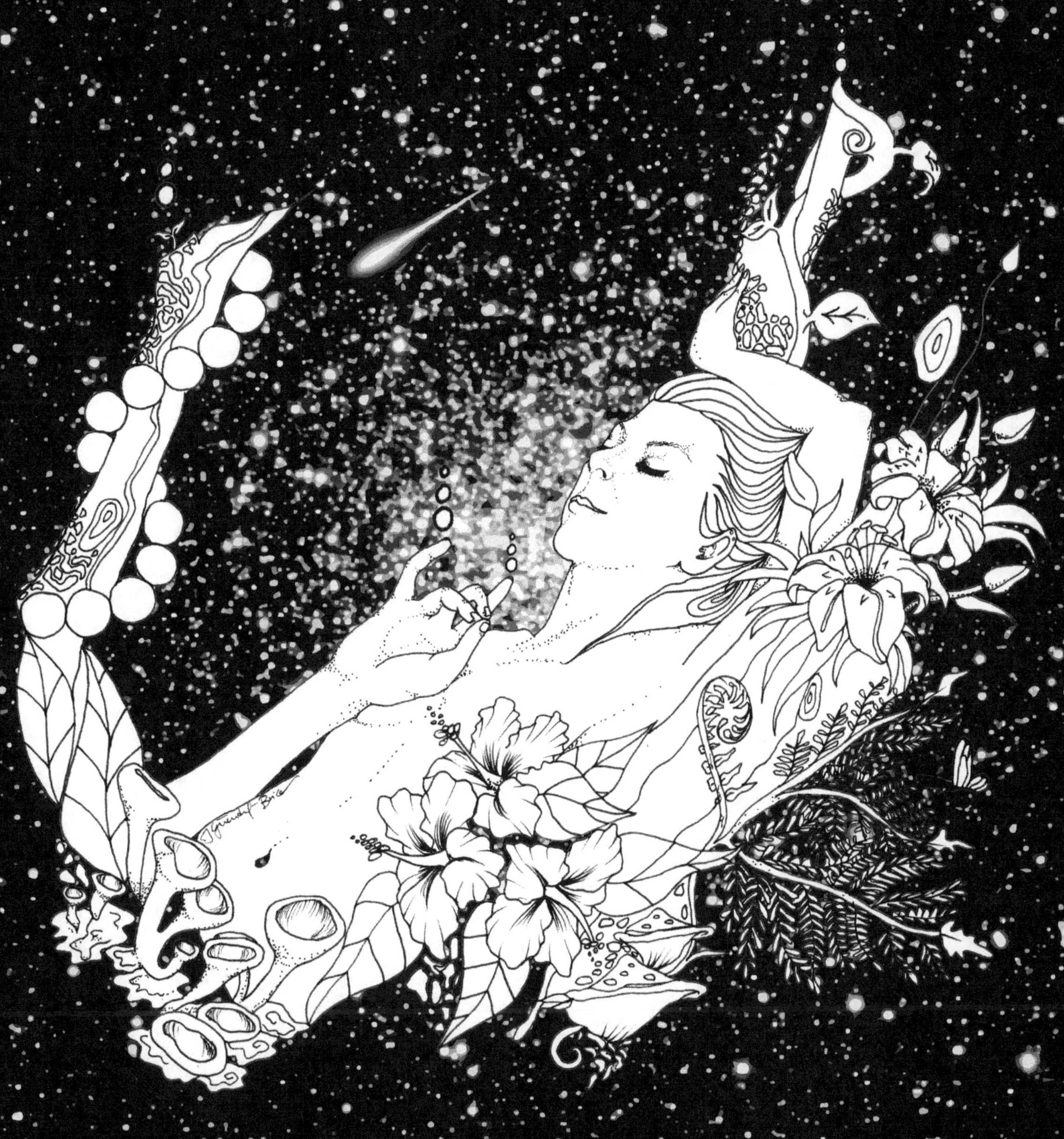

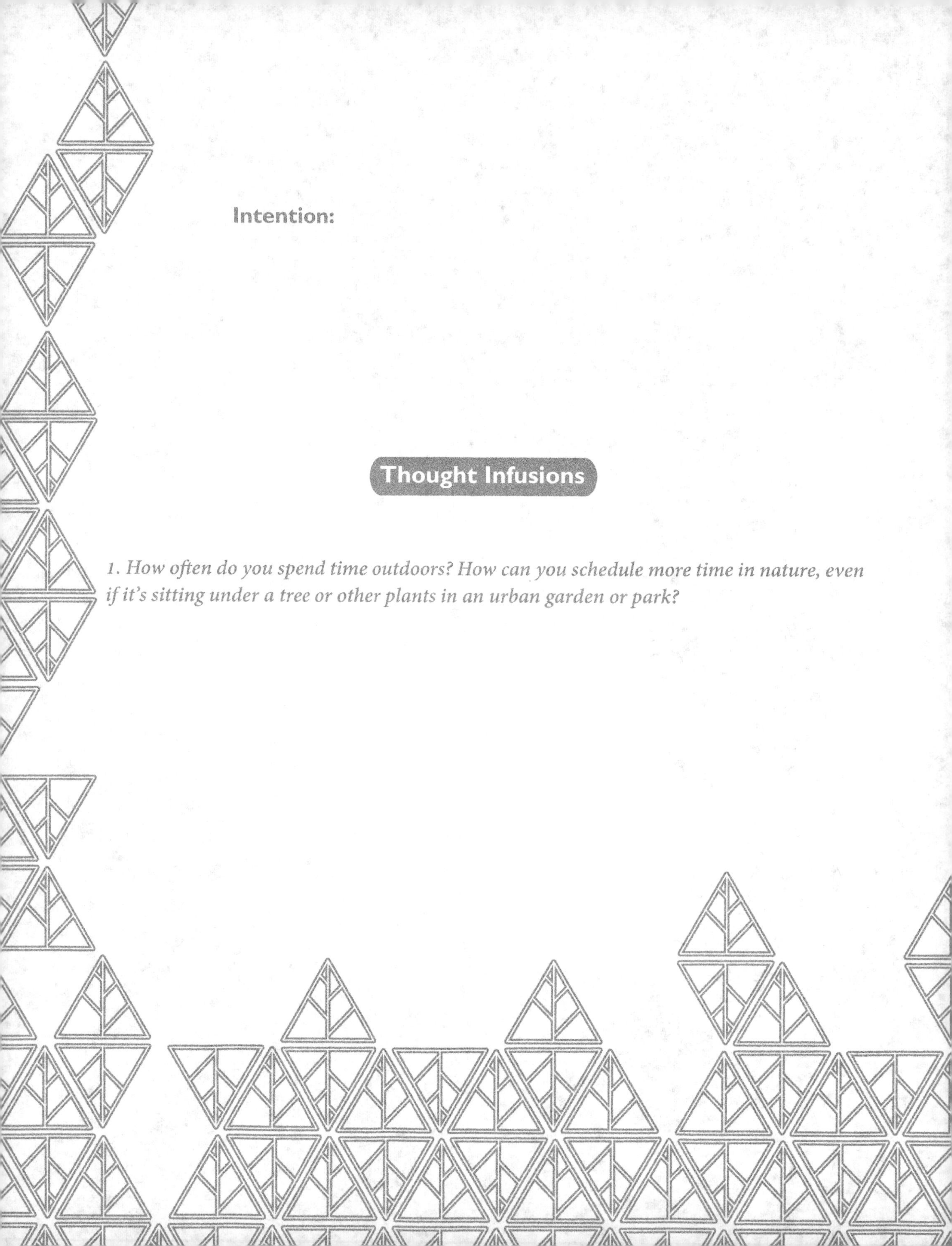

Intention:

Thought Infusions

1. *How often do you spend time outdoors? How can you schedule more time in nature, even if it's sitting under a tree or other plants in an urban garden or park?*

2. Think about your daily routine, how often do you really come into your body? Are you more in your mind? Let's see, observe yourself.

3. What other contemplative practices can help you balance your mind while grounding?

4. What new beginnings require your vision right now? How can you maximize your energy to see them through?

5. Contemplate your colored illustration. How does color change your initial perception of the image? What colors did you use? Look up #anewkindofcoloringbook and #puraprana, share your work. Explore other being's colors and see what new messages come to mind through observation.

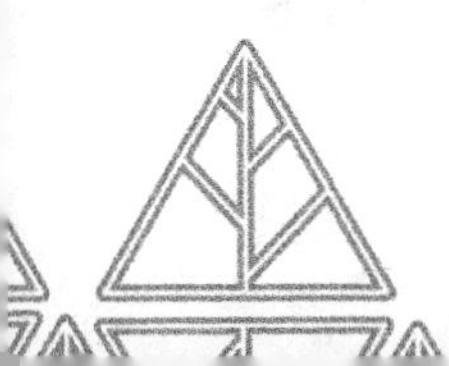

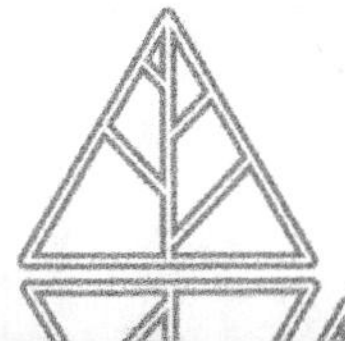

BREATHE

Mīra transliterates from Sanskrit to "ocean." In accordance with the qualities of flow and fluidity of the sacral cakra, mīra mudrā as its literal meaning, promotes the ease of movement of the sea. This flow translates to breathing as well, the easeful movement of air as we inhale and exhale every waking minute (the respiration rate for a normal adult at rest, ranges from ~12-20 breaths per minute). As we have discussed, proper breathing and breathing techniques are pivotal in the yogic tradition—as they should be in all our ways of life. The first thing we did when we were born was to breathe, and death will happen when our breath stops. There is autonomous breathing and then there is breath awareness and control. When we are aware of our emotions and mind-body-spirit, we're able to practice controlled breathing to improve our state of mind and well-being. *How will you use your breath to live your fullest, most vital, life?*

How | Join the tips of the little fingers and thumb pads, followed by joining the tips of the ring fingers. Extend the middle and index fingers. Hold or rest hands below navel.

Benefits | Helps balance the flow of breath and the flow of life. It influences both the root and sacral cakras, directing breath energy to the pelvis and abdominal areas,[26] grounding but flowing. Increases harmony and serenity, and helps release tension, worries, and emotions. Supports elimination and reproductive systems.

"Moments of reflection
rising with each breath.
A meditative rest of clarity,
a focus of mind
in this present time and space.
Allowing a thought to rise and dissolve...
a release of an expectation no longer to hold.
Exhaling attachments that no longer serve.
Letting go of the past as light fills our heart.

- Louisa Wargo (Lotus Rising) -

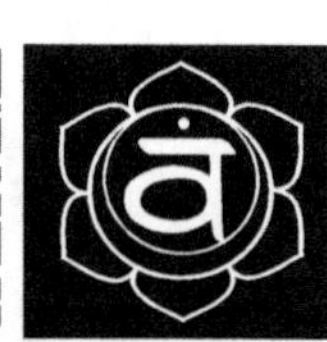

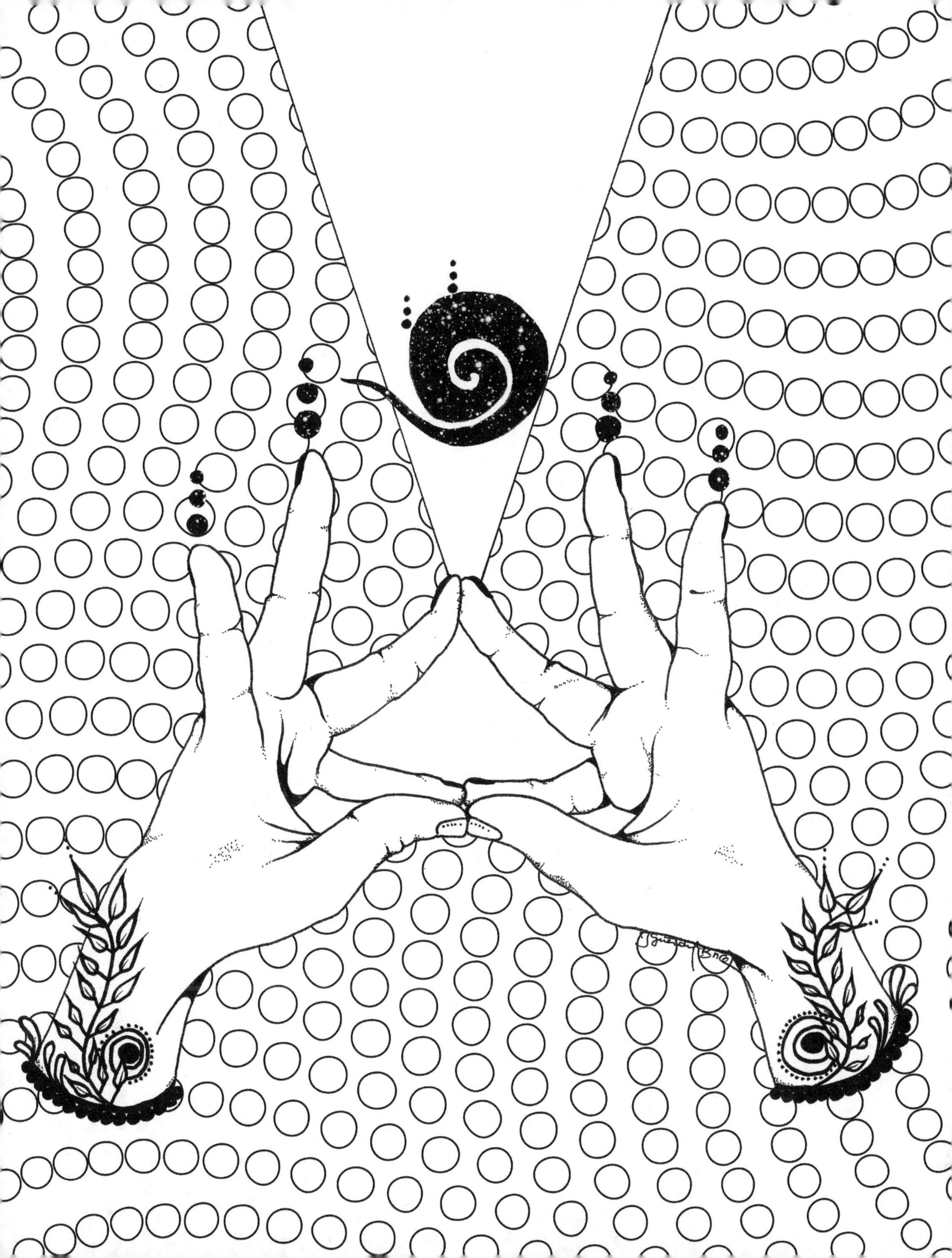

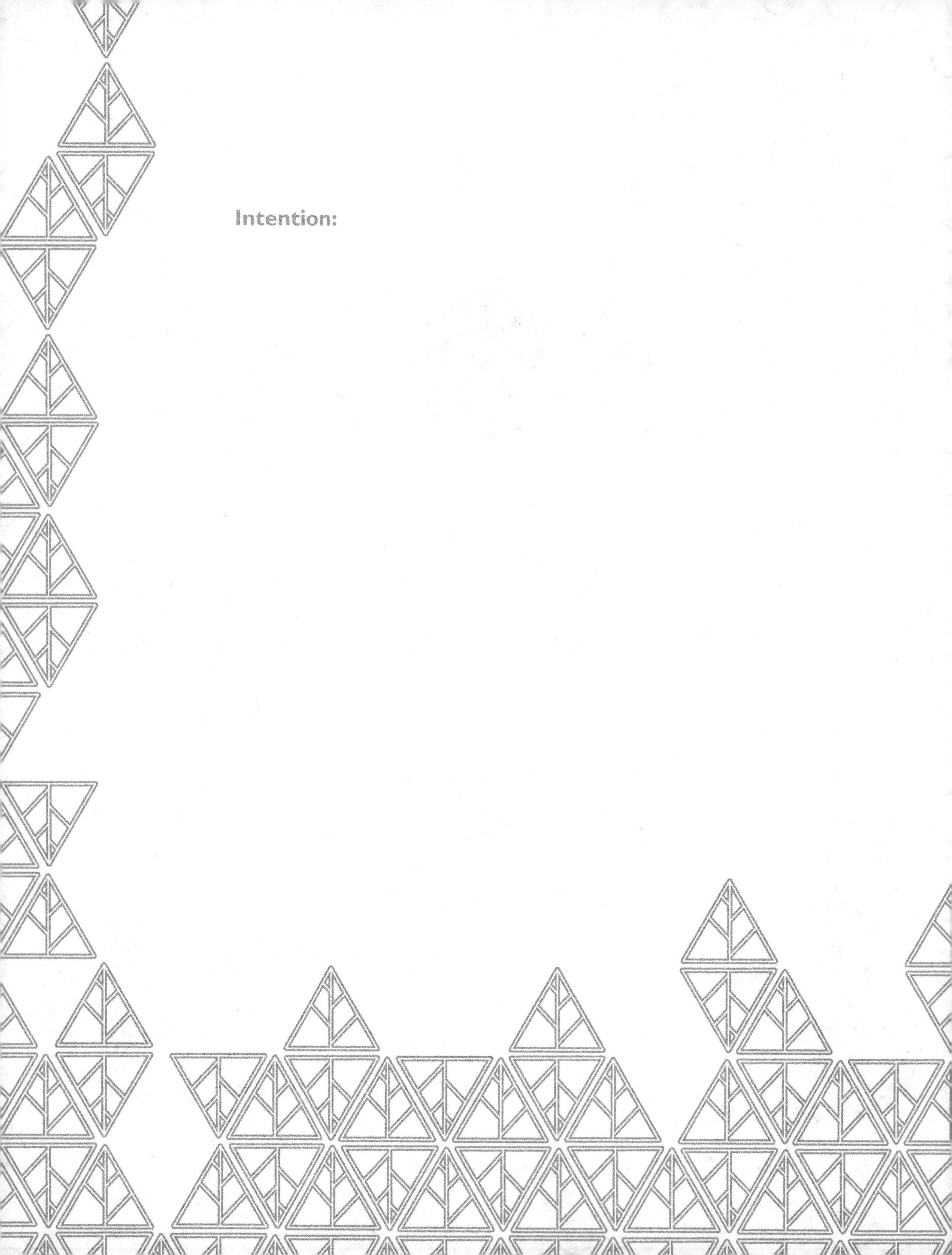

Intention:

Thought Infusions

1. For at least one day, monitor your breathing during your day. Does it change when you are driving? When you're at work? When you're in a meeting? When you're doing an activity you enjoy? Do you sigh when you are frustrated or overwhelmed? Think about how breathing is very much linked to emotions and actions.

2. Think of the vital nourishment breathing brings to your body. Take a deep breath and focus on gratitude. What words come to mind as you take that deep breath?

3. What lifestyle changes could you take to improve your respiratory and cardiovascular system health?

4. Contemplate your colored illustration. How does color change your initial perception of the image? What colors did you use? Look up #anewkindofcoloringbook and #puraprana, share your work. Explore other being's colors and see what new messages come to mind through observation.

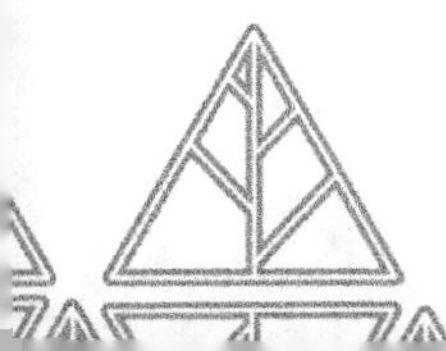

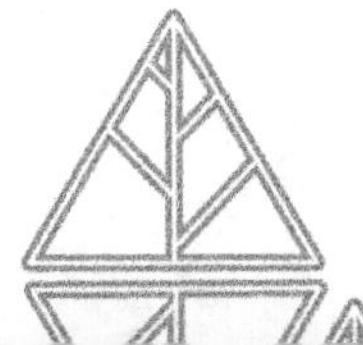

SEED OF LIFE

Yoni transliterates to “the womb and female reproductive system,” and represents “the seal of the inner source.”[22] This yoni mudrā maṇḍala incorporates powerful symbolism for meditation and healing energy channeling to the female reproductive organs and your creative centers (2nd, 3rd, and 6th cakras). Embedded in the center we find the “Seed of Life” universal stroke pattern, a symbol of creation and fertility. It functions as the blue print of the universe and the primary building block of the “Flower of Life” (page 155). Found across religious traditions and ancient cultures, it also represents the origins and everything that exists in this reality. Surrounding it are orchid and lotus flowers for love, beauty, strength and purity; while four placentas represent the sacred nourishment and protection derived from the intrauterine odyssey, as well as serving as a reminder of our life cycle.[29]

How | For the iteration illustrated, press all finger tips together facing upwards, press thumbs together and extend in opposite direction.

Benefits | Nourishes female reproductive and urinary systems, sensitizes sensory organs by creating inner silence, helps “unplug” from external influences and reduces stress.

As the moon folds into the night
and the sun creeps up to take its place,
a seed of thought is planted into your consciousness.
As the morning beckons
your mind to open to new possibilities,
a new life is awakening.
Given birth by the seeds of life
that flow from your soul’s desires
and a fluid stream of creativity.
Embrace this growth,
reach for your dreams and challenge your spirit
to drink from Mother Earth’s blessed nectar.

- Louisa Wargo (Lotus Rising) -

29. Loke YW. Life’s Vital Link: The astonishing role of the placenta. Oxford, UK: Oxford University Press (2010)

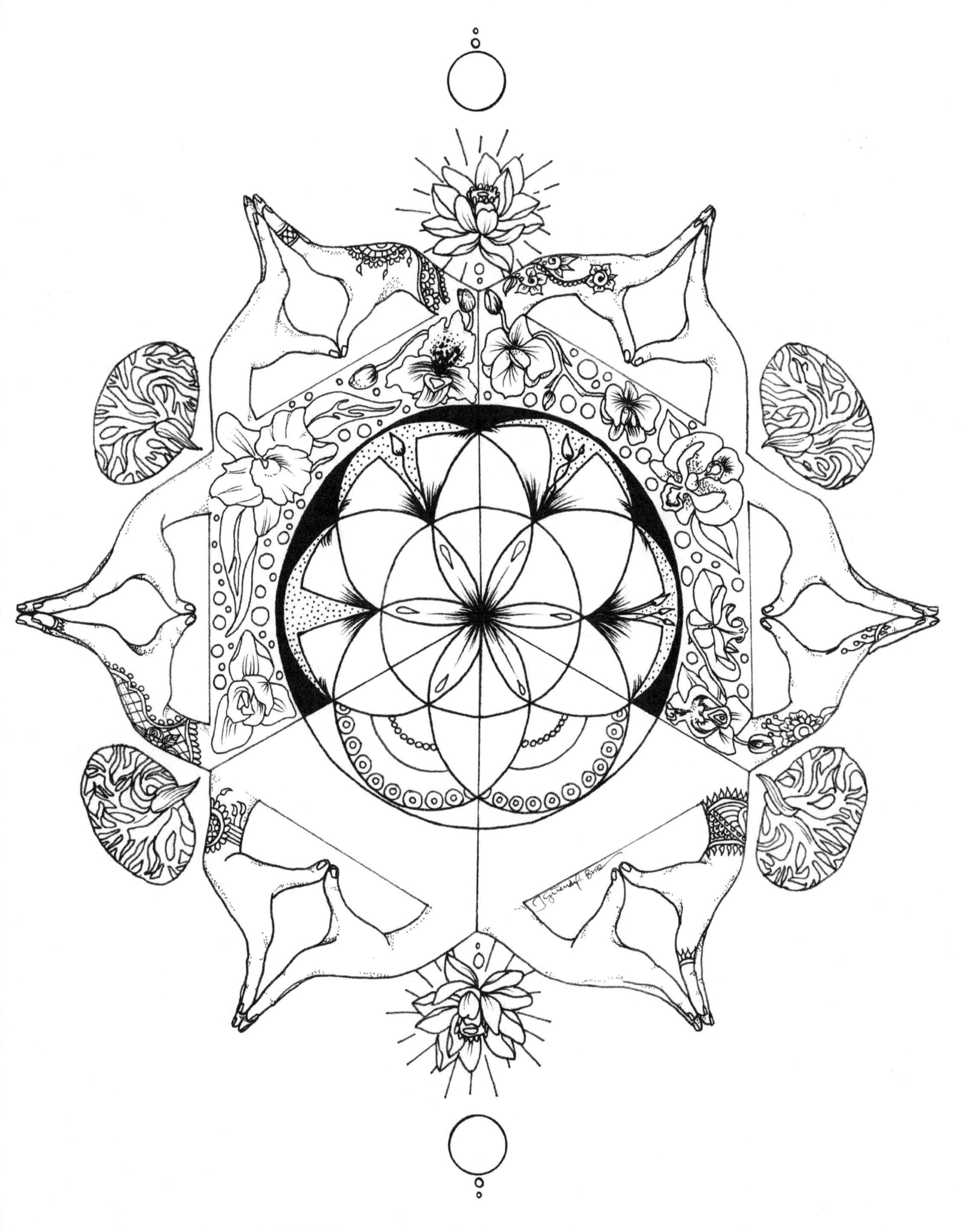

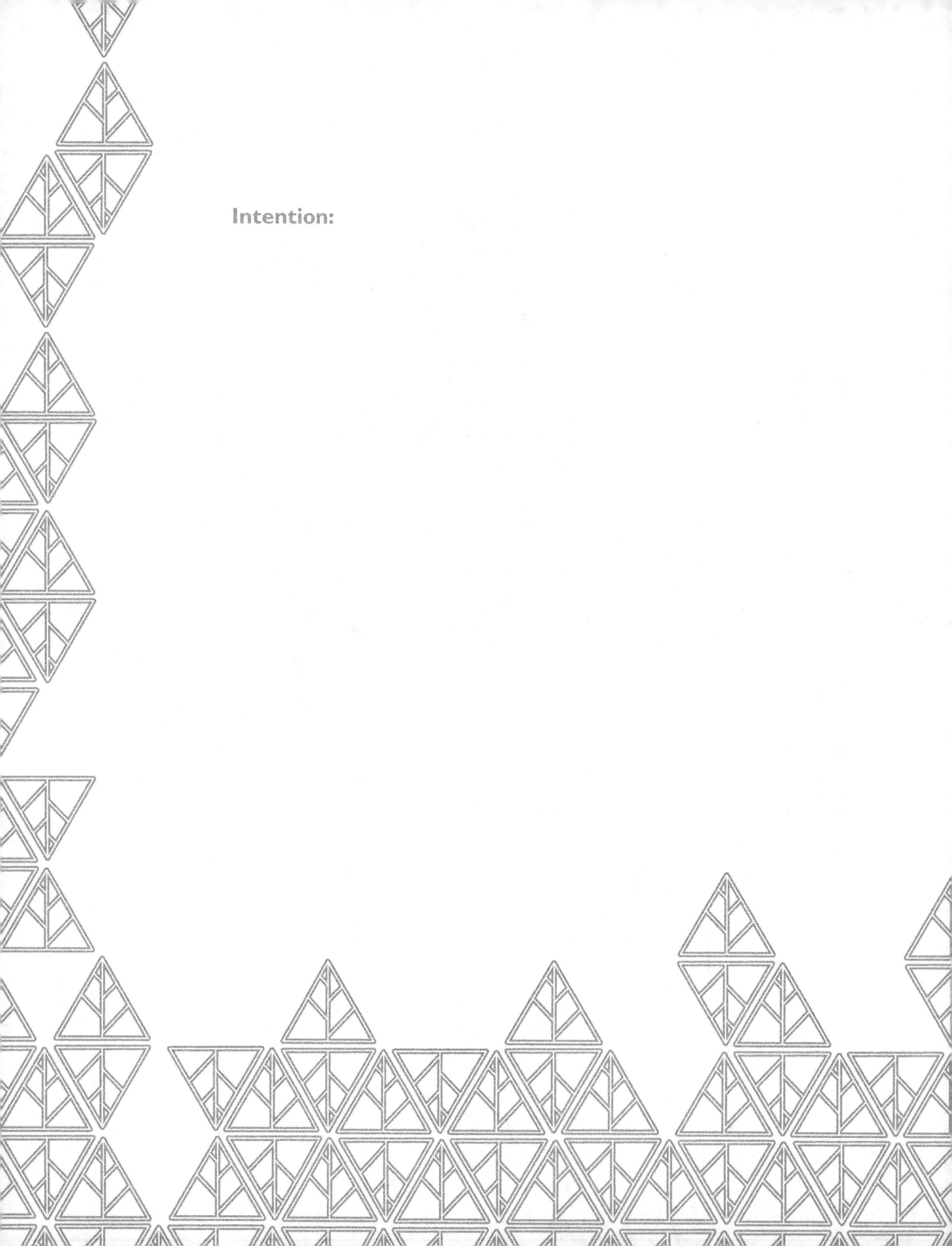

Intention:

Thought Infusions

1. How do you honor the creative capacity of your sacral cakra? Physically, energetically, spiritually, and emotionally? Which seeds do you plant with your hands: physical seeds, spiritual seeds, seeds of love?

2. How do you honor the sacredness of your womb, if applicable? Physically, energetically, spiritually, and emotionally? Note—Independent of biological gender, this center is believed to exist energetically at the sacral cakra.

3. The yoni holds the energy to manifesting your dreams, it is the portal to creativity and the imaginal realm. What lifestyle changes can you make to better connect to this energy to increase beauty, creativity, and pleasure? Tip: Explore the energies of your feminine cycles and rhythms.

4. Contemplate your colored illustration. How does color change your initial perception of the image? What colors did you use? Look up #anewkindofcoloringbook and #purаprana, share your work. Explore other being's colors and see what new messages come to mind through observation.

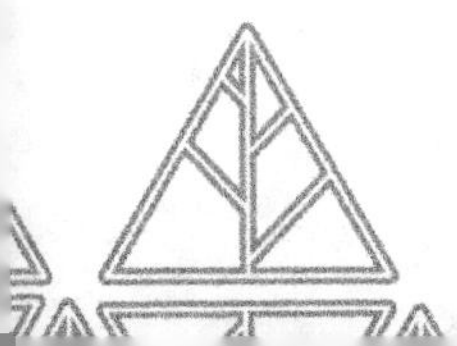
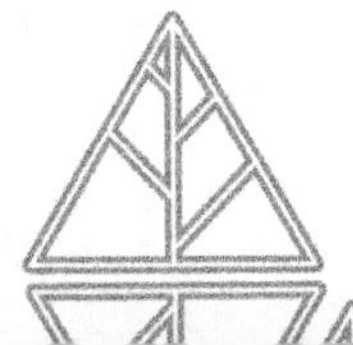

EBB AND FLOW

About 71% of the Earth's surface is water, of this, 96% is saline water in the oceans.[30] Water is a foundation for human existence, it's a precondition. Without food, we can last a few weeks. Without water, we can last a few days. Water is life, it's needed for healthy ecosystems and for human survival. Approximately 68% of the human adult body is water,[31] with infants at ~78% before settling to adult percentages by age one. The adult brain and heart are composed of ~73% water, our lungs are ~83% water, and our skin is ~65% water. Most of this water content is intracellular fluid, the remainder is extracellular.

Matsya transliterates from Sanskrit as "fish." This mudrā activates the water element,[26] awakening the qualities of fluidity, and inner refreshment and nourishment. The fish metaphor assigns underwater sand, mud or other type of dirt, to our life challenges (e.g., jealousy, anger, the ego, health); and asserts how the fish is able to swim in the cloudy water without getting tied-up in it.[8] This illustration aims to reflect movement, water flow. The starry night reflected in the water within the circle is inspired by puṣpa, which transliterates to "flowers." According to Swami Harshananda,[32] to the observer, the sun, the moon, and the stars, seem to rise from the waters of the ocean each day. They are the flowers of the water, and the one who knows them as such receives great blessings.

How | Place your right hand over the back of the left hand, keeping fingers together and extending thumbs outwards.

Benefits | Helps activate self-healing potential by cultivating fluidity, flexibility, and calmness. Helps release emotions and muscular tension, and support joint function. Evoking thoughts of swimming in such sacred element generates feelings of devotion, gratitude, and compassion.

Water is the driving force of all nature.

- Leonardo da Vinci -

30. Shiklomanov I. World Fresh Water Resources. In: Water in Crisis: A Guide to the World's Fresh Water Resources. New York, NY, US: Oxford University Press (1993)
31. Mitchell HH, *et al. **J Biol Chem.*** 158: 625-637 (1945)
32. Harshananda S. A Concise Encyclopaedia Of Hinduism. Bangalore, IN: Ramakrishna Math (2008)

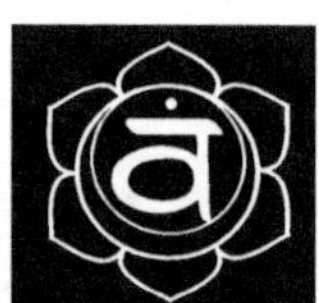

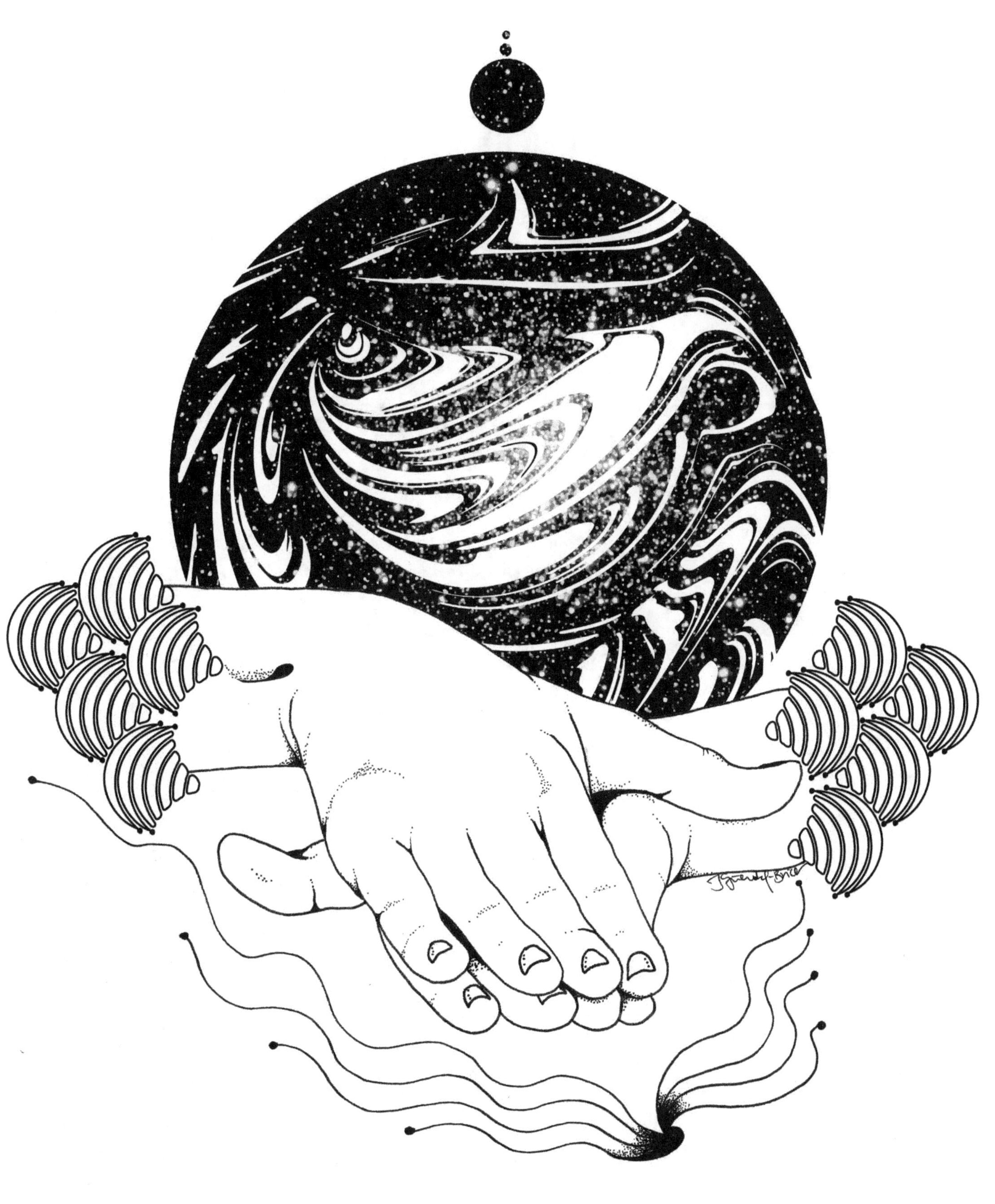

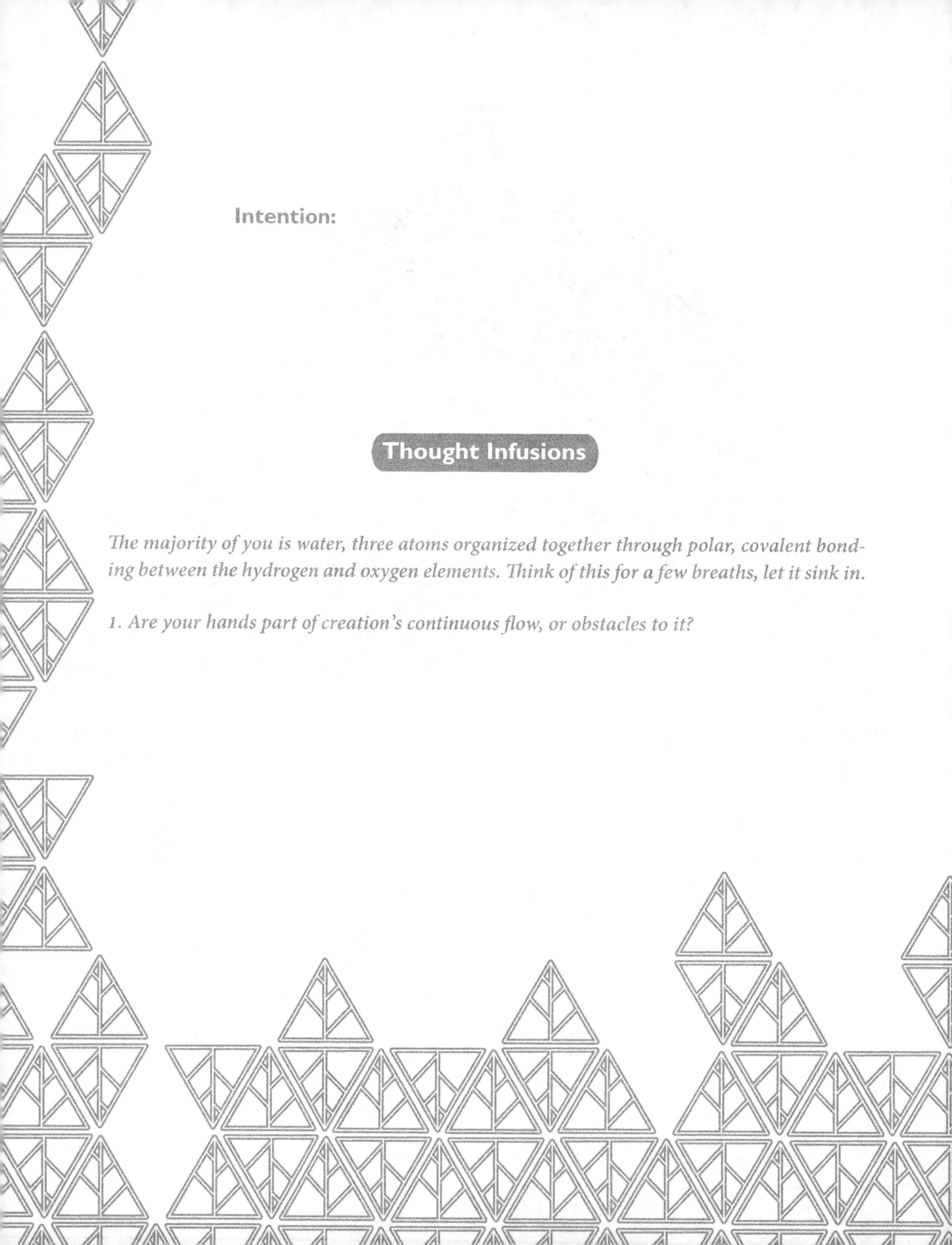

Intention:

Thought Infusions

The majority of you is water, three atoms organized together through polar, covalent bonding between the hydrogen and oxygen elements. Think of this for a few breaths, let it sink in.

1. Are your hands part of creation's continuous flow, or obstacles to it?

2. What does your spiritual belief system, if any at all, say or teach about water? Are there any particular prayers, meditations, rituals or ceremonies? What about fish symbolism? Explore.

3. Contemplate your colored illustration. How does color change your initial perception of the image? What colors did you use? Look up #anewkindofcoloringbook and #puraprana, share your work. Explore other being's colors and see what new messages come to mind through observation.

4. How can you approach the use of water in your life with more devotion? Turn your use of water into a contemplative meditation: be present, give thanks.

5. I was raised to be aware of my water usage, but it was until I moved to a location where we collect our drinking water from rain using a cistern, that I truly started to be hyper-aware of water conservation. Even more so in the post-disaster conditions that Hurricanes Irma and Maria brought in 2017 to the Caribbean region. Water is at the core of sustainable development, and access to clean water and sanitation is one of the most important United Nations sustainable development goals. Scan the code for more information. How can you get involved in efforts that aim to bring awareness of water conservation, rights, and access; to your community, city, country and world?

UN Water

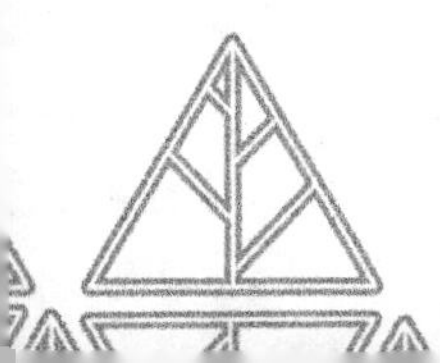

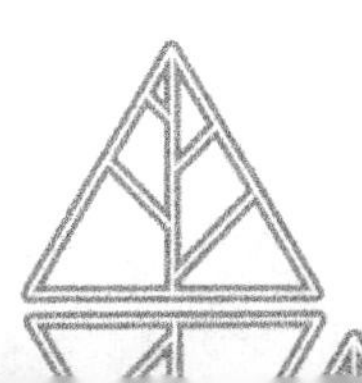

BENEVOLENT SUN

Sūrya transliterates from Sanskrit to "sun." As in the *Ebb and Flow* illustration notes (page 98), sunlight like water, is also a foundation for human existence. It's also a precondition. Sun symbology has been present as a constant in art, religion and spirituality, and even politics, throughout history. The sun is representative of Divine radiance, glory, brilliance, power and authority, happiness, life, spirituality, and hope.[30] In this illustration the sun rays are depicted as straight radiance bursts, while they are drawn in the classical alternately straight and wavy conformation in the next illustration, *Advaita* (page 106). As documented by Herdeg, when represented as a single sunbeam, the ray signifies "by the light of heaven,"[33] as is used extensively in my art. Sūrya mudrā channels radiant light and energy.

How | Use the thumb pad to cover the minor knuckle (closest to the nail) of the ring finger and extend other fingers in a heavenly direction.

Benefits | As assigned to the solar plexus cakra, it helps to fuel clarity, intrinsic power, confidence and self-esteem. It activates inner vibrancy, vitality, and luminosity, while helping reduce depression and mental fog. Representing the fire element or agni, it aids the digestive process of physical food as well as life experiences.

The hand of radiance
moves these restless thoughts
to a motionless repose.
The light of spirit
draws a peaceful ease
from tired bones.
Wrapped in a cloud of composed comfort,
a subtle message is heard.
Inspiration leads a quiet mind
to a state of knowing,
a confirmation of a Divine circumstance.

- Louisa Wargo (Lotus Rising) -

33. Herdeg W. The Sun in Art : Sun Symbolism of Past and Present, in Pagan and Christian Art, Polular Art, Fine Art and Applied Art. New York, NY, US: Graphis Press (1968)

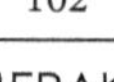

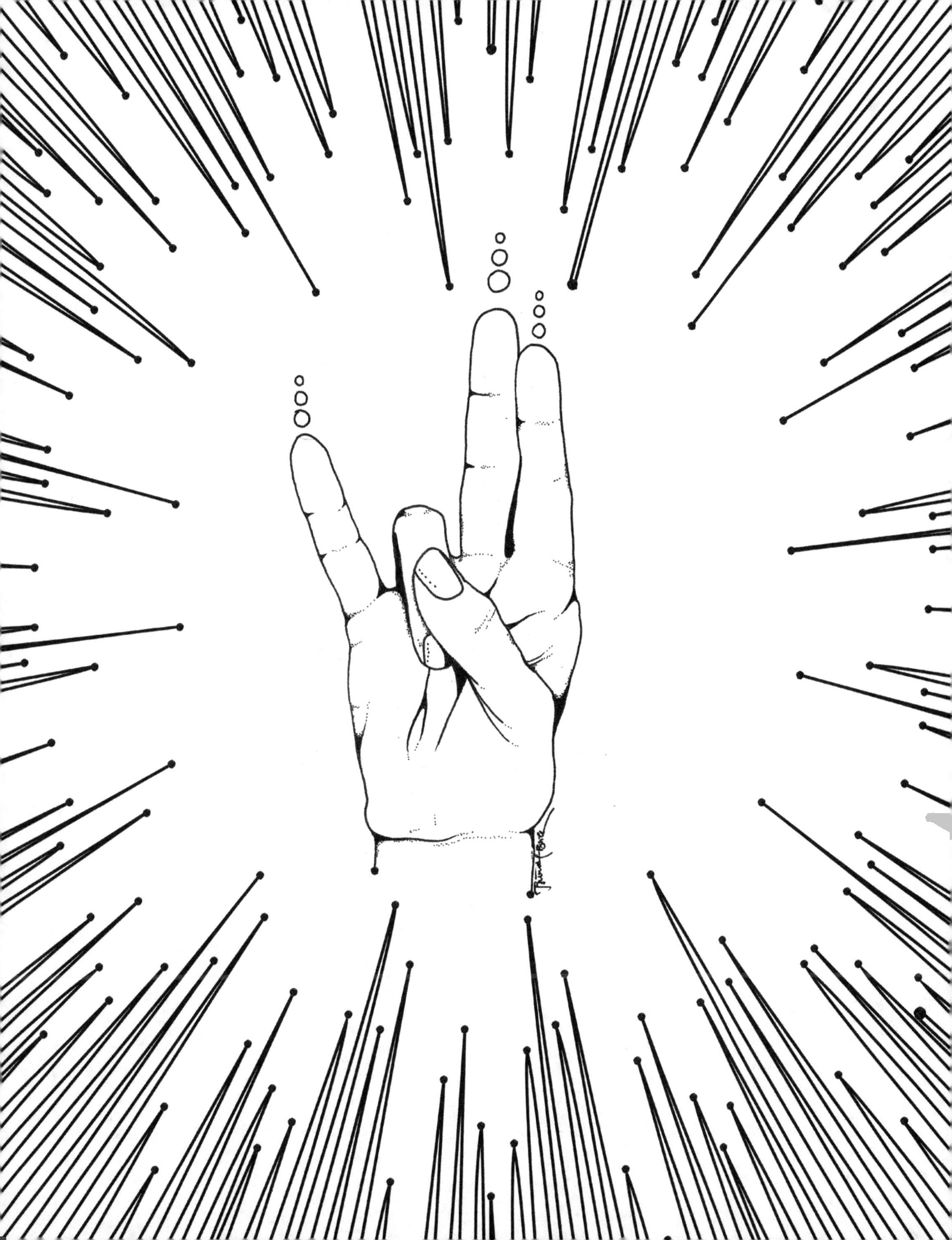

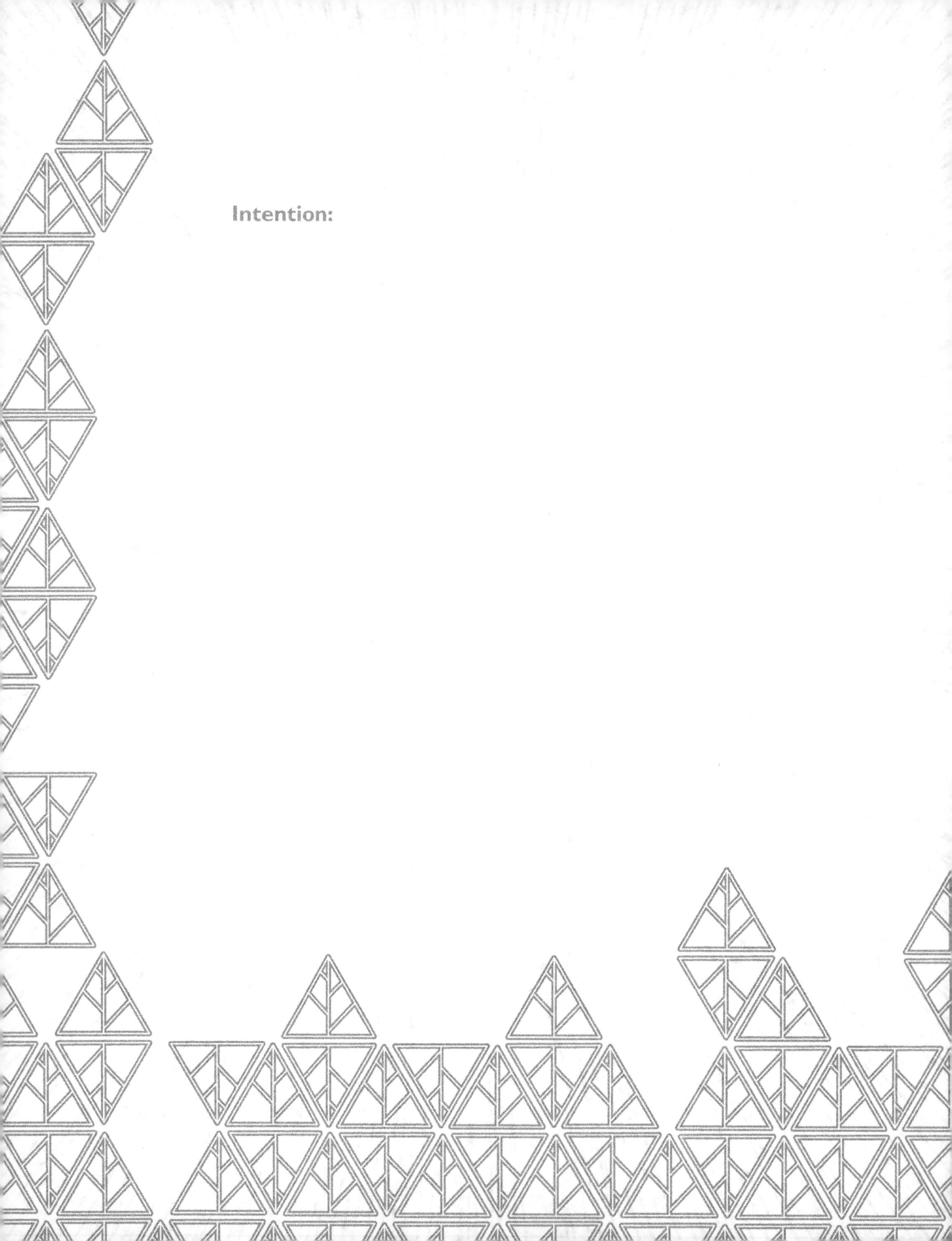

Intention:

Thought Infusions

1. How do you cultivate energy and vitality? What things drain your energy? How frequently do you react in ways that drain your inner vibrancy and vitality?

2. Do you feel confident in yourself? Where is there confidence, and where is it lacking? What barriers are present and how can you work towards regaining your personal power?

3. How often do you schedule some intentional outdoor time in the sun? Use this time to consciously breathe and absorb sunlight. Imagine your body metabolizing its radiance into vital energy.

4. Contemplate your colored illustration. How does color change your initial perception of the image? What colors did you use? Look up #anewkindofcoloringbook and #puraprana, share your work. Explore other being's colors and see what new messages come to mind through observation.

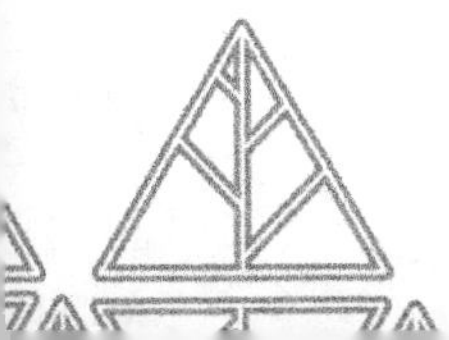
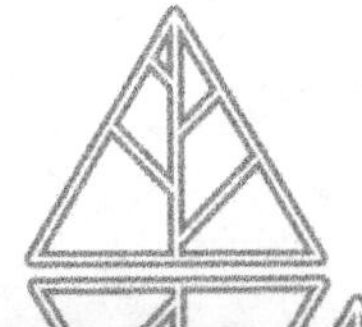

ADVAITA

Advaita transliterates from Sanskrit to "not two." It means non-dualism and represents a school of Hindu philosophy that is a practical guide to spiritual experience and self-realization.[34] Advaita promotes being pure awareness, adopting a non-dualistic way of thinking which translates into disposing of barriers generated by dogmas and rules. It is through self-knowledge that liberation or mokṣa can be achieved. Tejas transliterates from Sanskrit to "fire or illumination," this mudrā also channels inner radiance and bridges the 3rd and 4th energy centers.

How | Start with your hands in prayer position. Join the sides of the thumbs and index finger tips (index fingers arching over the thumbs). As you hold this gesture, visualize light within you, expanding to the rest of your body and outwards.

Benefits[26] | It directs breath to the heart, enhancing feelings of well-being and unconditional, devotional love. It supports connection to the Divine in your belief system. Its illuminating and radiant qualities support personal power and transformation.

When we practice individual mindfulness,
we discover compassion.
When we practice compassion in action,
we discover loving kindness.
When we practice loving kindness,
we discover humanity.
When we practice benevolence and being human,
we discover a deeper interconnectivity with each other.
When we practice with awareness of these sensibilities,
we discover being present with unconditional love.

- Vivia Astraia -

34. Deutsch E. Advaita Vedānta: A Philosophical Reconstruction. Honolulu, HI, US: University of Hawaii Press (1973)

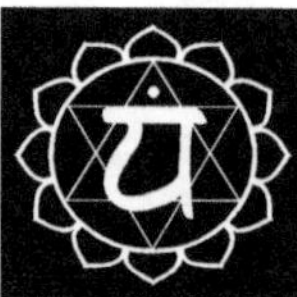

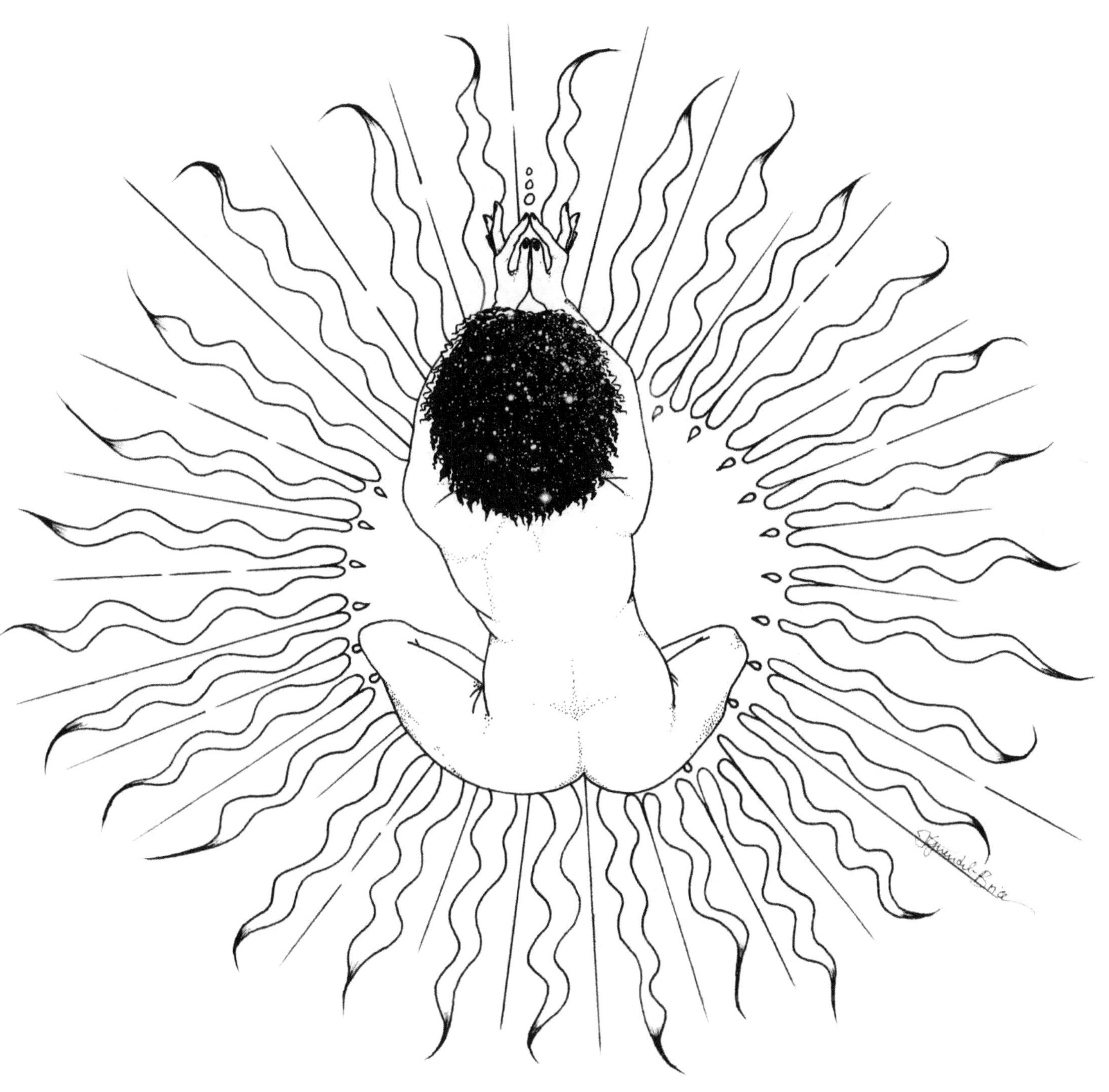

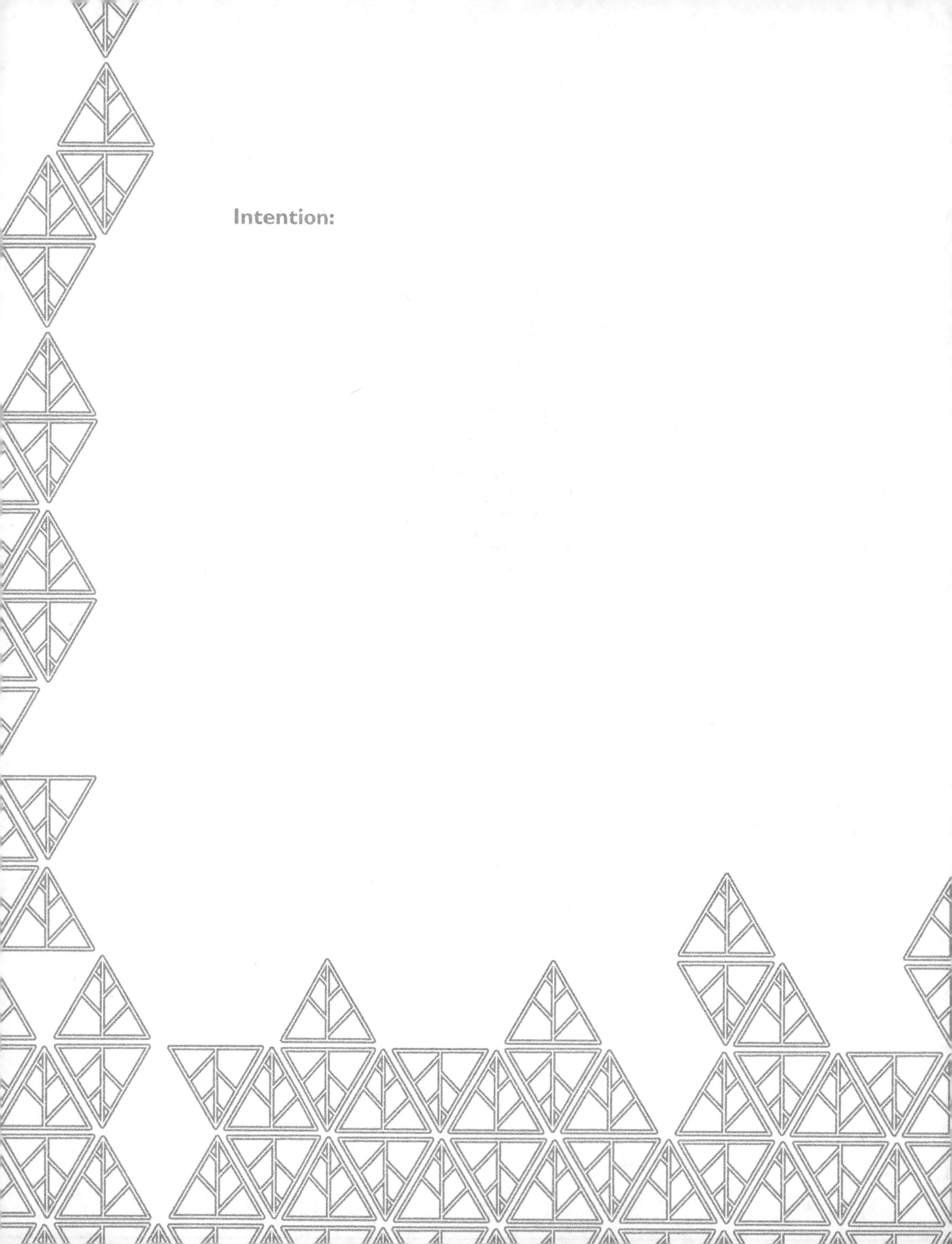

Intention:

Thought Infusions

1. When do you radiate the most? How easy or difficult is it to just be you? Are you comfortable with just being you and sharing who you are with others?

2. How do you cultivate constant presence and awareness throughout your day?

3. How do you connect with the Divine in your moment to moment, if applicable?

4. Contemplate your colored illustration. How does color change your initial perception of the image? What colors did you use? Look up #anewkindofcoloringbook and #puraprana, share your work. Explore other being's colors and see what new messages come to mind through observation.

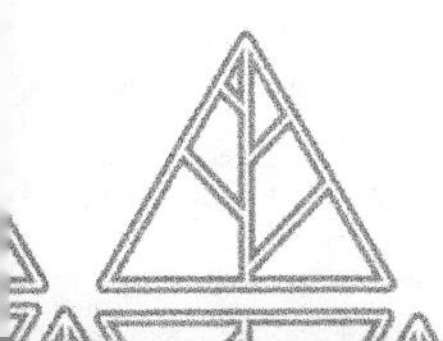

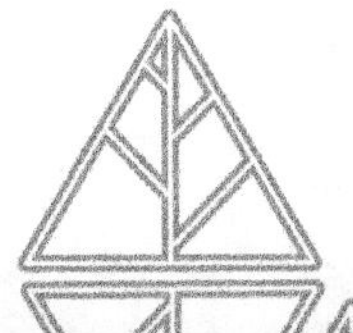

BUDDING BLOSSOM

In Āyurveda, padma or kamala transliterate to the color "lotus" and "lotus flower." It represents the budding and blooming sacred lotus flower, *Nelumbo nucifera.* As a powerful polyvalent symbol across cultures and spiritual philosophies, it's associated with purity in Buddhism, with beauty in Hinduism, and with the sun in Egyptian mythology, among others.[35] This mudrā represents creation and cosmic renewal, and holds the promise of transformation, perseverance, and growth to the practitioner. Kamala is pure creative force, the power to create beauty and abundance, and to see beauty everywhere in our lives.

How | Place your hands in a prayer, then open the middle three fingers and the cup of your palms to create the budding lotus. Continue to expand the mudrā while keeping the little finger and thumbs joined to form the full bloom (page 115). Inhaling and exhaling sequence may vary depending on intention (e.g., inhale as you open, exhale as you close).

Benefits | Increases compassion, gratitude, forgiveness, kindness while remaining rooted, empathy, and unconditional love. Nurtures the blossoming heart. Reduces tiredness and sense of loneliness.[21]

"Rising like a lotus,
aware of many realms
of the mind, body, soul.
All the earthly elements,
that make us whole.
In each new moment we can
acknowledge and dissolve old karma.
While planting seeds of wisdom.
Understanding the laws of cause and effect
through dharma.

- Vivia Astraia -

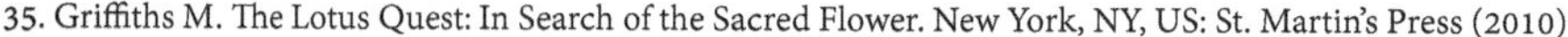

35. Griffiths M. The Lotus Quest: In Search of the Sacred Flower. New York, NY, US: St. Martin's Press (2010)

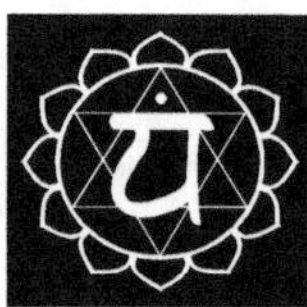

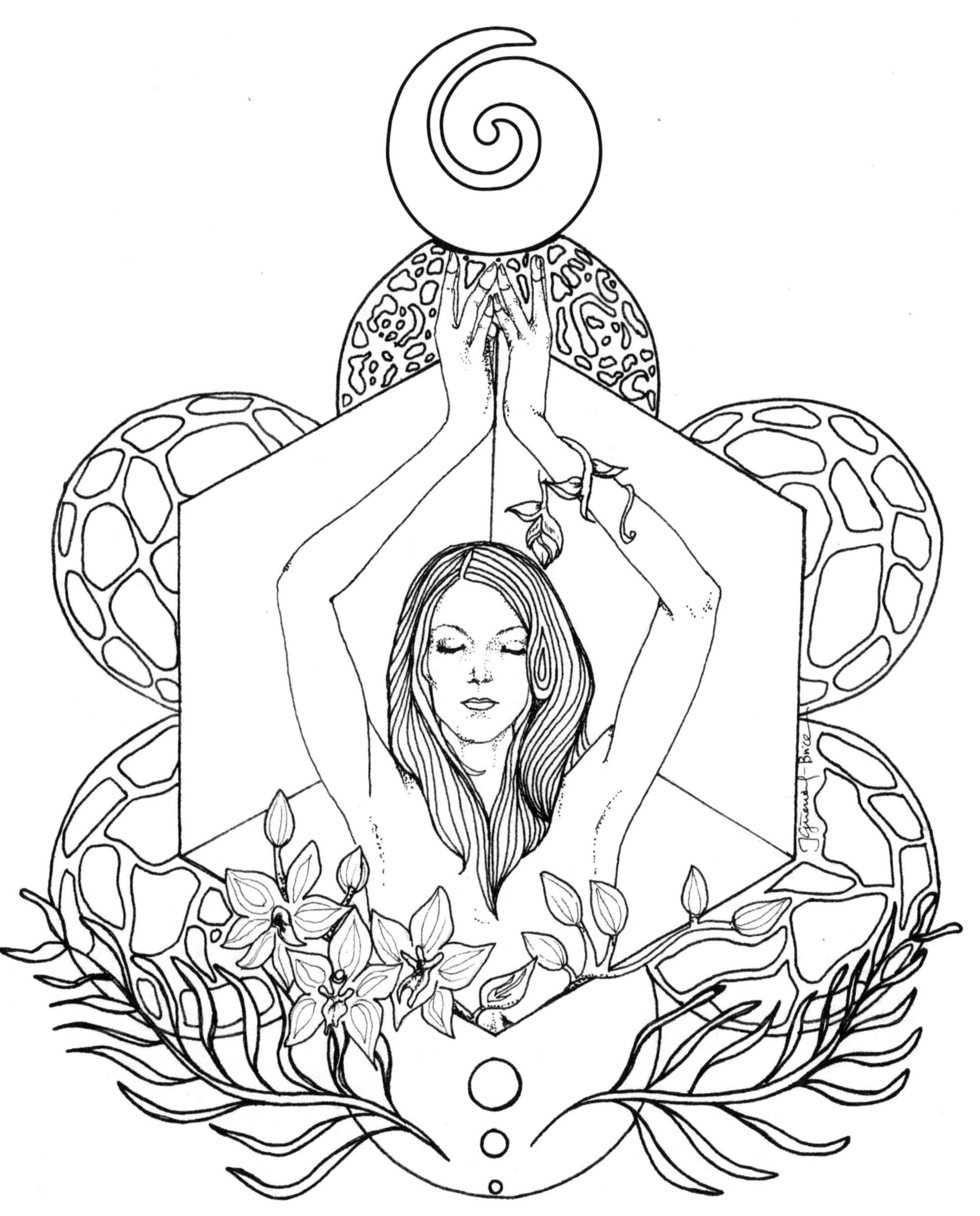

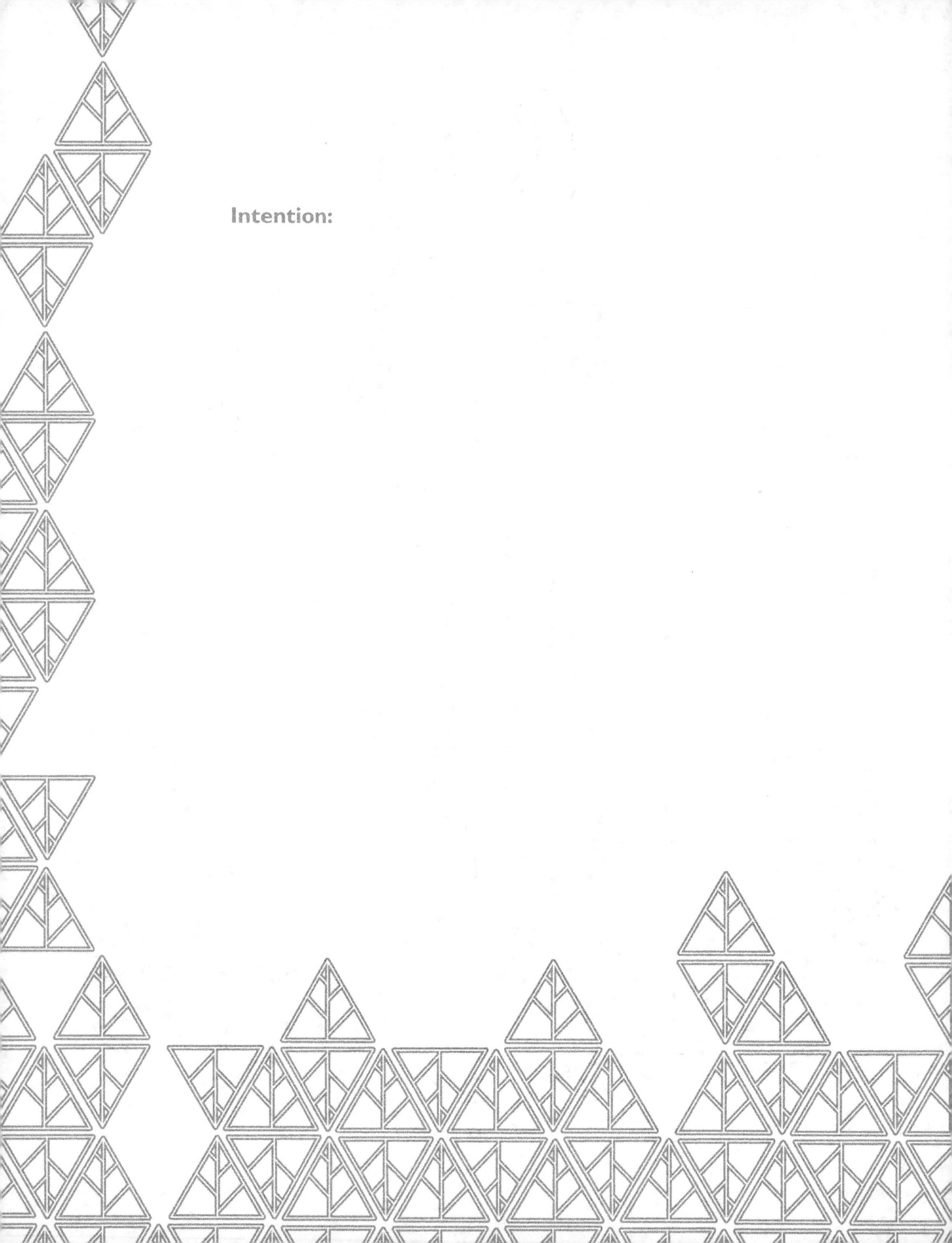

Intention:

Thought Infusions

1. How do you show love to yourself? How do you show love to others?

2. Are you able to freely give and accept love? If not, what do you think are some barriers? What can you change to overcome any challenges?

3. Thinking of your day to day, are you able to focus in finding beauty everywhere, in everything, and in everyone? If not, what mental shifts can you practice to focus in finding the beauty and positive?

4. Contemplate your colored illustration. How does color change your initial perception of the image? What colors did you use? Look up #anewkindofcoloringbook and #puraprana, share your work. Explore other being's colors and see what new messages come to mind through observation.

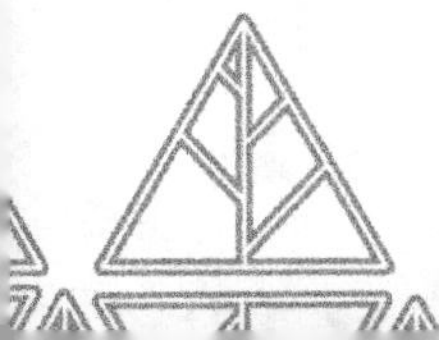

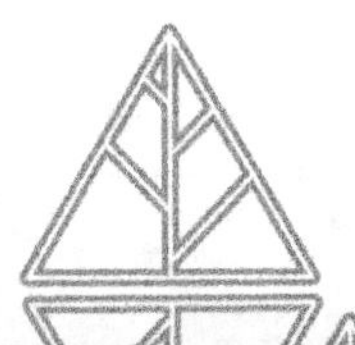

FULL BLOOM

Practicing padma mudrā (page 110) provides an opportunity to stand at the crossroads of your potential and infinite Divine inspiration. It allows for your inner perception and creativity to bloom, gather strength and certainty, in turn amplifying your visions into inspired action. Tap into your truth: *What did you come here to create and co-create?*

"Lotus is a symbol of purity and strength.
When we begin the first steps of a new journey,
it is important to ground in your body and root intentions.
Clarity of your vision with keen awareness & mindfulness.
Grounding with strength and grace,
as you get ready to embark
the next stages of this journey of blossoming and awakening.
Place both hands, in your expression of a closed bud shape,
centered in front of your chest.
Breath in deeply as you visualize a goal you wish to manifest.
Allow a moment to think of this seed intention.
With your mind's eye,
visualize any colors or symbols that represent this intention.
Be sure to keep your thumbs and pinky fingers connected.
As you exhale,
expand the other three fingers on both hands.
Create symmetry,
like the blossoming of a lotus flower.
Repeat a few times.
Breathing in with the closed bud.
Cultivating new Qì with every breath.
Charging and nurturing this vision and seed intention.
Exhale with full blooming lotus,
expanding and opening your heart more each time.

- Vivia Astraia -

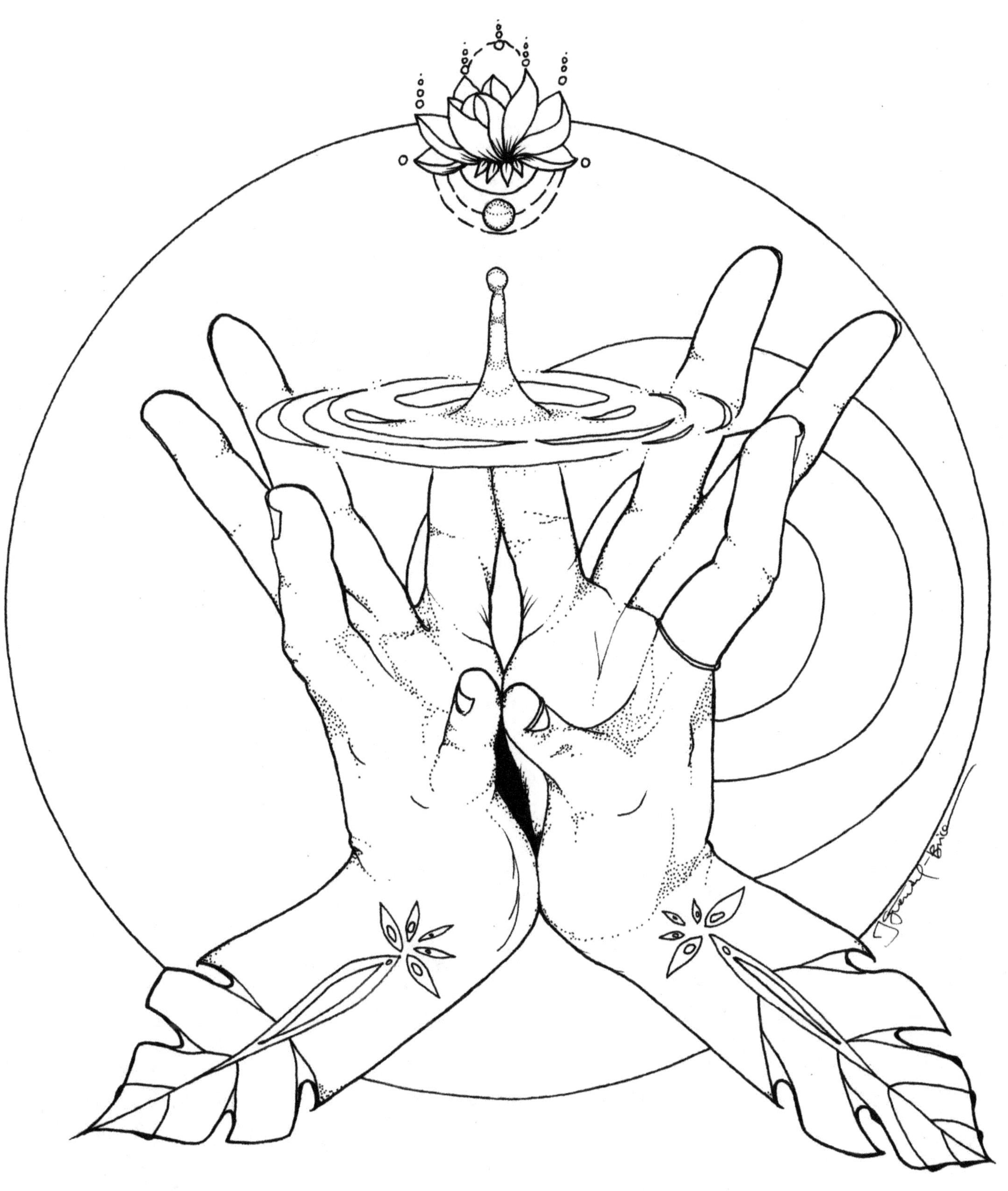

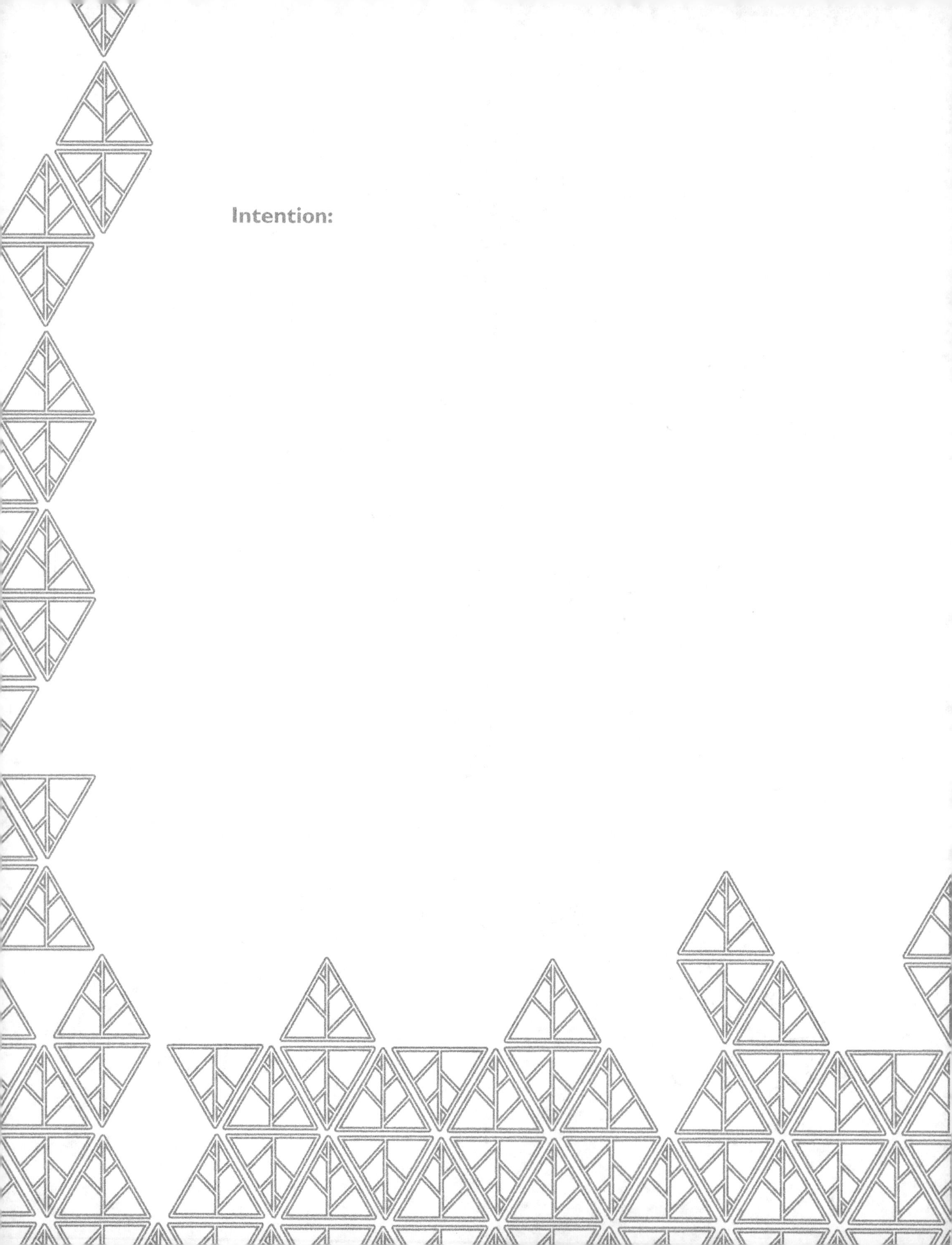

Intention:

Thought Infusions

1. As a symbol of purity, the lotus reminds us to keep our energy centers pure. Rangaraja Iyengar[8] explains that this mudrā uses the water and fire elements of little fingers and thumb to cleanse the heart and mind with water, and clean emotions by fire. How can you increase purity in your mind-body through intentional actions?

2. The lotus also symbolizes giving something, as well as receiving something (e.g., the blooming flower gives joy and beauty, and it also opens to the sun and receives its nurturing radiance). What things do you wish to give or are already giving that builds on your spirit? What things do you wish to receive? How can you use this metaphor in meditation and prayer to open to the Divine in your belief system to receive blessings?

3. How are you presently blossoming? What steps do you need to take to see yourself and your dreams truly blooming?

4. Contemplate your colored illustration. How does color change your initial perception of the image? What colors did you use? Look up #anewkindofcoloringbook and #puraprana, share your work. Explore other being's colors and see what new messages come to mind through observation.

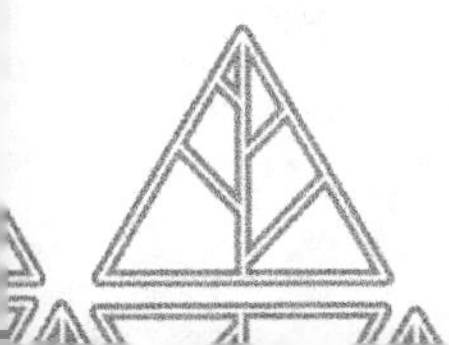

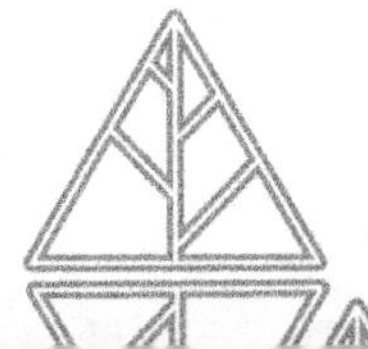

MĀṆIFEST

The blooming lotus is a mudrā of transformation. Here, we have the ultimate manifestation of the padma mudrā, alapadma. Alapadma transliterates to "fully blossomed lotus and happiness," and is the 20th single-hand dance gesture as described in the Abhinaya Darpaṇa (manual of the art of expression dating to the 5th and 2nd centuries BC).[36]

How | With a single hand, continue expanding your blossoming lotus mudrā to its fullest expression, the little finger points up and others are stretched and extended outwards mimicking an open flower.

Benefits[37] | Helps stimulate and activate all five elements in the body (page 46), boost vitality and happiness, and energizes body and mind. Supports the cardio-respiratory and immune systems.

"A time to interconnect within planes of synchronicity.
As you feel the pulse of connecting energies.
A rhythm of life that pulls from within.
A dance of solitude to a time well spent,
in meditative pause of collective rest.
Intentions set,
a manifestation of a soul's deep longing.
Open up the receptors of channeled thoughts,
receiving the Divine from within yourself.

- Louisa Wargo (Lotus Rising) -

36. Coomaraswamy AK, Duggirala GH. The Mirror of Gesture. New Delhi, IN: Munshiram Manoharlal (2010)
37. Pratishtha A. Let's Learn Kathak-I. Saharanpur, IN: Mokshayatan Yog Sansthan (2015)

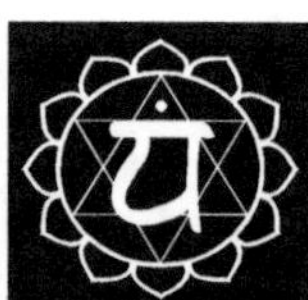

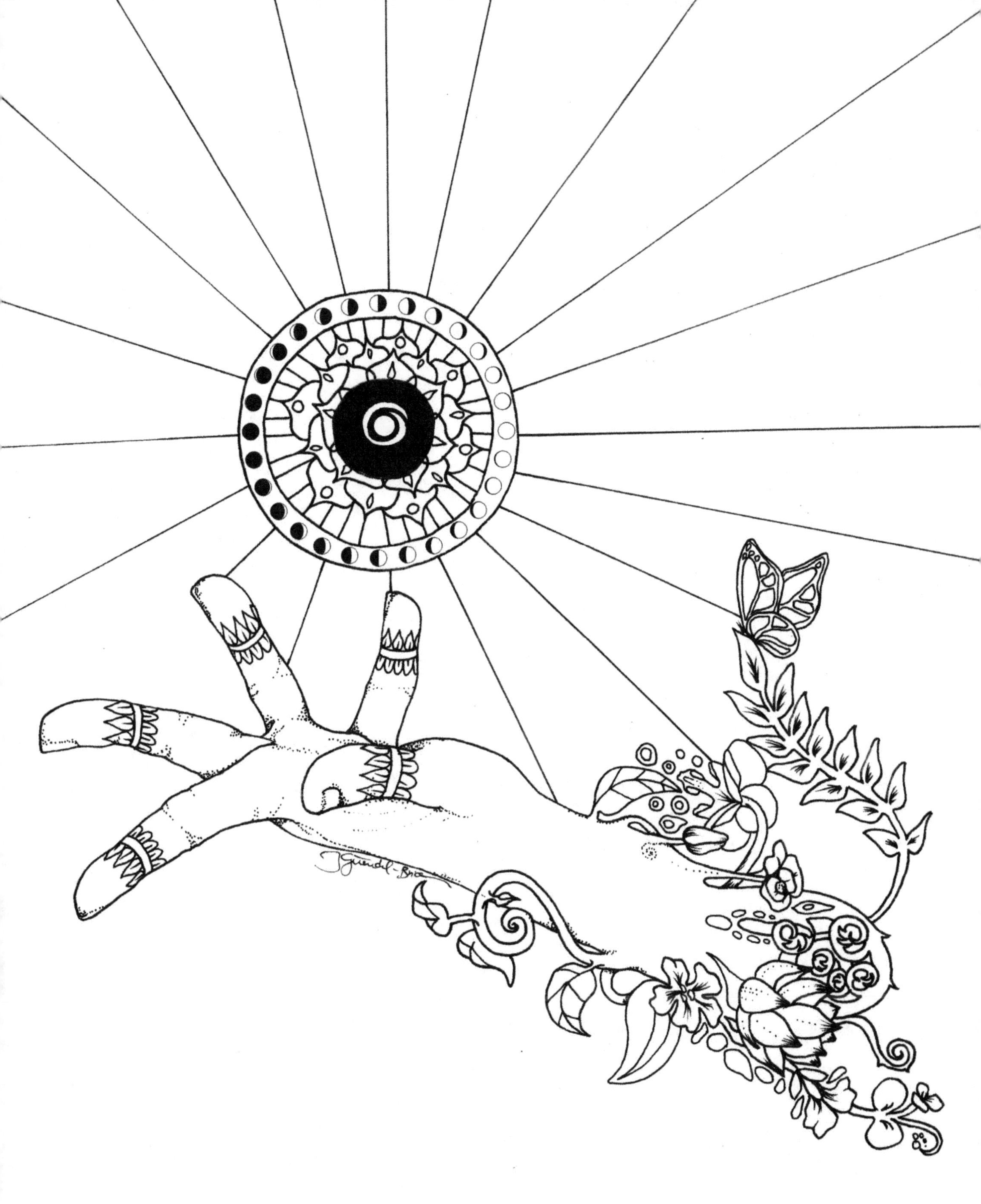

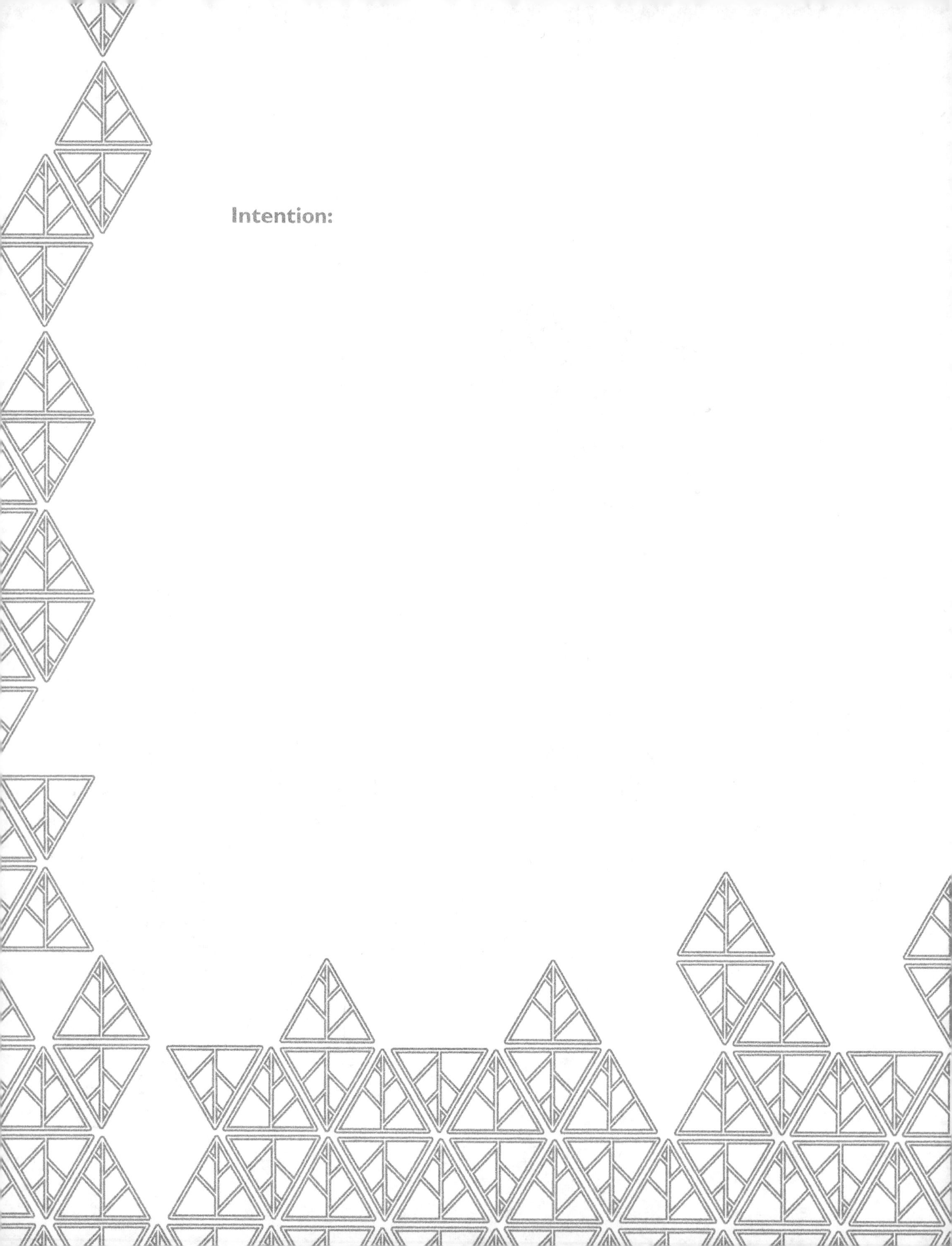

Intention:

Thought Infusions

1. How do you practice any form of "creativity in bloom" in your life, if at all?

2. How can you integrate all of the concepts touched upon with the padma and alapadma mudrās into your intentions of creating and co-creating?

3. Can you envision yourself at your fullest expression and the best version of self? Do you take the time on a regular basis to consciously put energy into your goals?

4. Contemplate your colored illustration. How does color change your initial perception of the image? What colors did you use? Look up #anewkindofcoloringbook and #puraprana, share your work. Explore other being's colors and see what new messages come to mind through observation.

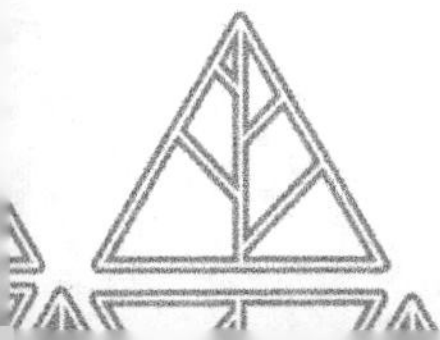

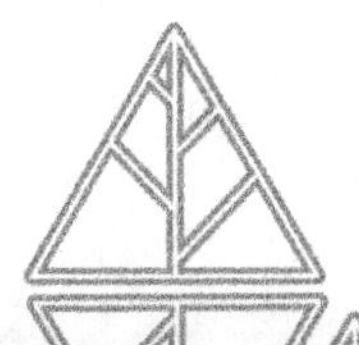

KINETIC ENERGY

Vajra transliterates from Sanskrit to "thunderbolt." The vajrapradama mudrā is the gesture of "unshakable trust and confidence."[26] It's extremely interesting to me that before I knew anything about this particular mudrā, my hands would intrinsically, quite often, gravitate to this gesture. This gesture also links the 3rd and 4th energy centers, as it deals with self-trust and confidence which again, go hand-in-hand with self-love. When you think of a thunderbolt, you think of intense and focused energy, and for example, in Buddhism the thunderbolt is seen as a weapon against self-doubt.[38]

How | Weave fingers together, crossing them. Thumbs extend outwards, place gesture over your sternum. I sometimes hold it at chest level and focus my gaze on the palms.

Benefits | Helps increase self-trust, openness, and enthusiasm. Helps release hopelessness, mistrust, and self-doubt, specially in times where circumstances may seem overwhelming. It directs energy to the heart center, reminding us to be kind to ourselves, and to believe in ourselves.

"Closing in on a dream,
interpretation is left to a wishful mind.
Holding the years that brought us to this moment,
nothing seems impossible to me now.
Every step that caused pain and every hour of doubt,
now folds into this present expectation that we fought for,
lays clearly in view.
This is our fate,
held in the hands of an ambitious hope.

- Louisa Wargo (Lotus Rising) -

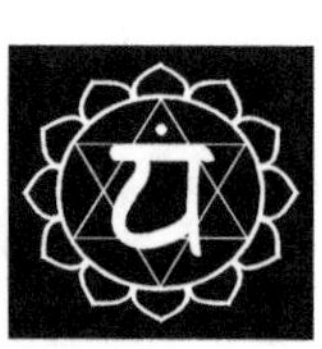

38. Burke C. The Yoga Healer. New York, NY, US: CICO Books (2017)

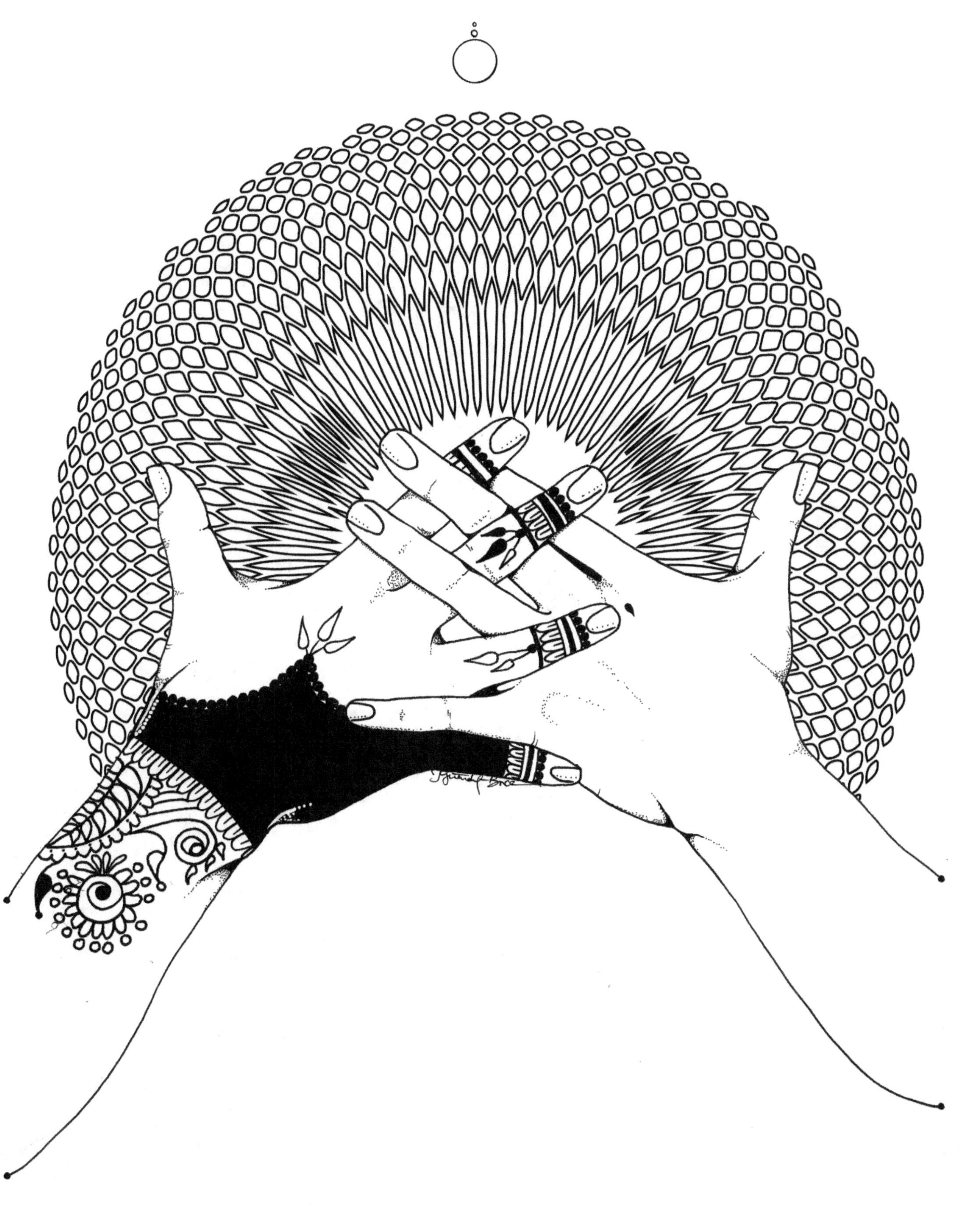

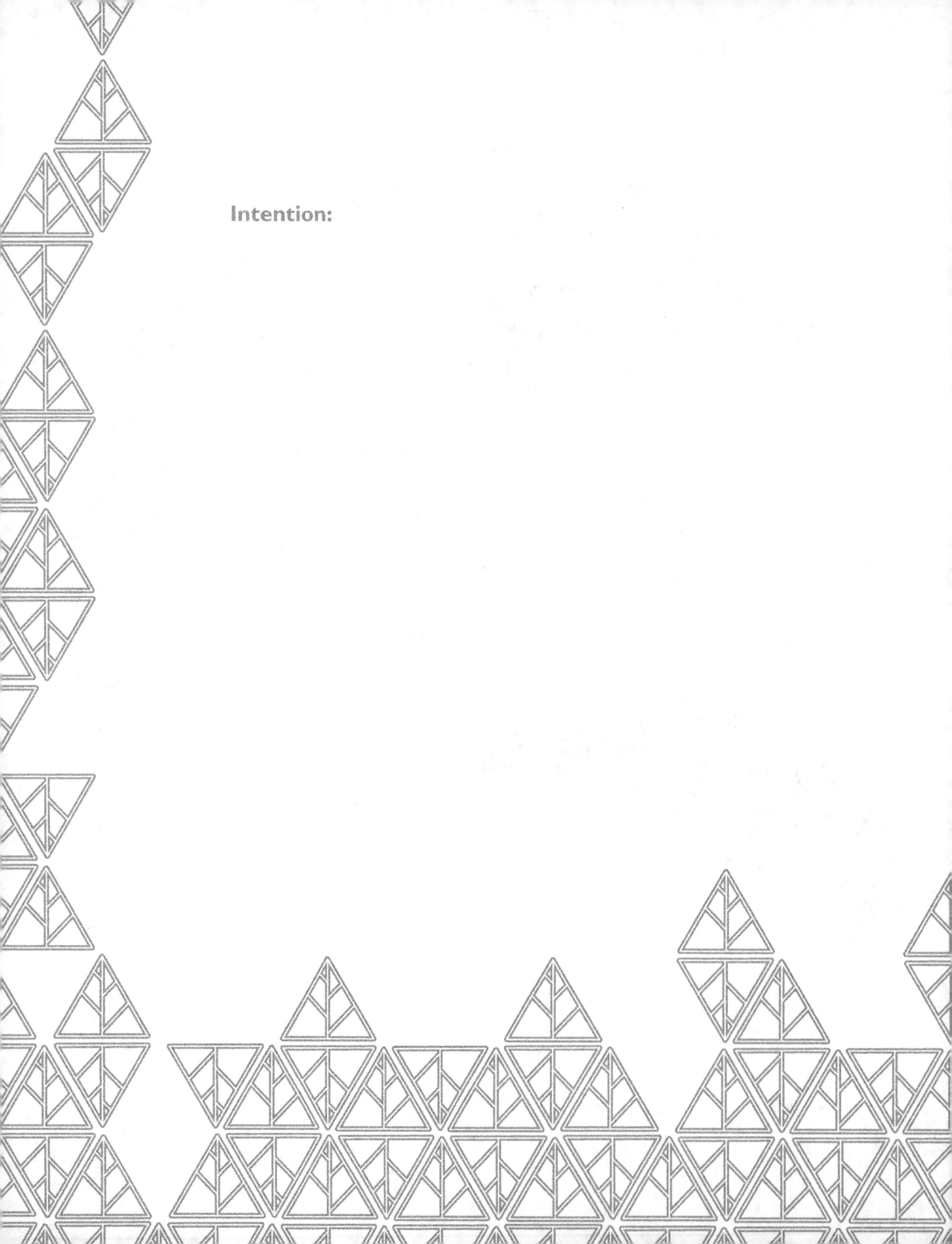

Intention:

Thought Infusions

1. Do you trust yourself when you think of your journey forward?

2. What are your current go-tos when self-doubt strikes? What are your reactions? In their exceptional book, Mudras of India,[21] Cain and Revital Carroll remind us that the Divine essence is always present within us, and they prompt for inquiry into whether we are present as well. Explore.

3. What are your inner gifts that you have consciously or unconsciously decided to keep in the shadows? What will be required from yourself (and others) to bring them out to the light, to be shared with the world?

4. Contemplate your colored illustration. How does color change your initial perception of the image? What colors did you use? Look up #anewkindofcoloringbook and #purapranа, share your work. Explore other being's colors and see what new messages come to mind through observation.

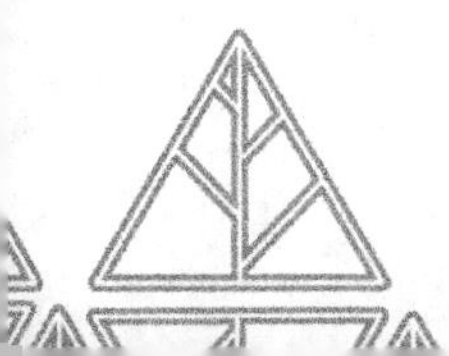

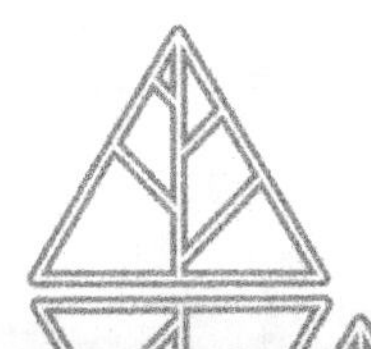

AWAKE

Uttarabodhi transliterates from Sanskrit to "realization and enlightenment," and it's the "seal of highest enlightenment."[22] The first time that I encountered this gesture was in a permaculture workshop: the facilitator was holding this mudrā as we were sitting in circle and she was speaking. Ever since I understood its meaning, I hold it before or during meetings, when teaching, or when speaking publicly, if the need arises. In his book, How to Attain Enlightenment,[39] James Swartz reflects upon enlightenment not feeling like anything, but instead, it's the realization and the knowledge itself, of the self being limitless and partless. To me, in the day to day, this involves self-trust, certainty, and the release of fear by using those qualities and knowledge. Illustrated is *Angelica archangelica*, a mighty plant ally that is transcendent and loving. It provides protection and guidance, increased intuition or inner vision, and helps root the sacred connection to the Divine. The root, seed, and fruit are used for herbal preparations. The flowers are used for vibrational essences.

How | Interlock hands at navel level, while connected index fingers and thumbs are left extended. Pair with breath work to refresh the mind and body.

Benefits | Like abhaya mudrā (page 78), it dispels fear and increases the experience of non-separateness with all. It directs breath to the heart center and ribs, nurturing qualities of both 3rd and 4th energy centers. Cultivates insight and inner silence, problem-solving capacity, and mental clarity. Similar to vajrapradama mudrā (page 122), it calls upon focused energy. Use it to connect with Divine inspiration before any activity that demands your creativity.

Beautifully and intricately woven
into the fabric of the universe.
Restfully abiding
in this present state of awareness.
Knitted together
with the Hand of God...
a collective embrace
from the Creator's gift.

- Louisa Wargo (Lotus Rising) -

39. Swartz J. How to Attain Enlightenment: The Vision of Non-duality. Boulder, CO, US: Sentient Publications (2010)

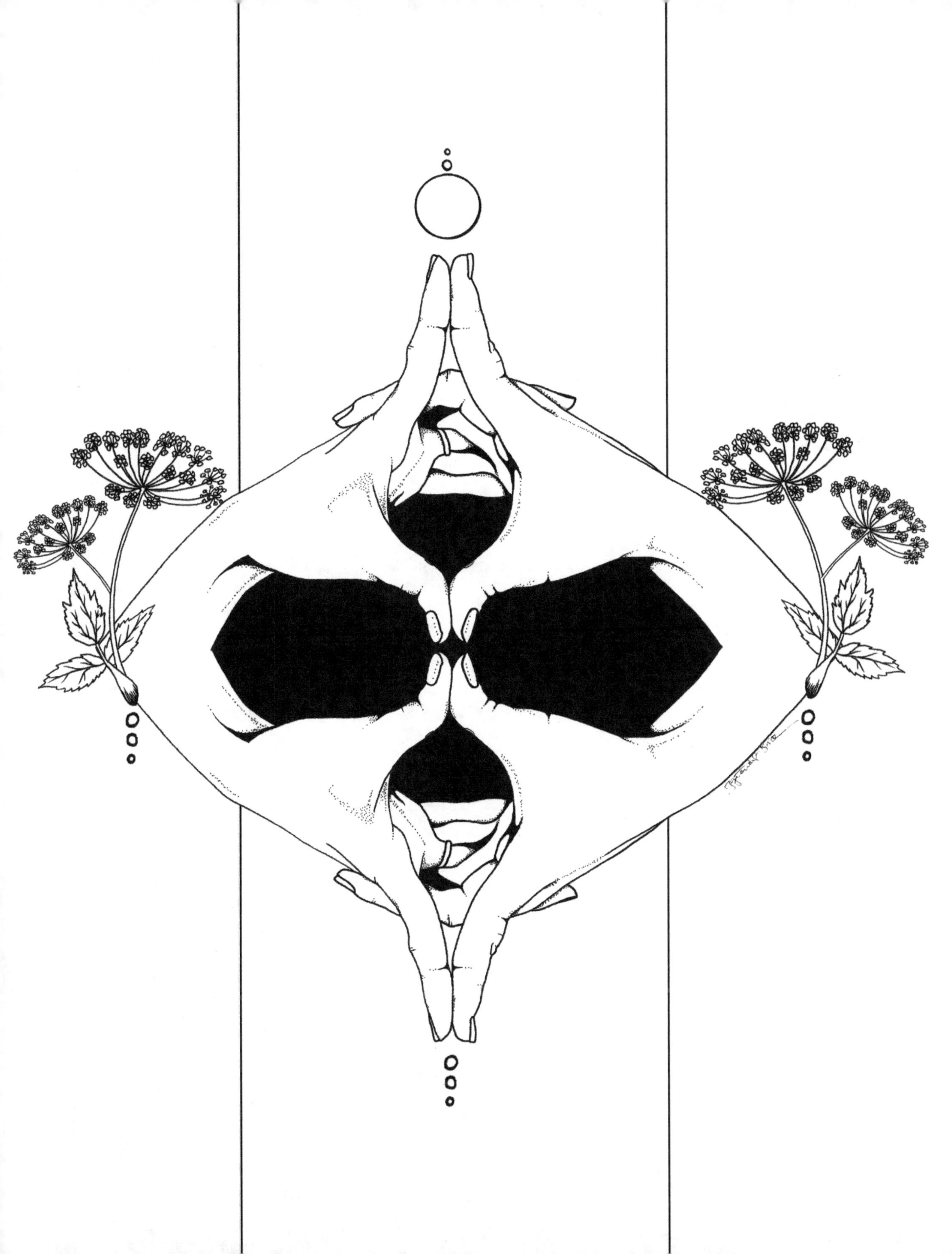

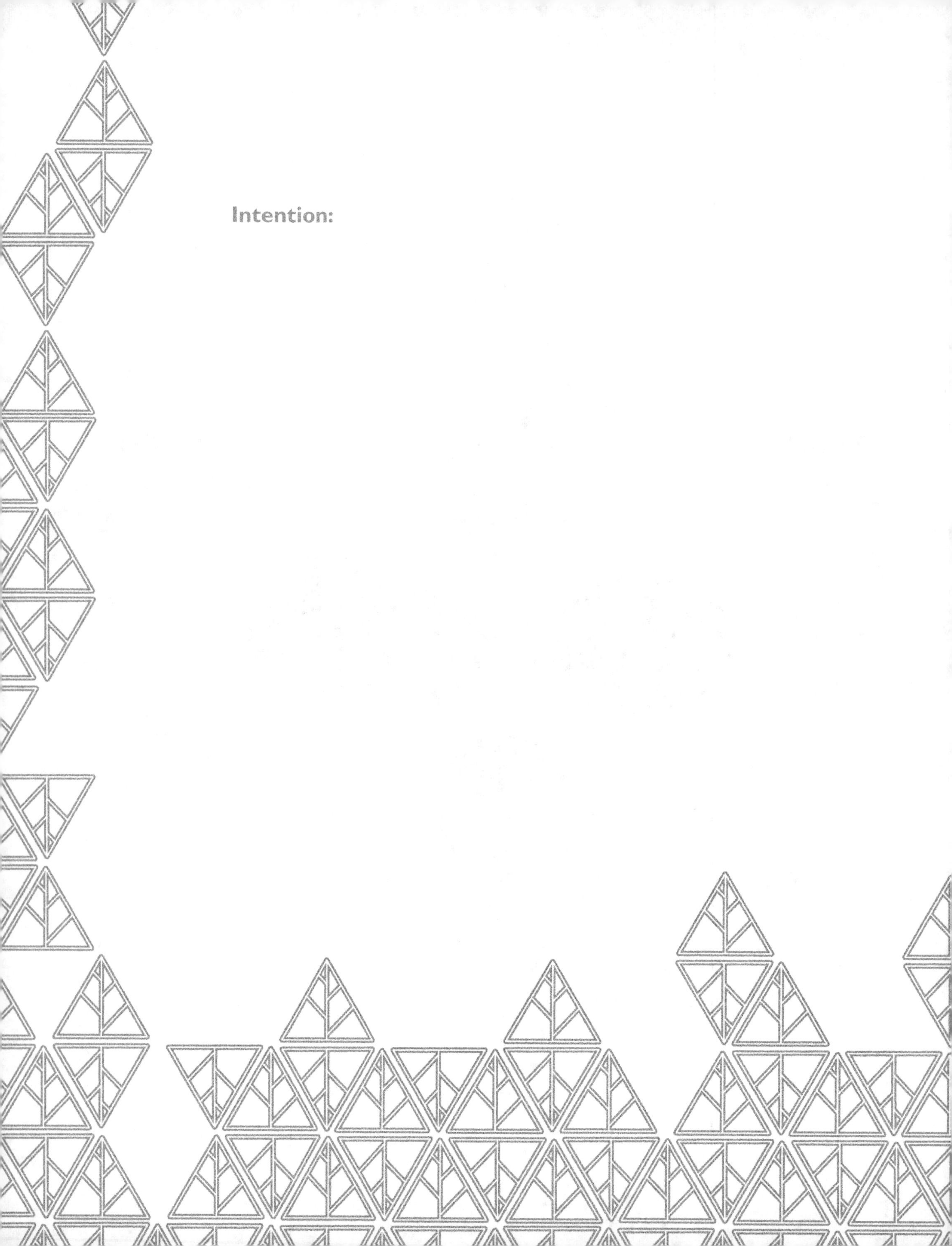

Intention:

Thought Infusions

1. How do you sustain insight and inspiration? Do you trust your insights?

2. Do you think you've had an awakening moment(s) in your life? Were your perspectives and perception changed? If yes, was there new knowledge that could no longer be ignored?

3. What contemplative practices do you already practice (or noted earlier), cultivate your Divine knowledge? How connected do you feel to your spirituality and belief system?

4. Contemplate your colored illustration. How does color change your initial perception of the image? What colors did you use? Look up #anewkindofcoloringbook and #purapranа, share your work. Explore other being's colors and see what new messages come to mind through observation.

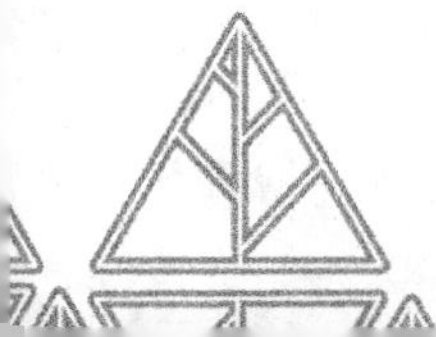

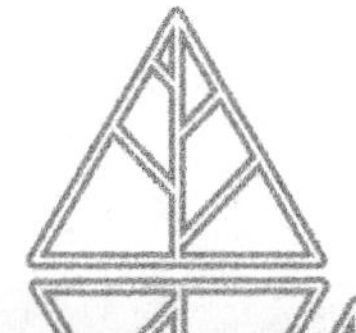

SANA

Kṣēpaṇa or kālī mudrā is a gesture of "pouring out and letting go."[22] In effect, kṣēpaṇa transliterates from Marāṭhī to "casting or throwing away," while Kālī is the Hindu goddess representing death, destruction, transformation, and ultimately, purification.[26] In a practical way, the deliverance from negativity in your life will have a transformative effect. "Sana" is Spanish for healing, so think of self-healing when setting your intention before practicing this gesture: *What aspects, experiences, or charged reactions and emotions do you want to destroy (or transmute) in order to move forward, heal, and grow?*

How | Interlace all the fingers and cross thumbs. Keep index fingers extended and touching fingertips. Gently press palms against each other and stretch your arm upwards from the chest level, reaching for the sky.

Benefits | Helps channel energy flow to the upper cakras and increase expansiveness. Use it to break negative thought patterns. Helps bring breath and awareness to the 5th energy center, releasing tension from shoulders, neck, and throat. Through transformation, new space is made for vitalizing energy. Stimulates elimination system.

There's a path that leads us through a valley,
pitted with stories that hold our grief.
We can choose a slow walk that visits each chapter
or we can kick dust as our feet move with purpose
to the parts yet unwritten.
It's a matter of choice and decision
made with a hand holding loosely
on to what determines our fixed state of concentration.
The power we possess
is only limited by the belief in ourselves...
held in our own heart and fed by the words we speak.

- Louisa Wargo (Lotus Rising) -

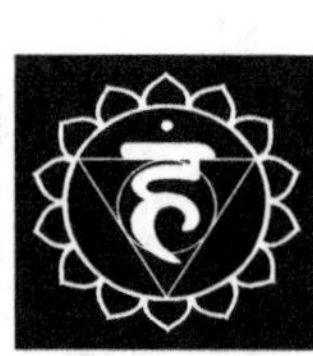

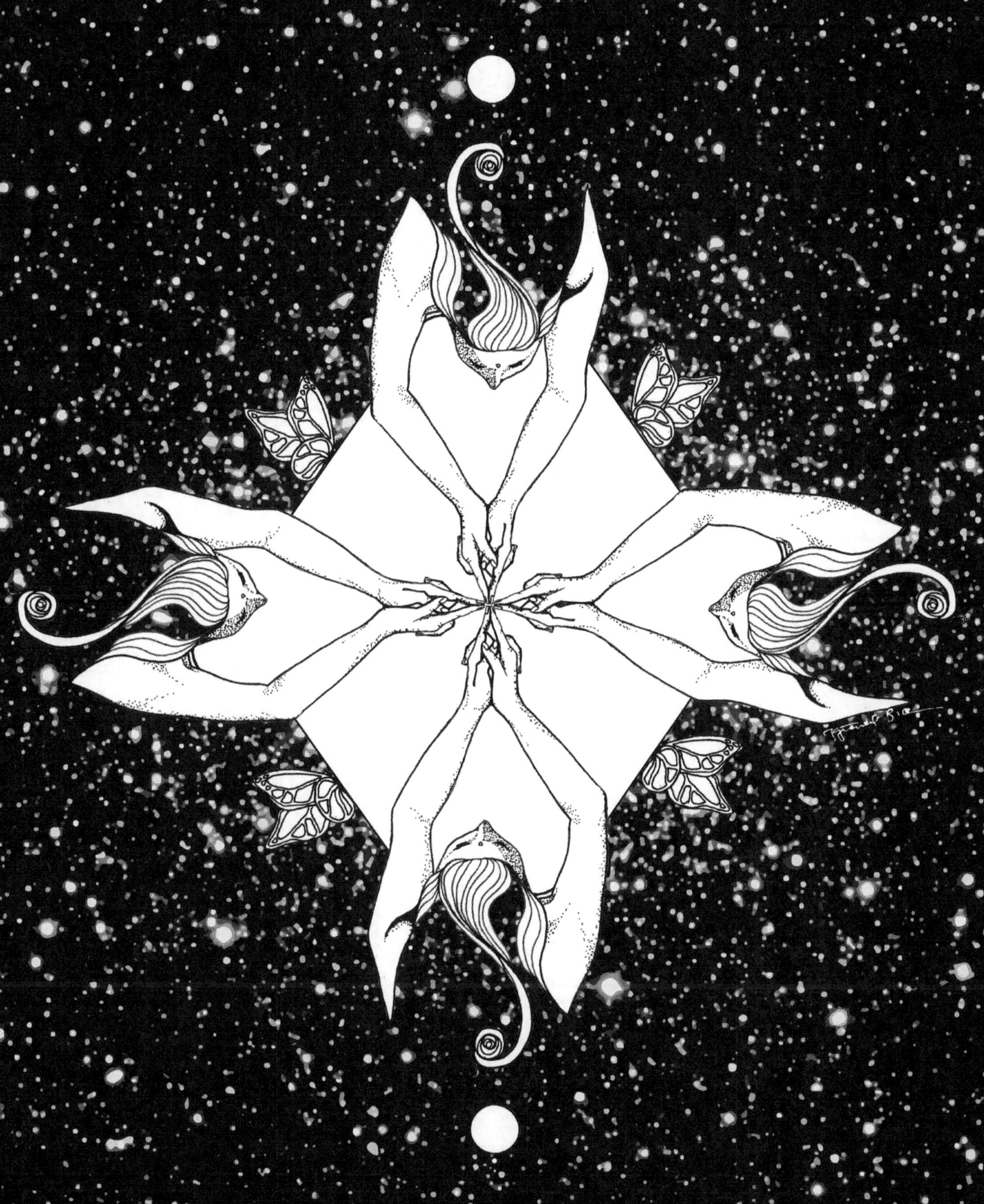

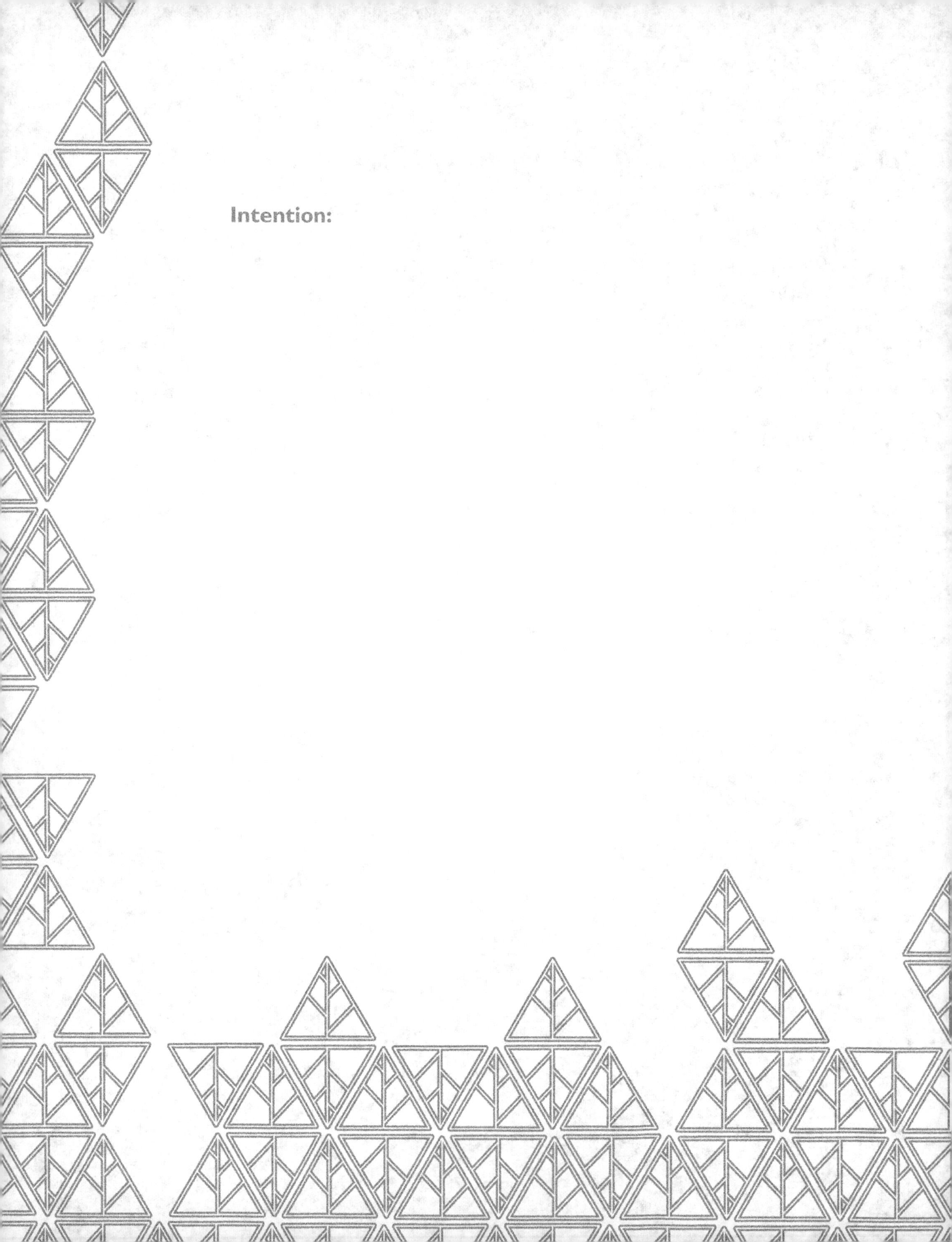

Intention:

Thought Infusions

1. What negative ruts and thought patterns do you gravitate towards? If you haven't fully looked at your negative patterns, take at least one week to observe the way you react or carry-on about your day, you could be surprised at what you find. Take note of any charges you encounter at any time, be it in thought, emotion, verbal, or by action. Always seek support and professional help if you think there are things that you may not be able to handle alone.

2. How frequently are you aware of how your energy is reaching others? Is it constructive or destructive? Are you a co-creator, builder, sustainer? Or a destroyer?

3. Contemplate your colored illustration. How does color change your initial perception of the image? What colors did you use? Look up #anewkindofcoloringbook and #puraprana, share your work. Explore other being's colors and see what new messages come to mind through observation.

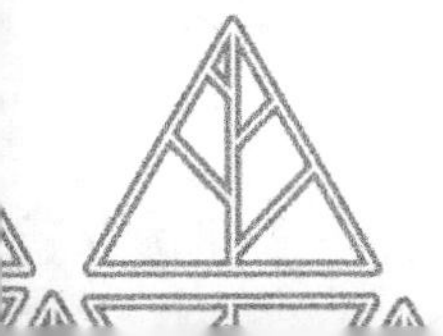

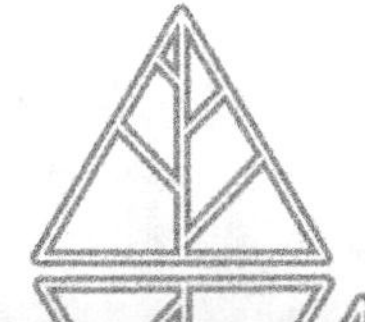

FORGING PATH

Garuḍa transliterates from Sanskrit to "eagle or mythological bird," and this concept is regarded as such in various traditions such as Hindu, Buddhist, and Jain mythologies. Garuḍa is deemed the king of birds (beheld as such in the indigenous Americas) and a creature of great strength and compassion, carrying the sun on its golden wings from east to west (very much like in Aztec mythology).[40-41] Resembling an eagle, Garuḍa and equivalents are also actively used as a cultural and national symbol in Cambodia, India, Indonesia, Japan, Mongolia, Myanmar, Nepal, Suriname, and Thailand. Likewise, eagle symbology is vastly used across many other cultures including those in Africa and Oceania, and other belief systems such as Christian symbolism and Greek mythology. Garuḍa mudrā carries uplifting and activating energy, it is a great gesture to practice for inspiration and creative processes.

How | Interlock your thumbs with your right hand on top of your left while extending all other fingers, palms facing inward.

Benefits[8, 22] | Activates energy flow and is energy balancing. Supports the cardiovascular system. It helps ease nerves and increase sense of calm. Supports mood balance and helps discern subconscious or hidden aspects of the mind.

Dancing with the creative spirit of fire
and its nurturing force.
Sparking new vision, inspired from source.
Ascending from our ashes
of old karmic patterns.
Shining a brighter light within.
Feeling the alchemical churning
as a phoenix fire burning
deeeeeeeep inside the old layers dissolve with combustion
during this healing process of transmutation.

- Vivia Astraia -

40. Choskyi VJ. ***Buddhist Himalaya.*** 1(1): 7 (1998)
41. Werness HB. Continuum Encyclopedia of Animal Symbolism in World Art. London, UK: Cotinuum International Publishing Group (2003)

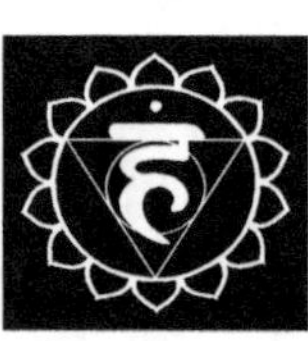

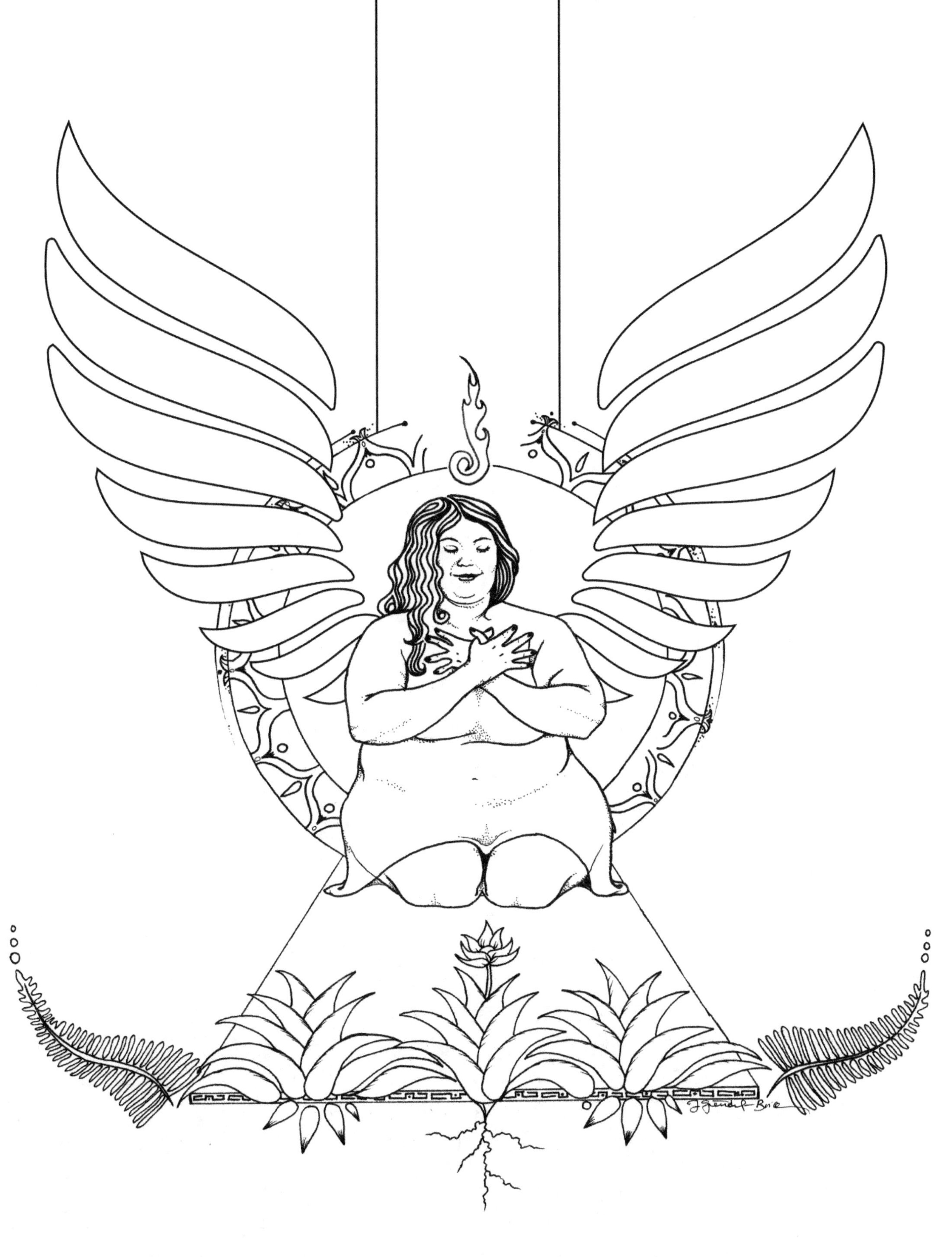

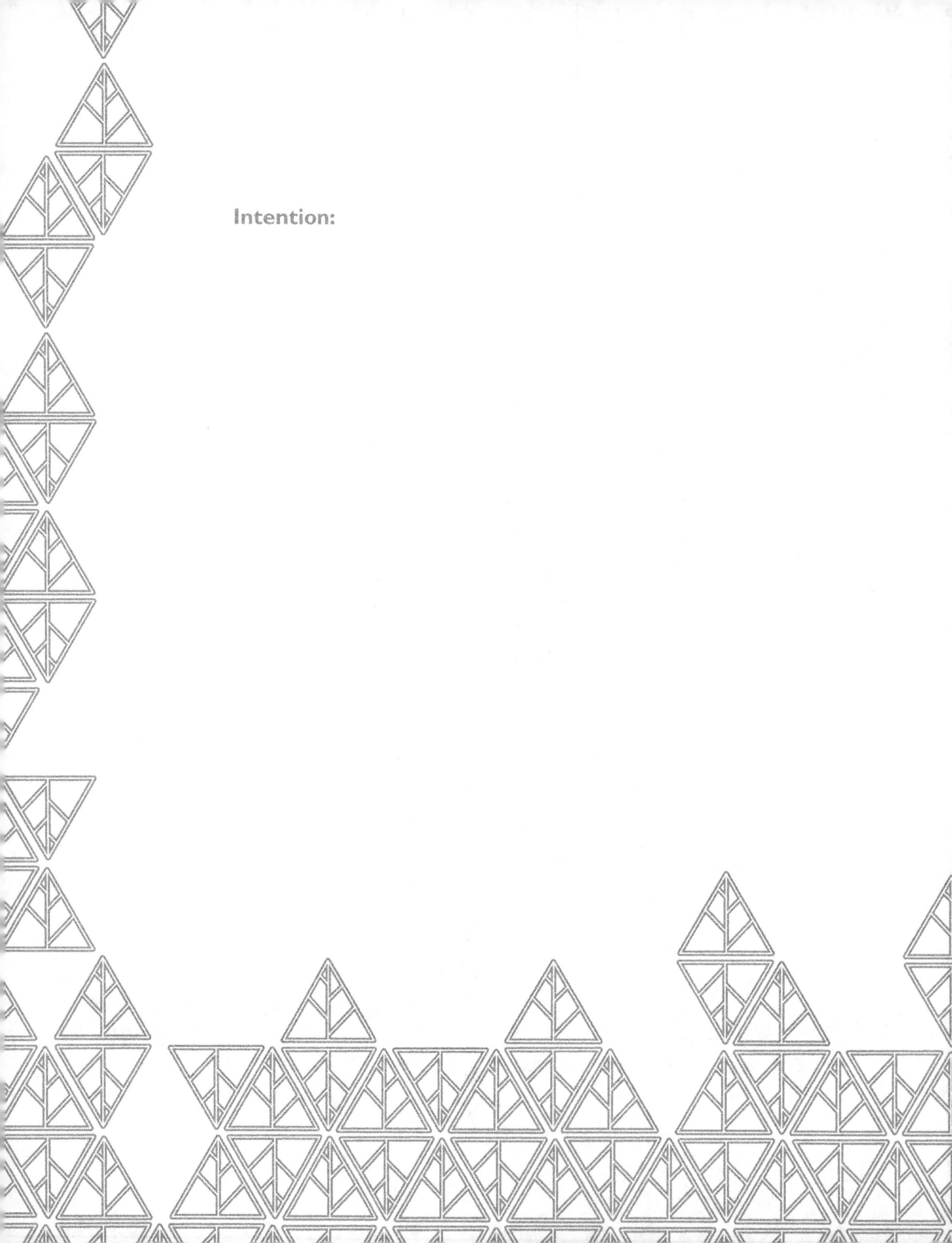

Intention:

Thought Infusions

1. As illustrated, garuḍa mudrā evokes expansion and openness. How can you embody expansion and openness as you move through the present moment? Imagine the sensation of being a bird, stretching out your wings, and soaring into your journey or any task at hand.

2. Do you forgive yourself? How frequently do you sit with yourself to heal the wounds that are often self-inflicted?

3. Garuḍa is often depicted as the devourer of snakes. The snake in this instance symbolizes feelings and thoughts that you may or may not be fully aware of (e.g., jealousy, helplessness). For at least one week, practice awareness of your needs and feelings, thoughts, and actions. Awareness of these processes brings freedom through the understanding of how you digest life, and how your mind reacts. Scan the code to access the best resource I have learned about for needs and feelings.

Feelings List

4. Contemplate your colored illustration. How does color change your initial perception of the image? What colors did you use? Look up #anewkindofcoloringbook and #puraprana, share your work. Explore other being's colors and see what new messages come to mind through observation.

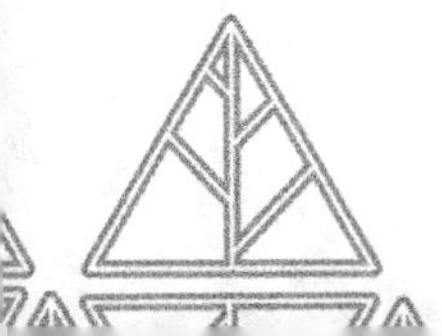

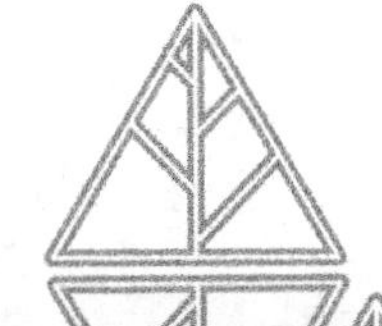

Qì

Qì is often translated as the equivalent to primordial life force or prāṇa, yet "(...) Chinese thought does not easily distinguish between matter and energy. (...) Qì is somewhere in between."[42] It's the thread that connects all beings, and the central principle in Chinese traditional medicine, martial arts, and overall Chinese culture. Qì is usually described as a flowing force, however, there is a balance between flowingness, stability and structure. Qì is able to provide both. Hākinī is the goddess that represents the "power or śakti (shakti)" of ājñā, or the 6th energy center.[43] Hākinī mudrā exclusively works on the holistic integration of being and the power of the mind.

How | Join the tips of all fingers and thumbs, hold space for a sphere within the palms.

Benefits[8, 26] | Helps balance the bicameral brain. Increases cognitive ability, retention, and concentration. Harmonizes all aspects of our being, increases health potential and the ability to heal at all levels of the HEF (page 30). Awakens intuition and the sense of unity. Relaxes and supports the respiratory system.

Mudrā Keys
Serene Ease
Neuro-Circuitry
Expands
Neuro-Plasticity
Activate—Pulsate—Elevate

- Vivia Astraia -

42. Kaptchuk TJ. The Web That Has No Weaver: Understanding Chinese Medicine. Pennsauken, NJ, US: BookBaby (2014)
43. Shumsky S. Awaken Your Third Eye: How Accessing Your Sixth Sense Can Help You Find Knowledge, Illumination, and Intuition. Pompton Plains, NJ, US: Career Press (2015)

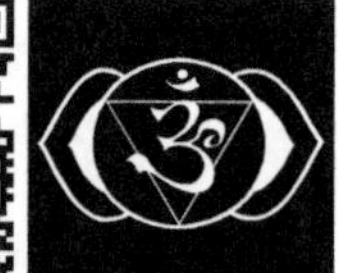

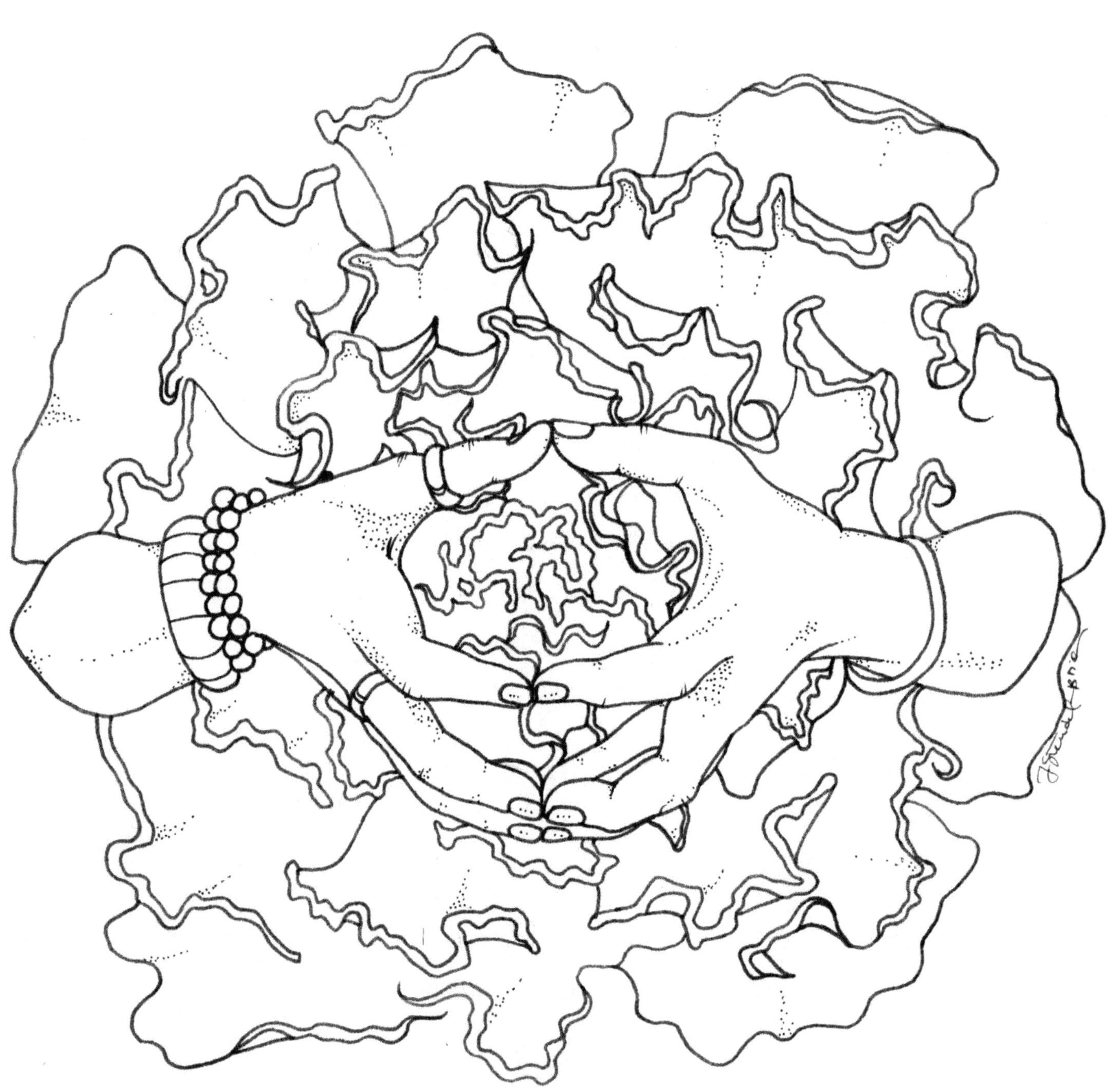

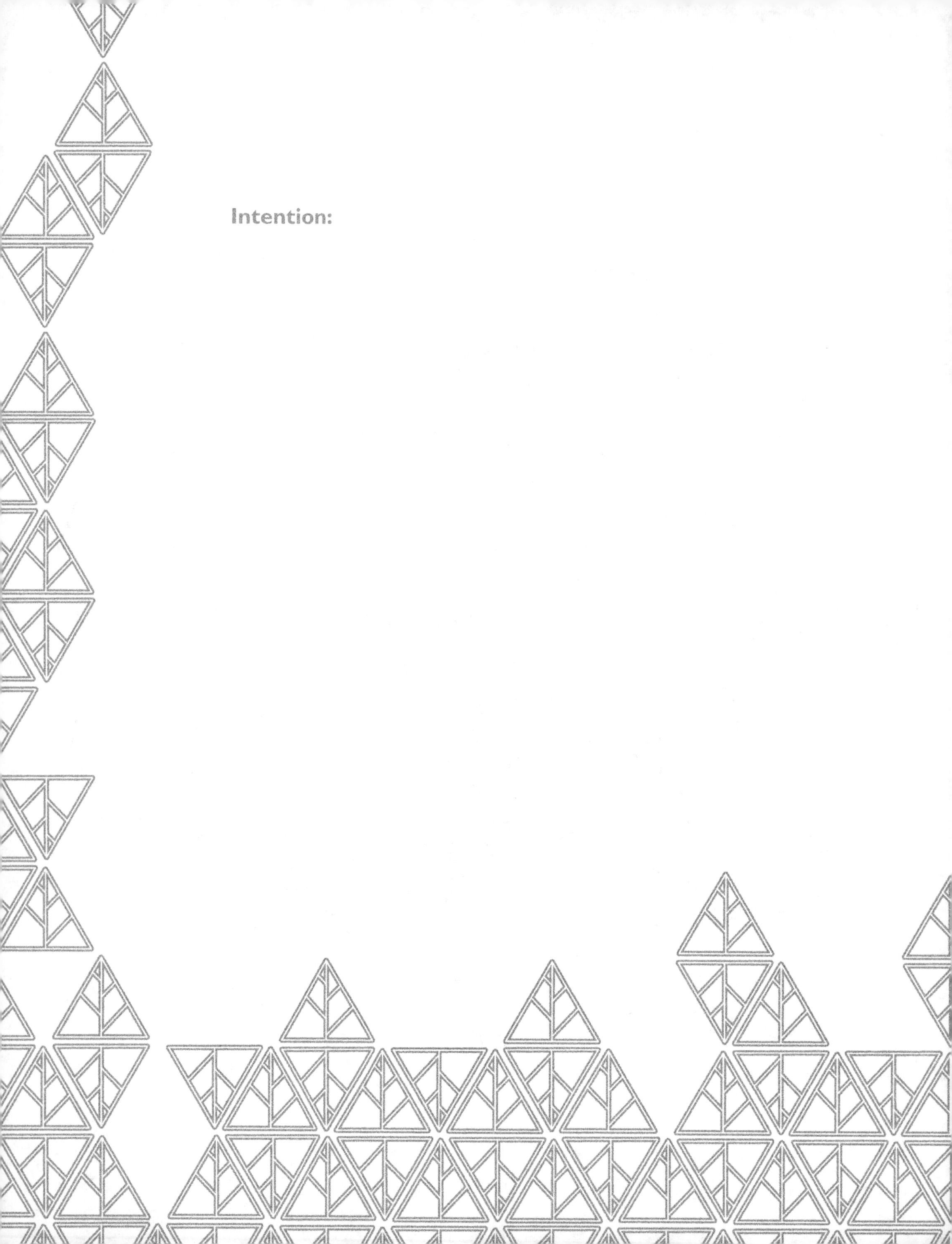

Intention:

Thought Infusions

1. How is your relationship to your inner sense of knowing and guidance?

2. How can you strengthen the power of your mind? What steps can you take towards that goal? Can you perceive any barriers? If yes, what can you do to work on those barriers?

3. Tactile sensing, mindfulness, and meditation have all been associated to neuroplasticity, or the brain's ability to re-wire itself based on behavioral changes that include emotions, thoughts, and actions. What changes can you make to optimize your positive growth?

4. Contemplate your colored illustration. How does color change your initial perception of the image? What colors did you use? Look up #anewkindofcoloringbook and #puraprana, share your work. Explore other being's colors and see what new messages come to mind through observation.

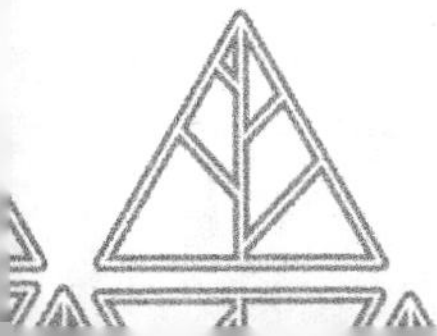

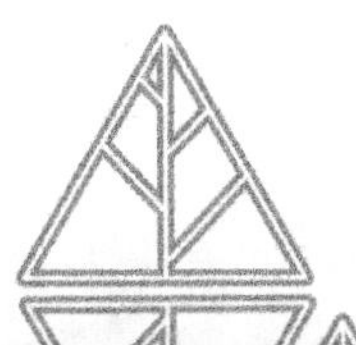

OPEN

Gyān transliterates from Sanskrit to "knowledge and wisdom." Gyān mudrā is the "seal of knowledge and consciousness," and an ancient gesture of spiritual progress characterized by peace and calmness. It's also known as jñāna (knowledge and omniscience) mudrā.Like many other mudrās, gyān can be found depicted in religious and spiritual iconography throughout. This mudrā also supports the root cakra (page 50) through its ability to help alleviate fear (similar to abhaya mudrā, page 78), the expansion of knowledge, and the ability to recognize the Divine in all living and non-living things—all is sacred.

How | Join the tips of the thumb and the index finger, relax the remaining fingers. Point fingers downward to focus on root cakra (called chin mudrā), point fingers towards the sky to stimulate third eye cakra aspects (gyān or jñāna mudrā).[22]

Benefits | Activates root cakra and helps decrease tension and depressed feelings. Helps increase openness to the Divine and focus during meditation. Stimulates the brain, nervous system, and pituitary gland. Helps increase receptivity and the forging of a path to increased clarity, wisdom, and universal knowledge.

**"Embracing the full spectrum of life:
not having attachment to pleasure
nor aversion towards pain.
To be open,
with compassion,
and ready for anything.**

- Vivia Astraia -

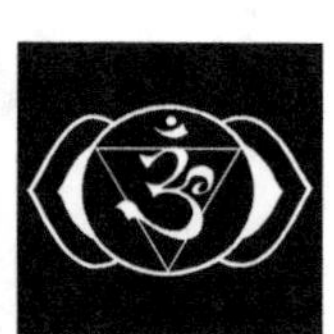

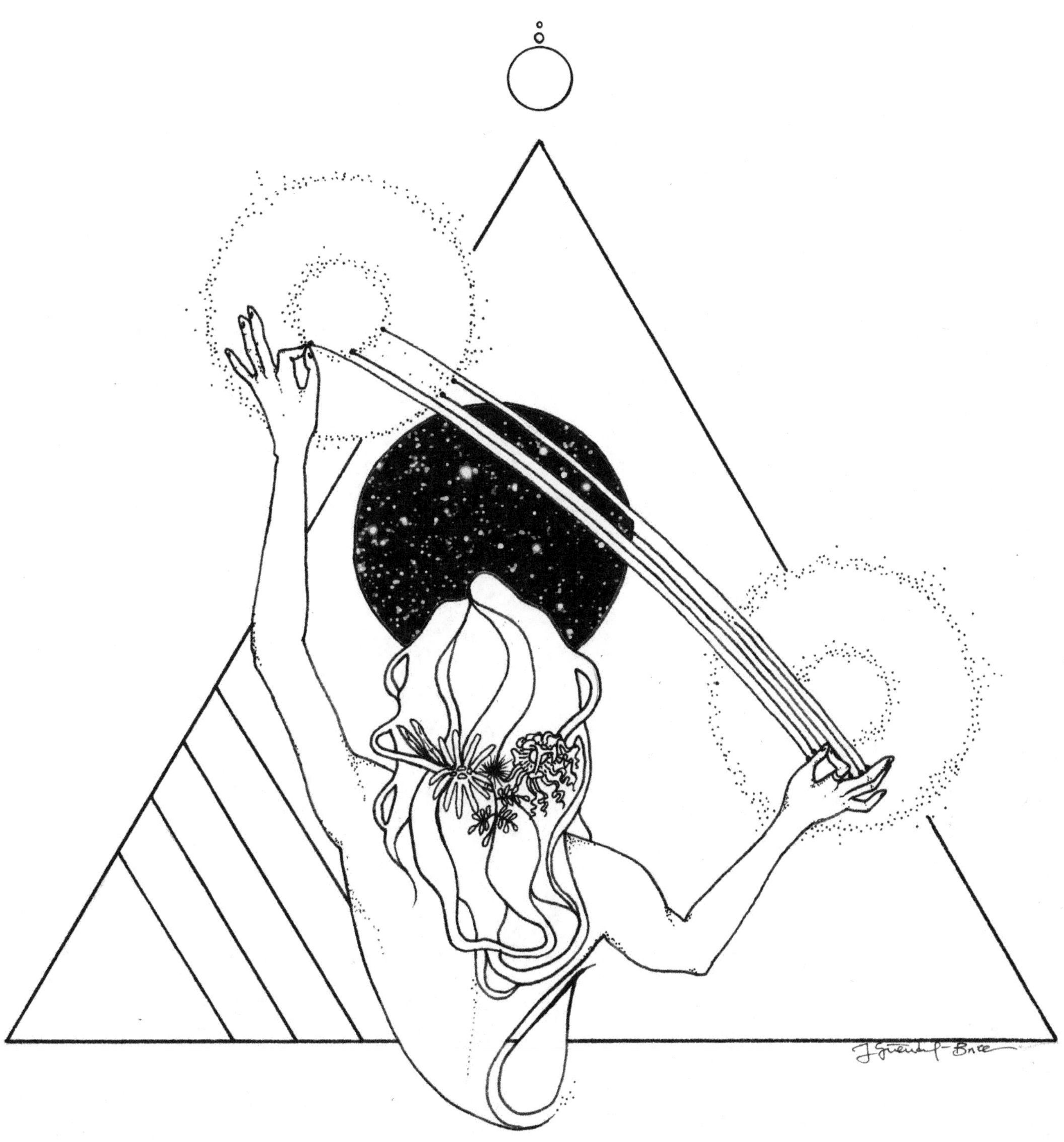

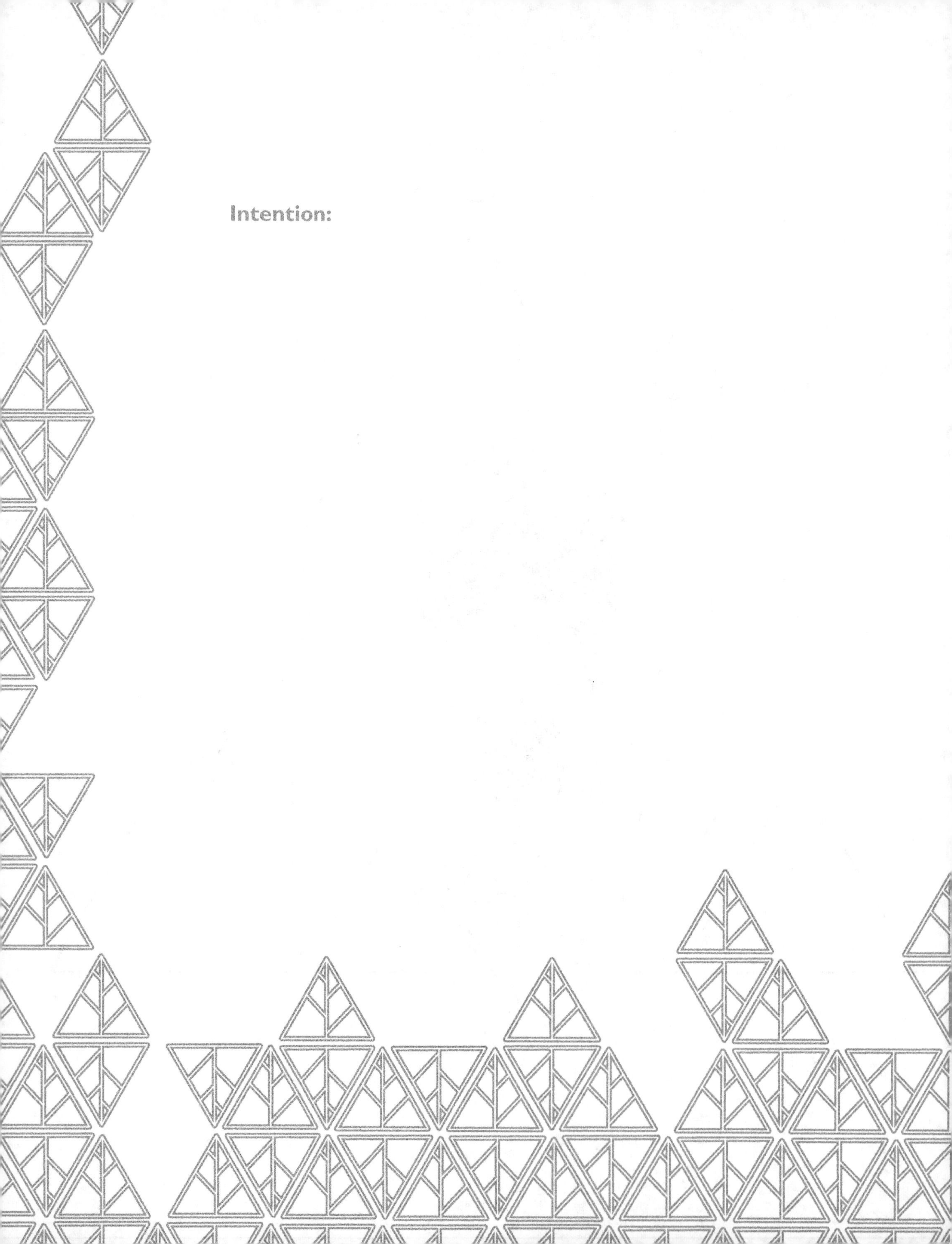

Intention:

Thought Infusions

1. Do you feel encouraged to be imaginative or to develop intuitive thinking? If not, what are the barriers and how can you overcome them?

2. Do you often stop to acknowledge the sacredness of all creation or existence? If not, what steps or lifestyle adjustments can you make to give yourself the space to be more present and receptive?

3. Thoughts and inner visualizations are a powerful thing. Once you have a thought it will appear as an image, which then feeds through your lower energy centers and moves upwards in the path of manifestation. Are you conscious and selective about your thought patterns? Are they kind to yourself and others?

4. Contemplate your colored illustration. How does color change your initial perception of the image? What colors did you use? Look up #anewkindofcoloringbook and #puraprana, share your work. Explore other being's colors and see what new messages come to mind through observation.

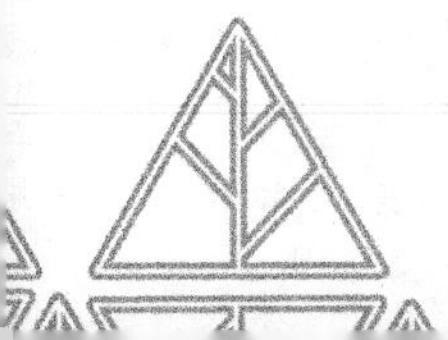

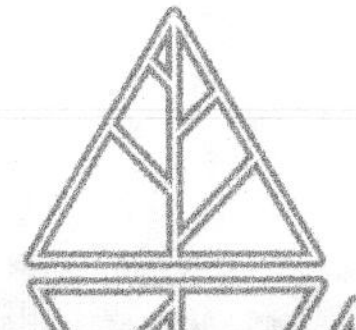

INWARD

Sākṣī transliterates from Sanskrit to "witness or observer." Sākṣī mudrā of the inner self provides a space to dwell with your spirit, to raise your vibration as you grow to understand the universal life force within you and all around you. This mudrā bridges the heart cakra to the upper cakras, collectively working on our doors of perception so we can see everything as it is, Infinite.[44] Sākṣī is a key element of reflection, whereby self-study is actionable through detached observation of the inner world: thoughts, emotions, physical sensations, and belief systems.[26]

How | Join all fingertips from opposite hands including the thumbs. Create a space at the center of this union where you concentrate your energy to practice this meditation. Clap and rub hands together and come into form, bring your hands to eye level and look into your space using your eye of contemplation. Press thumb knuckles between brows.

Benefits | Quiets the mind to allow for communion with the Divine, scatters the illusion.

"I'm resting in that place
where rivers flow to a gentle home,
where a whisper is heard
above a peaceful rain.
This is where I come to recline
in simple thoughts of precious mind.
All worries melt into an ocean far away,
as this is a refuge for a needed time.

- Louisa Wargo (Lotus Rising) -

44. Blake W. The Marriage of Heaven and Hell. New York, NY, US: Florence Press (1911)

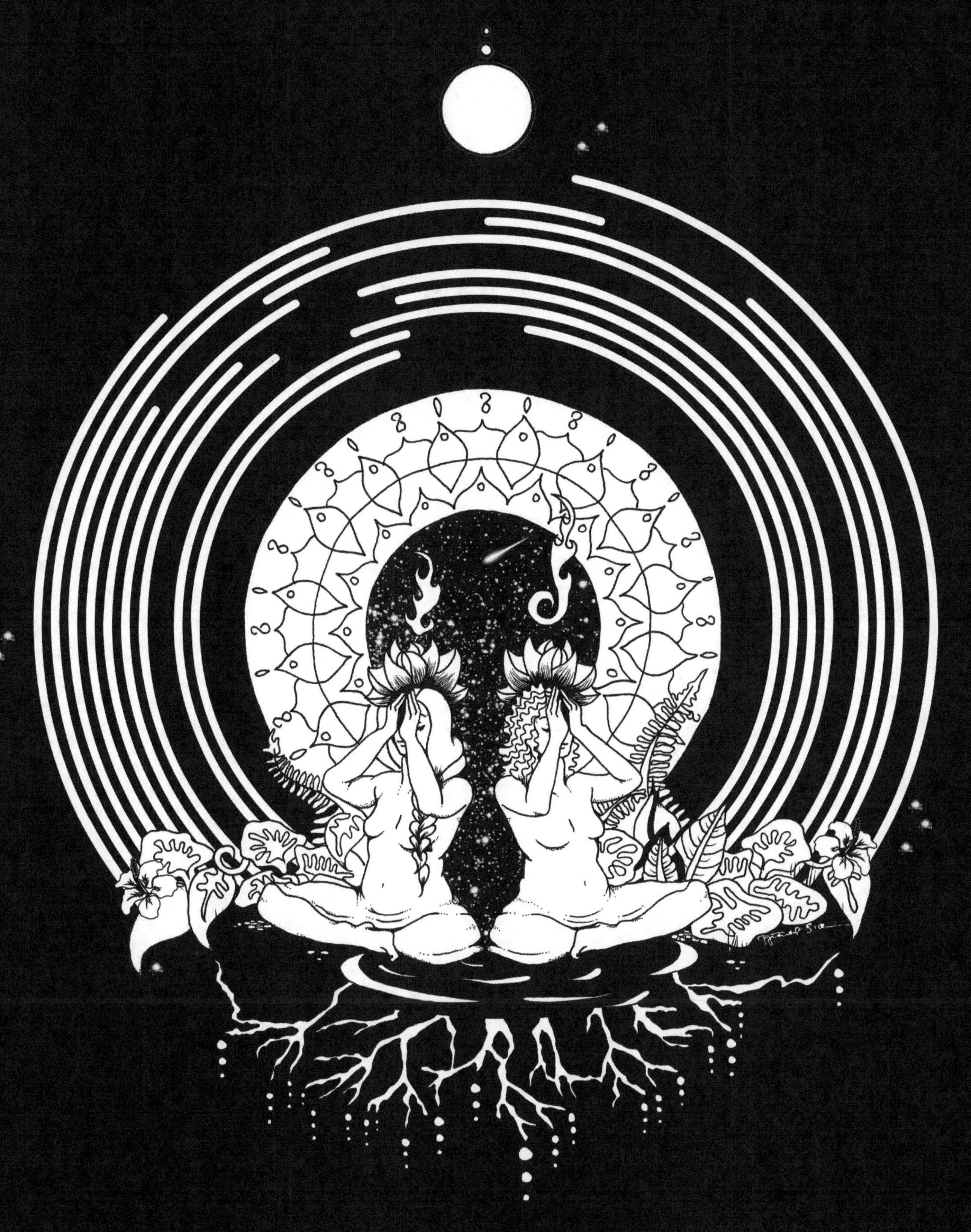

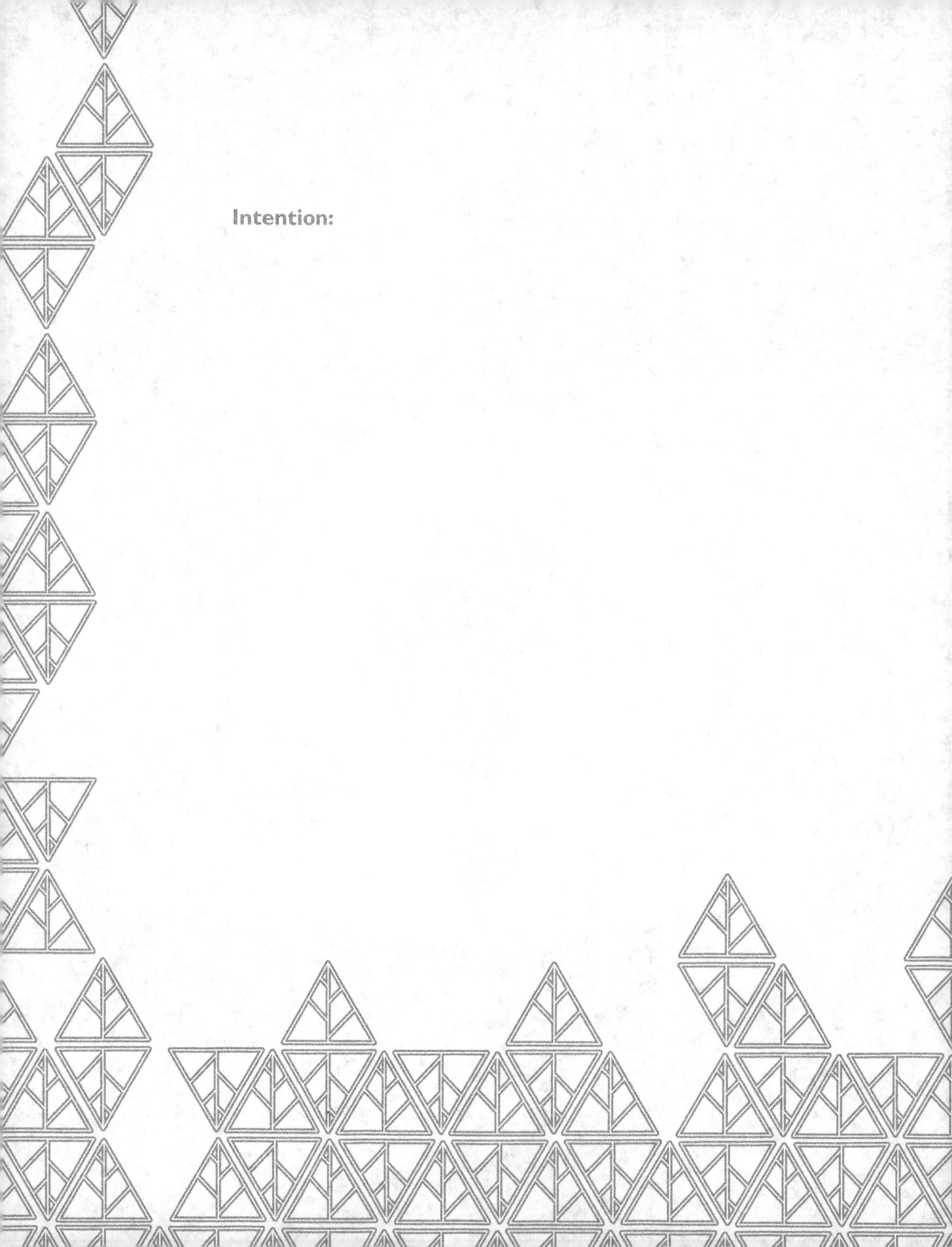

Intention:

Thought Infusions

1. We see the world, each other, and ourselves as filtered by our illusions (and belief systems). What identifiable societal and cultural programming can you identify in yourself? Think of illusions, indoctrinations, education, etc. How do these affect the way you internalize, measure, and see the world, your life, and others?

2. How does your inner guidance and intuition (from Qì illustration journal prompts, page 141) tug at you and your perceived reality?

3. Independent of practice or belief system, how often do you seek alone or quiet time to sit with yourself and direct your sight and inquiry inward? What contemplative practices do you use?

4. Contemplate your colored illustration. How does color change your initial perception of the image? What colors did you use? Look up #anewkindofcoloringbook and #puraprana, share your work. Explore other being's colors and see what new messages come to mind through observation.

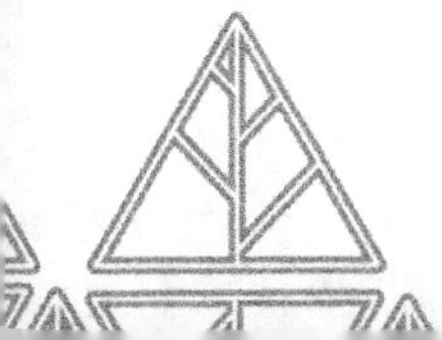

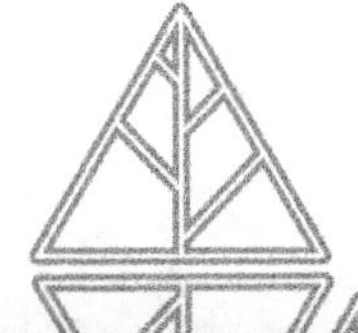

MYSTIC METAPHOR

Kāleśvara transliterates from Sanskrit to "time," in observance of the Hindu deity that rules over time. Kāleśvara mudrā is one of contemplation, a perfect complement for the very same practice that represents this third eye activity and this contemplative art meditations book. Similar to sākṣī mudrā (page 146), kāleśvara mudrā promotes self observance and aids in identifying and clearing conflicting thoughts.[22]

How | Join the middle finger tips and unite the joints of the index fingers. Join your thumbs and bend the remaining fingers inward.

Benefits[45] | Helps clear conflicting thoughts, decreases anxiety and brings inner calm, and supports memory and concentration. Aids in the elimination of addiction and addictive behavioral patterns. Set your intention and visualize obstacles in your journey that need to be overcome before you meditate with this gesture.

What is the single most important minute of your life?
The next minute and the next, and the next.
Visualize the *Temple of Dreams*.
Feel the depths of the wellspring of your heart.
Envision your innermost heart's desire.
Generate the frequency of this vortex.
Breathe in the essence of this portal.
Bathe in the quintessence of your soul's happiest place.
Your future self is there already.
In this minute, you have made the quantum leap.

- Vivia Astraia -

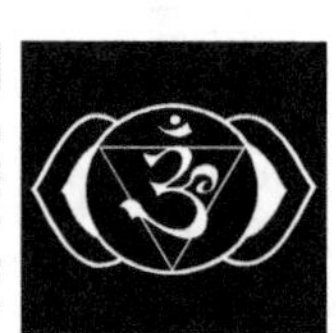

45. Sen RS. The Keys to the Best You. Bloomington, IN, US: Balboa Press (2014)

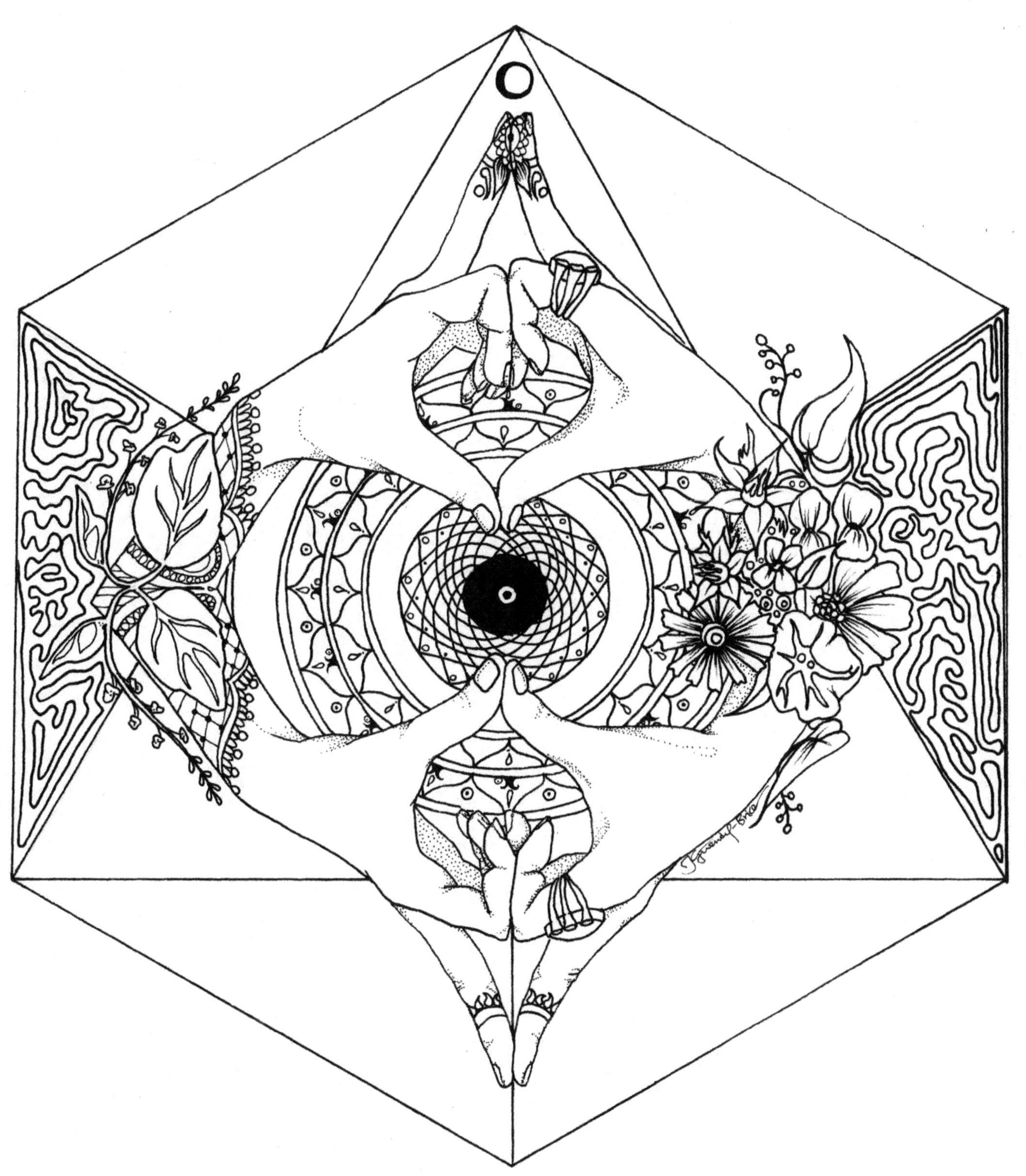

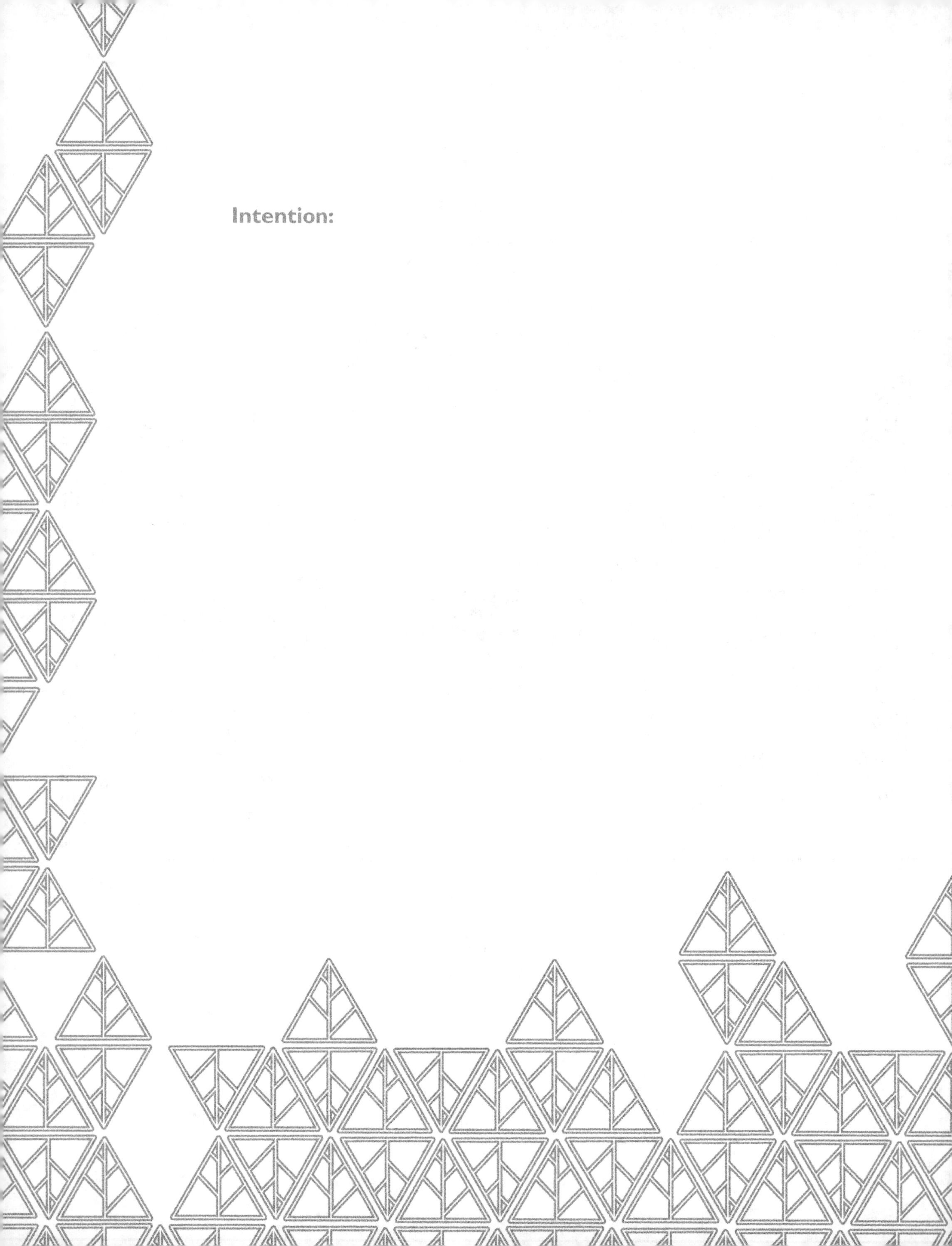

Intention:

Thought Infusions

1. What are the main negative behaviors that you identify in yourself and would like to overcome? What are the most predominant conflicting thoughts?

2. What contemplative practices do you wish to include or already include in your routine that can build on your sacred practice and help open or balance the 6th energy center? A few examples include chromotherapy and creative visualization (art therapy, page 18), guided imagery and visualizations, attending art or creative events, reading and daydreaming.

3. Contemplate your colored illustration. How does color change your initial perception of the image? What colors did you use? Look up #anewkindofcoloringbook and #puraprana, share your work. Explore other being's colors and see what new messages come to mind through observation.

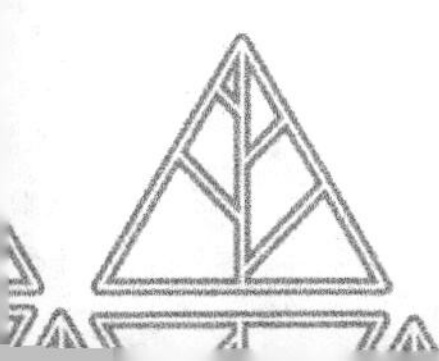

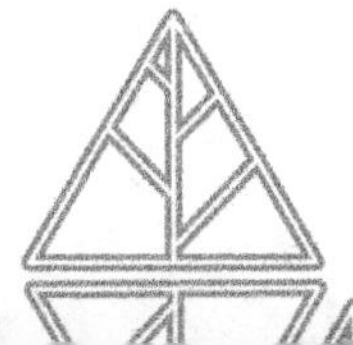

CULTIVATING LIFE

In Chinese philosophy,[42] including traditional Chinese medicine, martial arts and exercise; yīnyáng represents dual contrary forces that are in reality, interconnected and interdependent as present in all things. Yet, despite their perceptual dualistic nature, yīn and yáng are part of an indivisible oneness as represented by the iconic symbol (illustrated, derived from the Chinese cosmological philosophy of Tàijí). Yīn represents feminine and receptive qualities, while yáng is masculine and forceful energies. In Chinese Buddhism, shǒuyìn (手印) transliterates as the equivalent of mudrā to "hand seal or symbol,"[46] and yīnyáng transliterates to dual opposites "light-dark or negative-positive" (page 20). The dharmacakra mudrā represents the "gesture of turning the wheel,"[22] and evokes the conformation of the yīnyáng symbol. Shǒuyìn practice has similar energetic effects on the practitioner since yīnyáng interactions, according to the hand gesture and finger conformation, will result in different patterns of Qì flow in the body.

How | Join the finger tips of the thumb and index finger while spreading the remaining fingers. Invert the gestures in opposite reflection of each other.

Benefits | Helps balance the feminine and masculine energies, as well as all energy centers. Promotes grounding, and the observation of oneness from the dualistic reality. Promotes harmony through the intersection of limits and boundaries of opposites with the potential to create and expand.

The fragility of life opens like a spring blossom.
a victim to the pain of borrowed time.
The meaning of a circumstance lays hidden
amongst the endless threads that weave together from birth.
To embrace one's mortality
is to embrace a fate born from an acceptance
that our existence is continually unfolding
through an eternal universe.

- Louisa Wargo (Lotus Rising) -

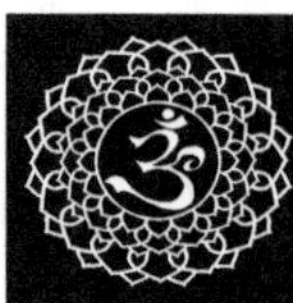

46. Soothill WE, Hodous L. A dictionary of Chinese Buddhist terms with Sanskrit and English equivalents. London, UK: Kegan Paul-Trench-Trubner (1937)

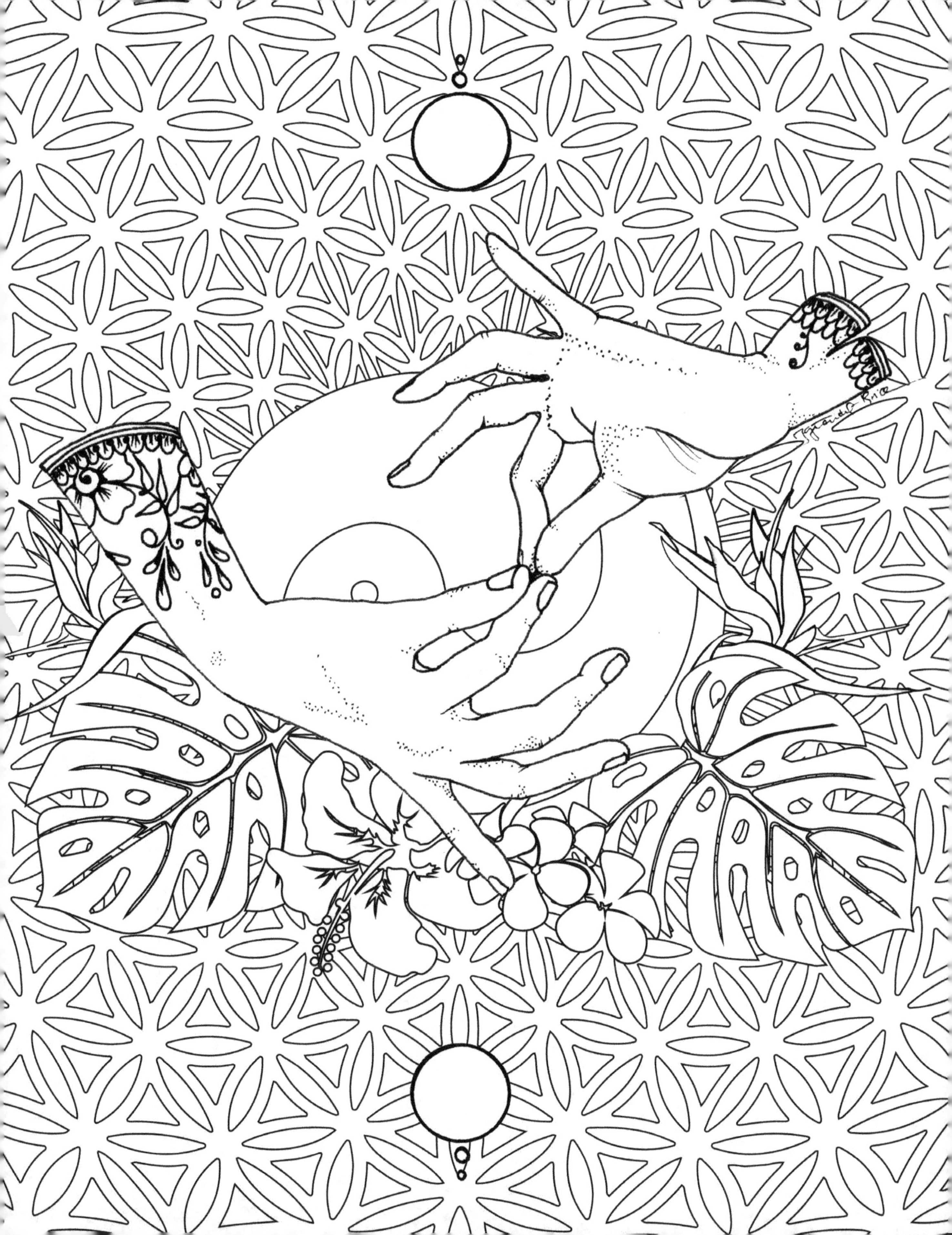

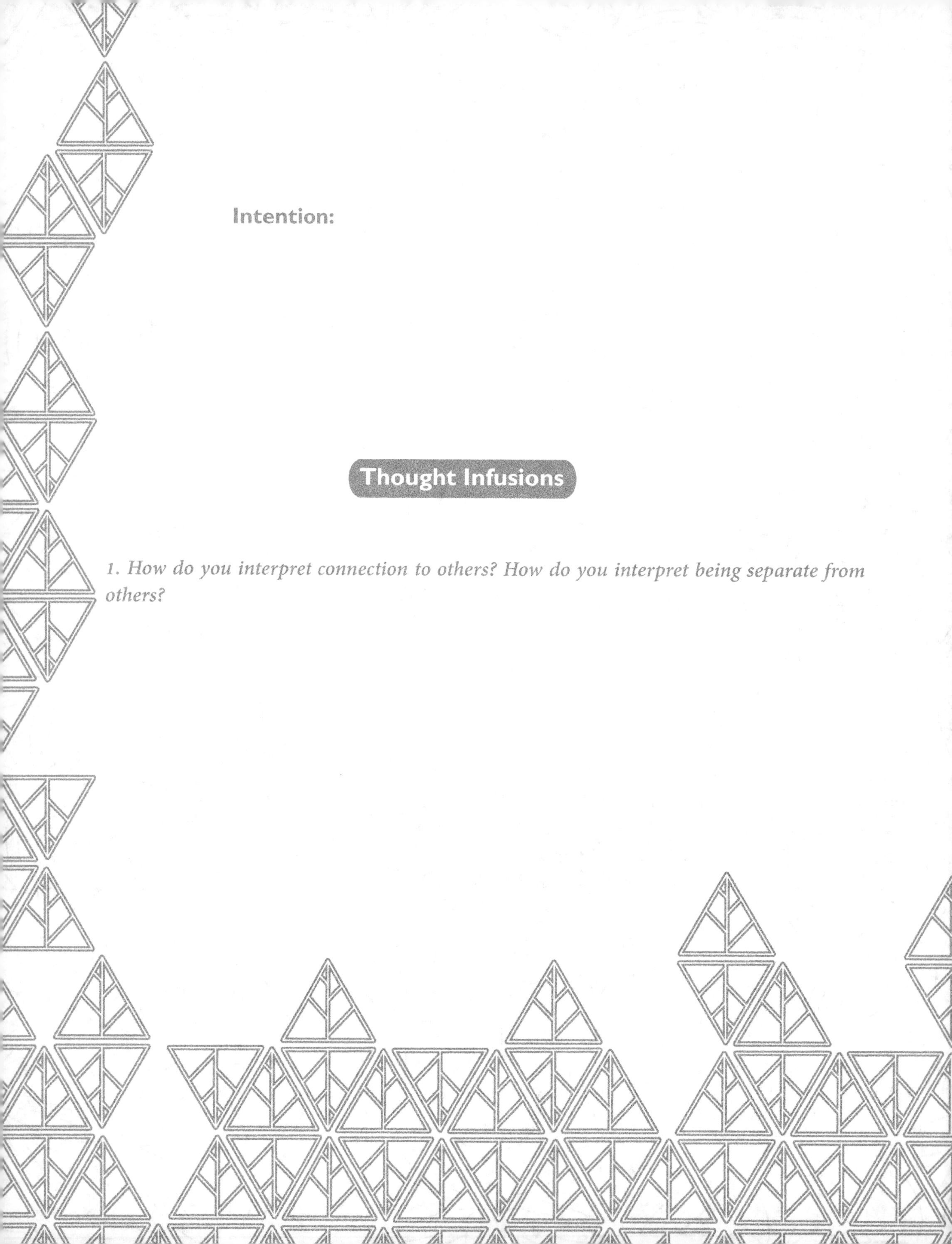

Intention:

Thought Infusions

1. How do you interpret connection to others? How do you interpret being separate from others?

2. Our reality and lives are immersed in dualism, there is night and day. Darkness and lightness. Black and white. Evil and good. The unjust and the righteous. Death and life. We are ruled by this dichotomy, can one truly live without the other?

3. How does your belief system support unity between all creation or existence?

4. Yáng is associated with the left brain hemisphere, while yīn is associated with the right side of the brain. How can you apply the principles of yīnyáng to your creativity?

5. Contemplate your colored illustration. How does color change your initial perception of the image? What colors did you use? Look up #anewkindofcoloringbook and #puraprana, share your work. Explore other being's colors and see what new messages come to mind through observation.

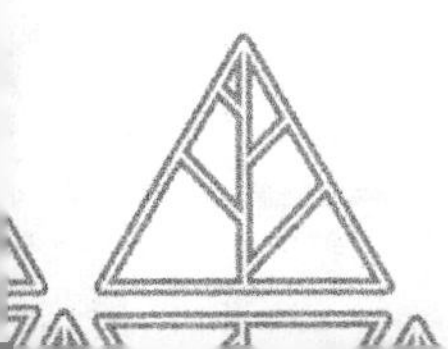

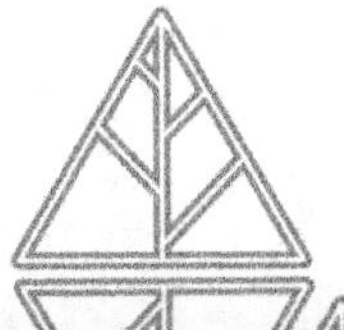

AMÉN

The añjali mudrā is most commonly associated in the Western world as a symbol of prayer, worship, and benevolence, and it's vastly used in religious iconography throughout the globe. In Eastern cultures it's used as a greeting, it transliterates from Sanskrit as "to offer or salute." The Purāṇas (ancient Sanskrit literature) describe añjali as a mode of worship with two hands. Añjali mudrā is a symbol of respect for what and who you hold sacred. It's also the first joint-hand gesture as described in the Abhinaya Darpaṇa.[36] Amén in Spanish stands for "amen," an affirmation added to the end of a prayer or hymn that can be loosely translated as "so shall it be."[47]

How | Inhale and bring your palms together. Rest the thumbs lightly on your sternum. Exhale and hold.

Benefits | Reduces stress and anxiety and opens the heart. Helps to increase flexibility of the arms, wrists, hands and fingers. Honors your blessings. Helps to re-energize and move towards a positive state.[8]

A murky hold on a fragrant awakening.
A time of inward growth in a place of darkness.
Transcending the rebirth,
the unstained arrival of a risen life.
As the lotus emerges from the depths of the mud,
its unfolding petals are drawn to the distant light.
Look up my sweet,
embrace this timely journey.
Take hold of this moment as intentions are set.
My love,
awaken and reach for your heart's desires
as the lotus inspires your deepest yearnings.

- Louisa Wargo (Lotus Rising) -

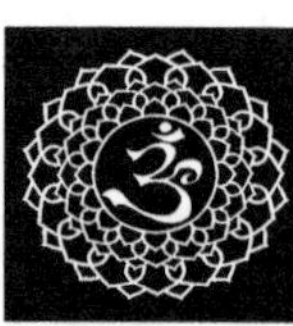

47. English Oxford Living Dictionaries. Available from: http://en.oxforddictionaries.com/definition/amen (as retrieved August 2016)

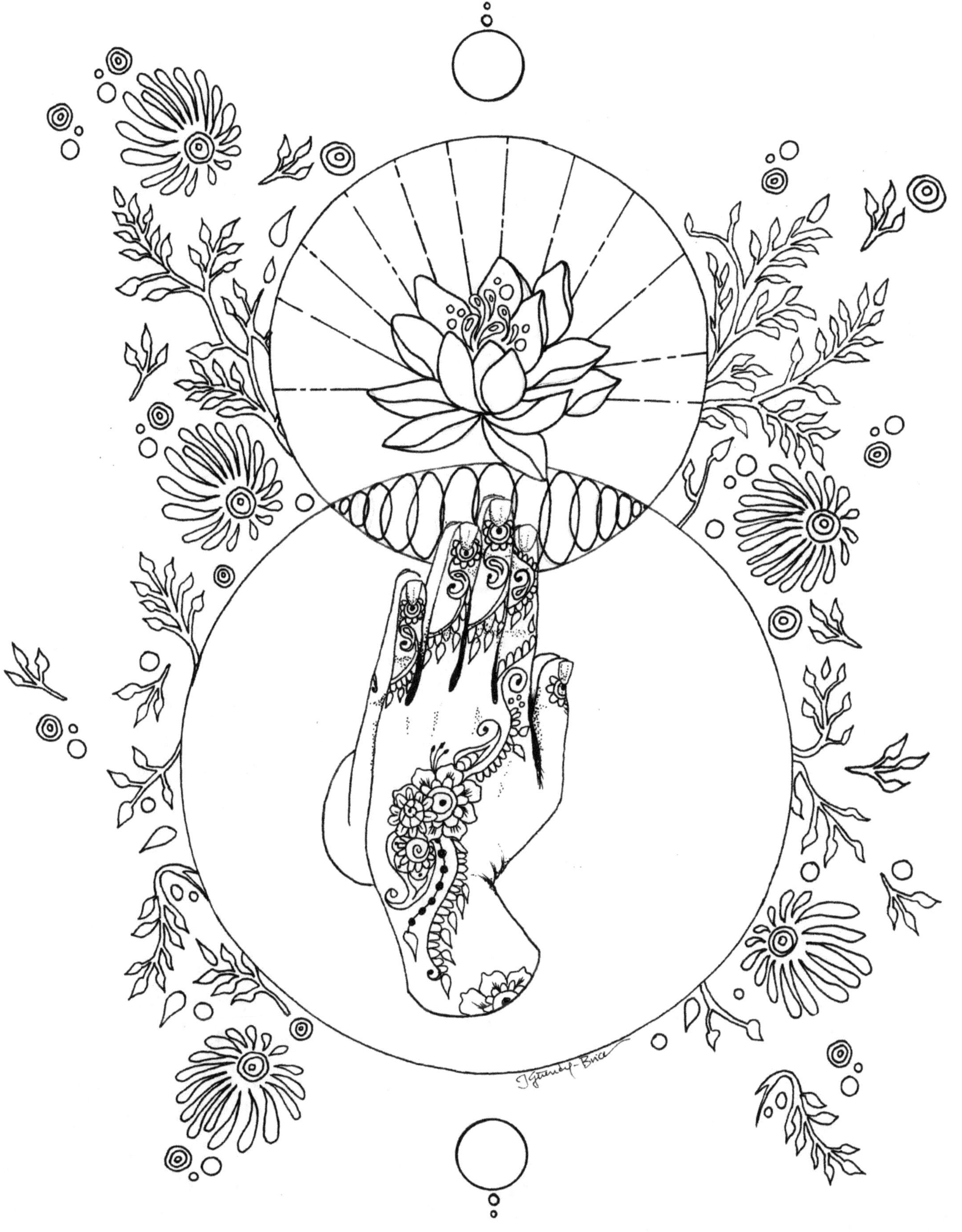

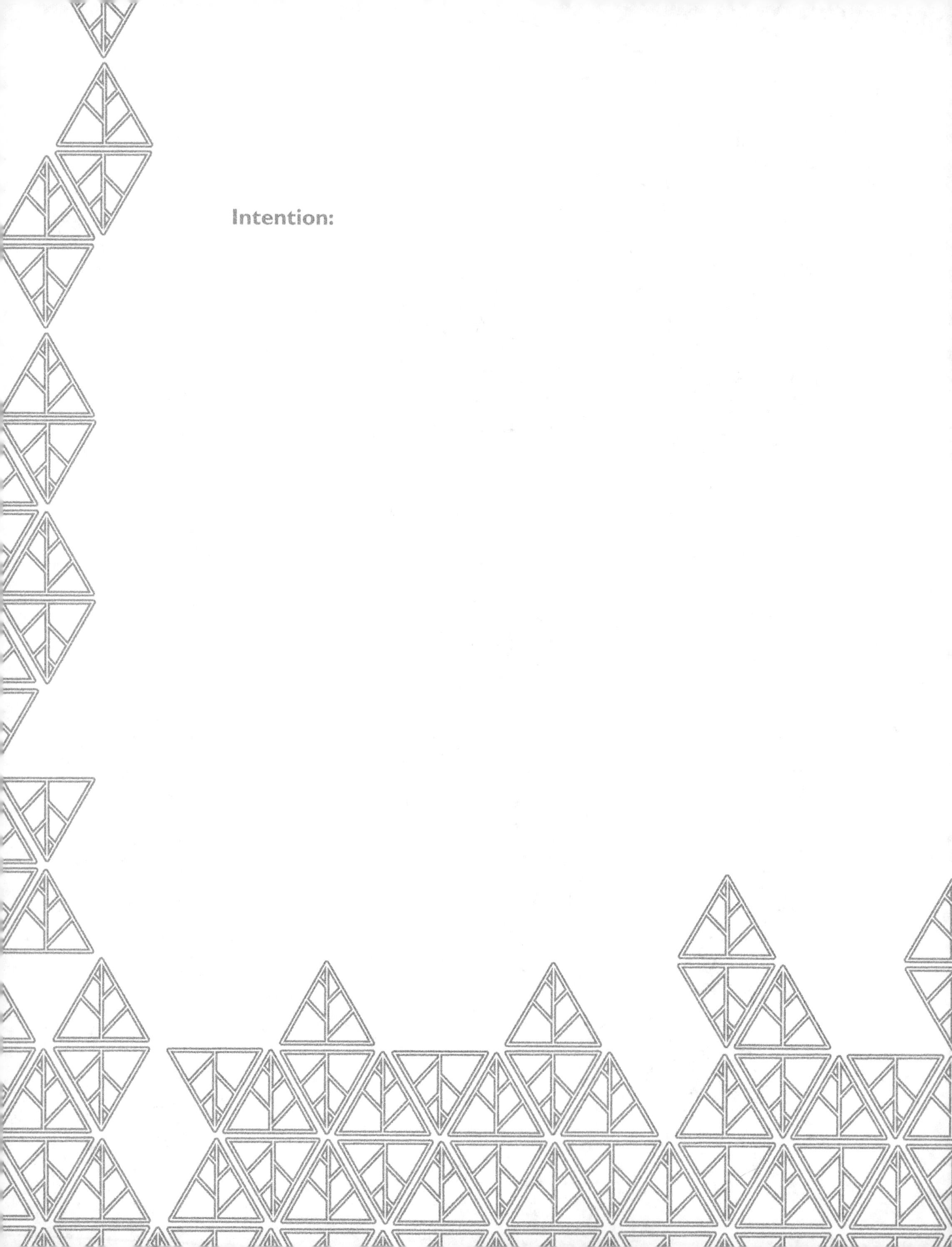

Intention:

Thought Infusions

1. What are your gratitude rituals? How often do you pause to acknowledge all your blessings? How can you improve gratitude mindfulness to increase inner joy and abundance?

2. How do you honor your blessings?

3. What actions do you take or what do you practice when you catch yourself on a downward-slope or trending towards negativity? How do you uplift yourself?

4. Contemplate your colored illustration. How does color change your initial perception of the image? What colors did you use? Look up #anewkindofcoloringbook and #puraprana, share your work. Explore other being's colors and see what new messages come to mind through observation.

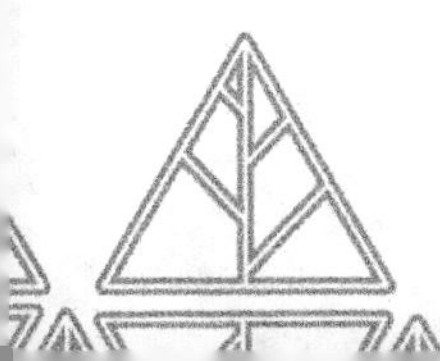

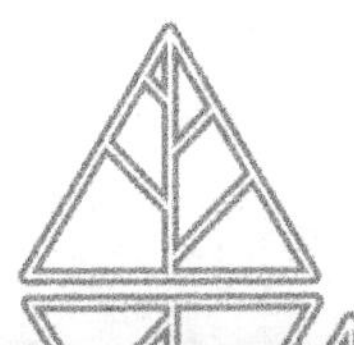

TREE OF LIFE[48]

Puṣpapuṭa mudrā is one of the joint-hand gestures as described in the Abhinaya Darpaṇa and Nāṭyaśāstra, meaning "handful of flowers."[36,49] In this illustration, it is detailed together with the *Tree of Life*, a sacred cosmic tree myth or archetype that spans across cultures and philosophies. Buddha meditated under a bodhi tree (*Ficus religiosa*), under which he is thought to have attained enlightenment. The bodhi tree is equivalent to aśvattha in Hindu mythology, the eternal tree (*F. religiosa*). In Christianity this tree conceptualizes the pure state of humanity, free from the original sin. In the Celtic tradition it represents the Druid belief in the link between heaven and earth. Trees are important cultural symbols, with more than 75 countries officially recognizing a national tree. To me, the most iconic and memorable include the oak (United States of America), the maple (Canada), the Lebanon cedar (Lebanon), the Guanacaste (Costa Rica), the Baobab (Madagascar), the Japanese cherry blossom (Japan), and the Indian banyan (India). It symbolizes perseverance: sprouted from seed, its full majesty now boasts deep roots, a strong foundation (trunk), and everlasting growth and fruition at its branches. It accepts the nurture of the sun's energy while embracing the Earth for its nutrients and water, in turn, giving life. It is a gentle reminder of our connection to Mother Earth, from which we draw both physical and spiritual sustenance.

How | Join your hands at the little fingers and cup them so as to form a recipient space.

Benefits | Both offers and receives. It is described for offering lights, twilight water, and flowers; or receiving or carrying of rice, fruits, flowers, foods, wealth, and carrying or removing water.

You are the bearer of seeds.
Find one, loose one.
You hold the balance between
destruction, co-creation, and stewardship.
Plant them.
Nurture them.
Protect them.
Only you can help them grow.

- Iréne de Brice -

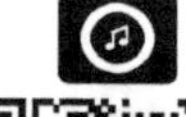

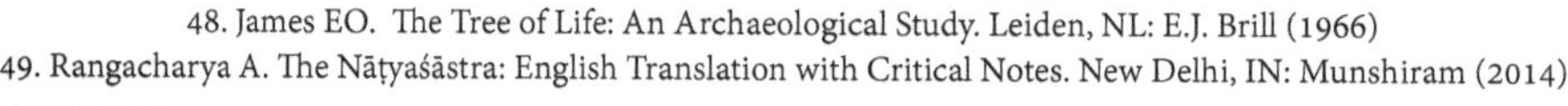

48. James EO. The Tree of Life: An Archaeological Study. Leiden, NL: E.J. Brill (1966)
49. Rangacharya A. The Nāṭyaśāstra: English Translation with Critical Notes. New Delhi, IN: Munshiram (2014)

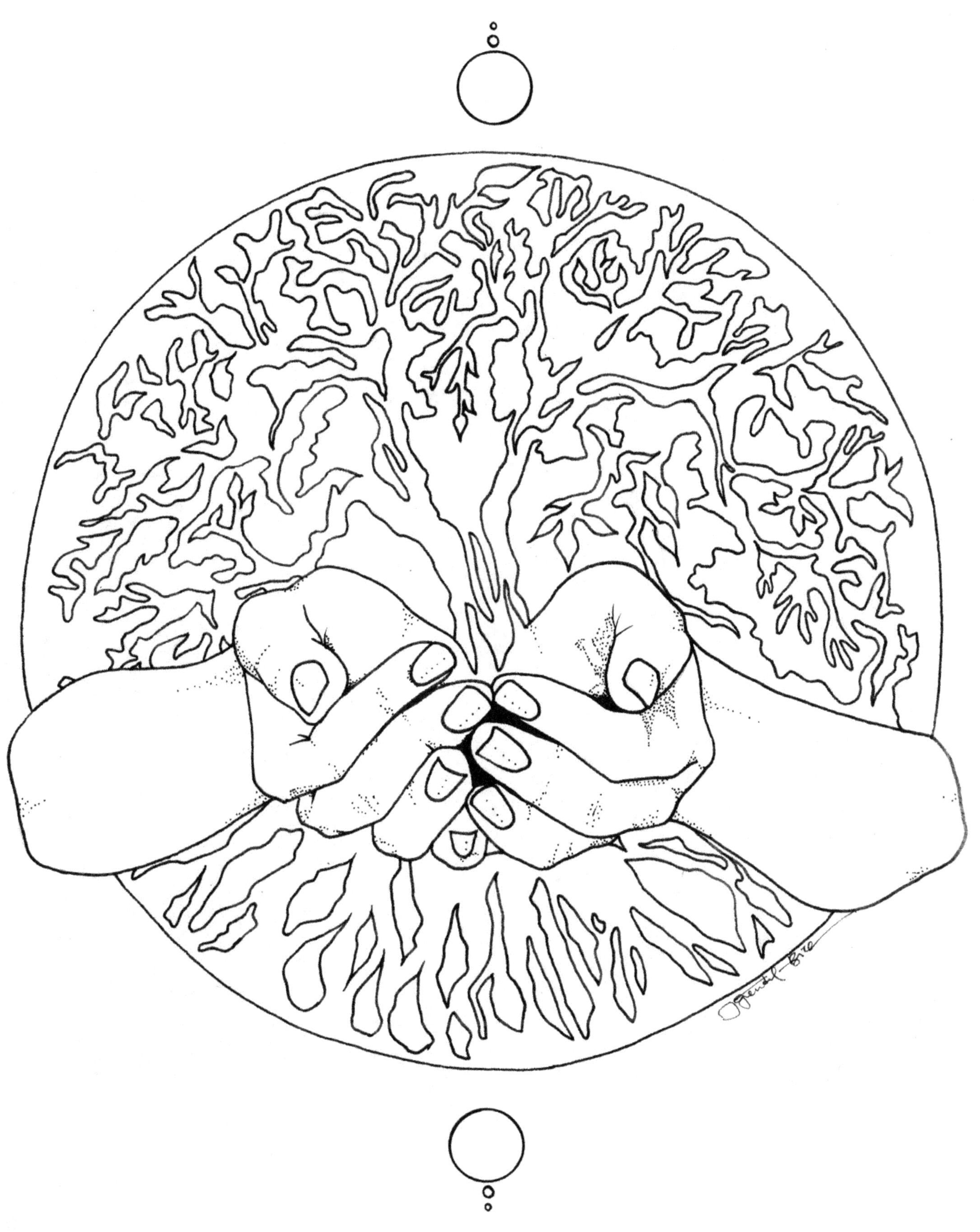

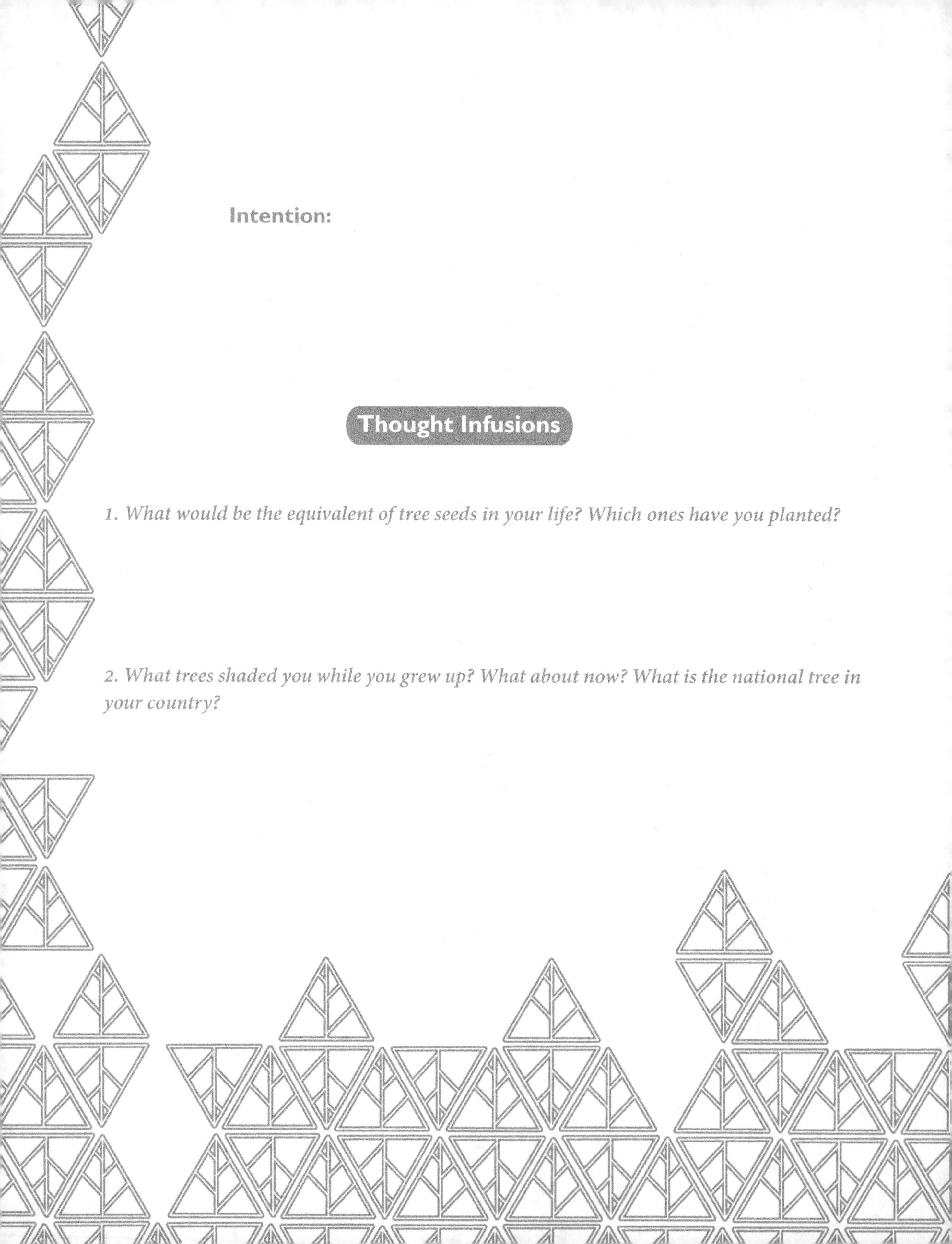

Intention:

Thought Infusions

1. What would be the equivalent of tree seeds in your life? Which ones have you planted?

2. What trees shaded you while you grew up? What about now? What is the national tree in your country?

3. An early childhood movie that also had a profound and almost mystical effect in my life (and I could even say it shaped the way I view, commune with, and revere nature), is Fern Gully: The Last Rainforest (1992). I recommend it to anyone, specially to families with children.

How is your relationship with trees? With the closest forest, if you are lucky to have one nearby? With nature? How do you integrate it in your life? Take a look at the passage below, beautifully written by Dr. David Haskell. How does it translate to, or mirror, our lives?

"Standing in a forest, we are surrounded by billions of conversations. The connections that make up the forest come in many forms. So, unlike the human brain, forest thought is diverse in its nature, but no less complex, agile, intelligent, or creative. Indeed our own 86 billion brain neurons — being structurally and functionally quite uniform, all serving the same organism — produce thoughts that are surely monotone and narrowly focused when compared to those leaping from decentralized connections among cell types drawn from the entire tree of life."[50]

4. Contemplate your colored illustration. How does color change your initial perception of the image? What colors did you use? Look up #anewkindofcoloringbook and #drapurprana, share your work. Explore other being's colors and see what new messages come to mind through observation.

50. Haskell DG. Listening to the Thoughts of the Forest. Originally published in ***Undark Magazine***, available from: http://undark.org/article/listening-to-the-thoughts-of-the-forest (as retrieved November 2017)

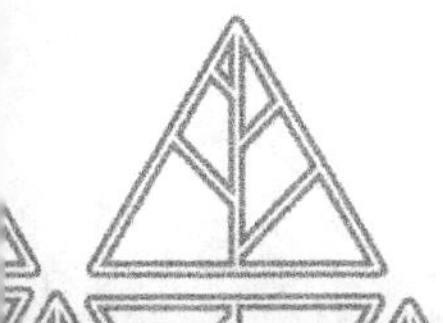

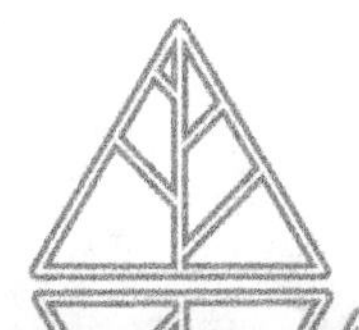

DANCE OF LIFE

Life is dynamic, a constant flow of interactions and lessons. Everything changes with each waking second. You learn, adapt, and progress in your journey. Seek the light, be the light... but don't forget that rich, fertile, and sacred darkness is needed to sprout new life. Seek love, give love. Take action when needed, be love in action. That is all that matters in this cosmic dance. Every day you awaken, give thanks, give praise. The last maṇḍala, to wrap up these stories, blends in multiple mudrās and symbolism that we have covered. At the epicenter of this message is a fractal geometric pattern (universal stroke), representing the mathematical cosmic order that everything in the universe follows, in its turn creating endless possibilities for us to cease.

Release, let your body move its way across this place.
Let it be that branch that begs to bend with ease.
Let it go, don't hide in your own self judgment.
It's just a disguise for radical non acceptance.
Now breathe... Exhale, repeat.
Peel back those layers of restraint.
Can you feel it?
You are free, you are found,
you are tasting the drink of self expression.
Spin, twirl... Like a morning bird chasing the sky.
Boundless. Safe.
Welcome to yourself.

- Louisa Wargo (Lotus Rising) -

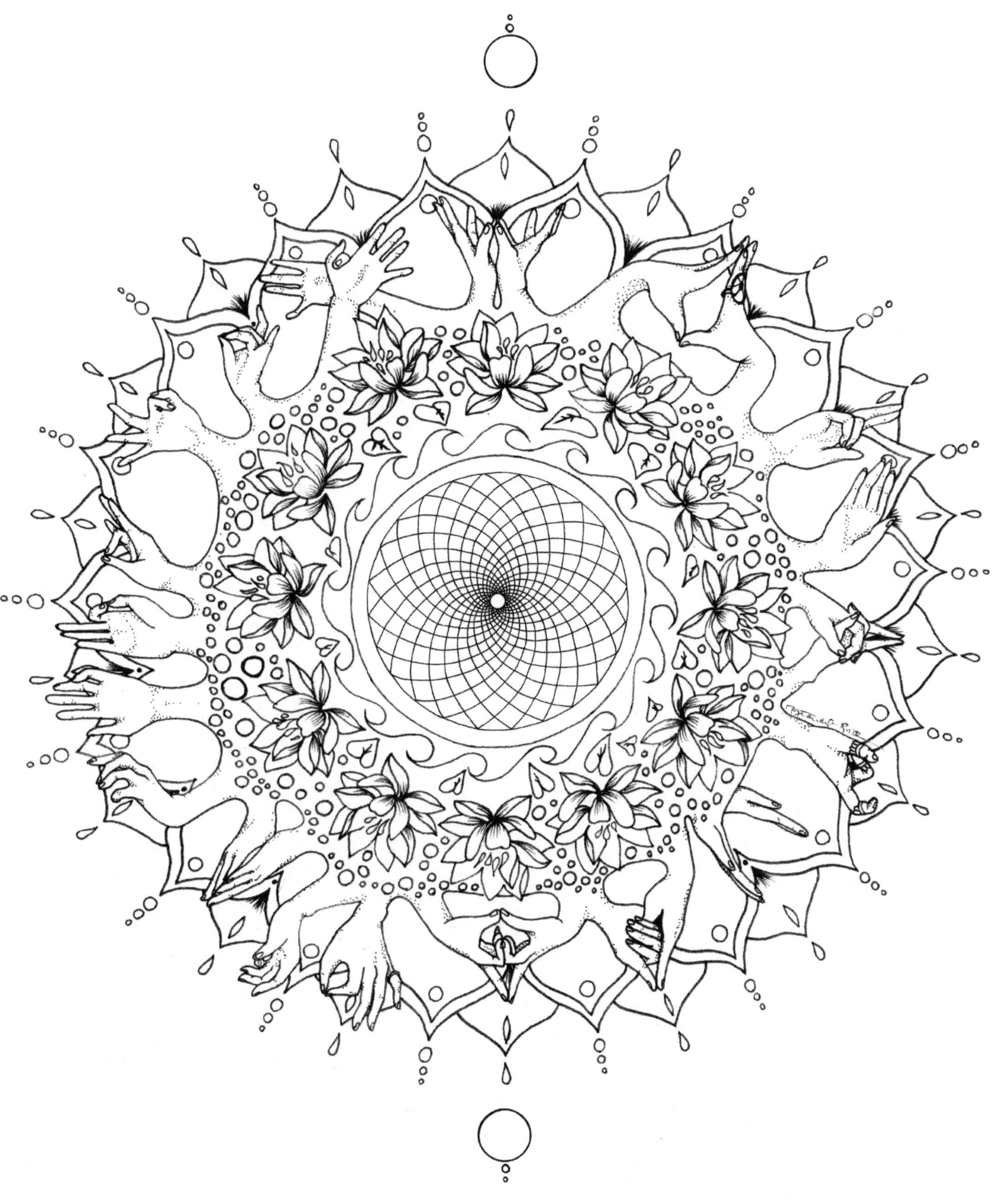

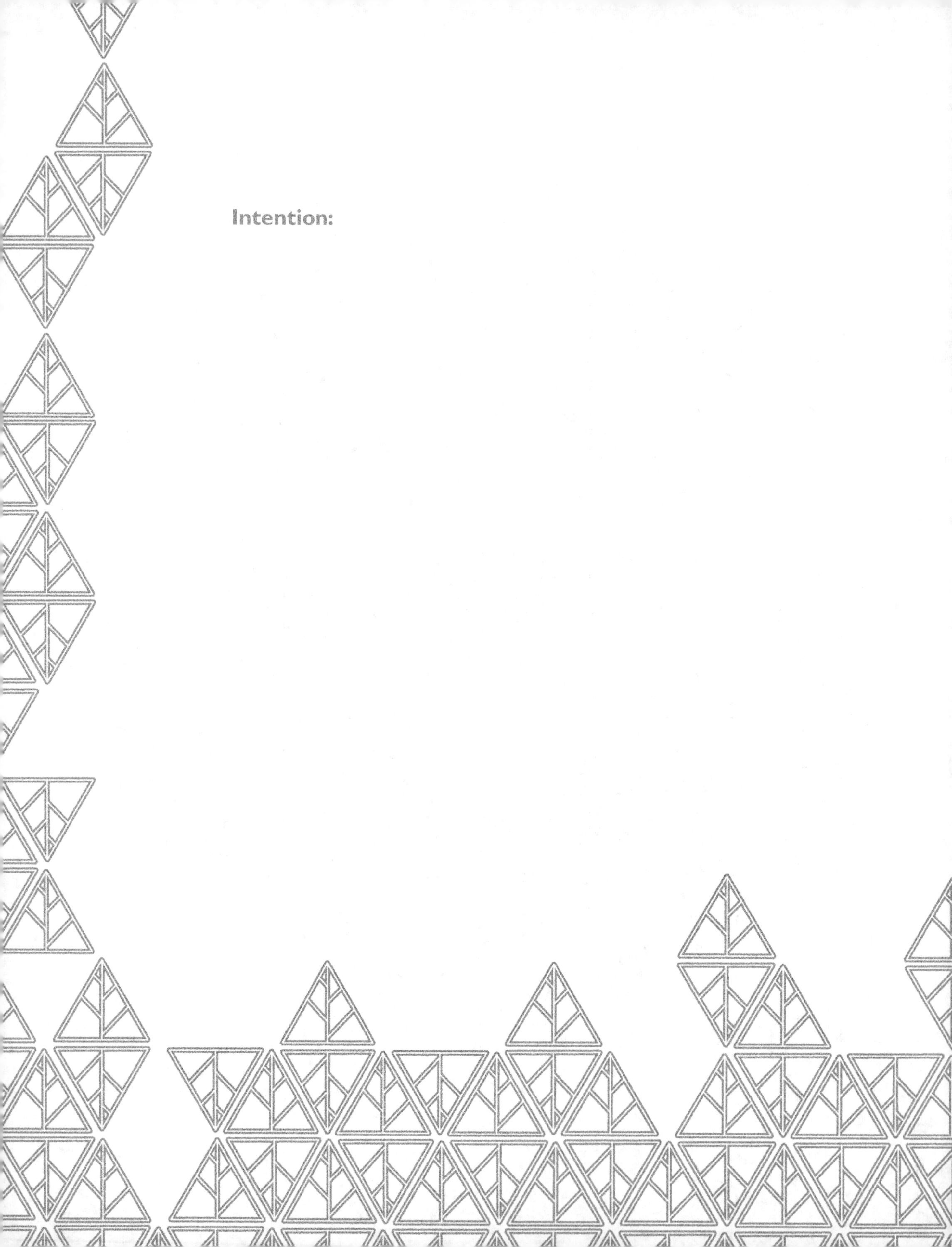

Intention:

Thought Infusions

1. Do you resist the flow of the dance of life? How do you embrace it?

2. Movement, as part of contemplative practices, is primordial to human health at all levels of mind-body-spirit. Movement, including dance, has been woven into belief systems throughout all time. How do you practice movement in your life? If there is limited movement present, what changes can you make in your lifestyle to allow for that intentional movement to be present?

3. Contemplate your colored illustration. How does color change your initial perception of the image? What colors did you use? Look up #anewkindofcoloringbook and #puraprana, share your work. Explore other being's colors and see what new messages come to mind through observation.

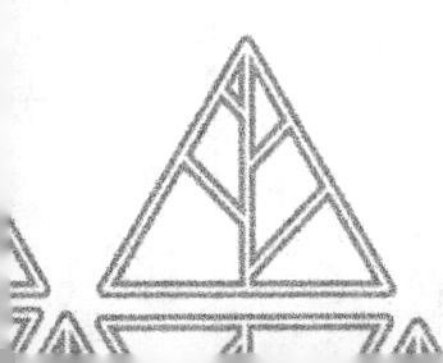

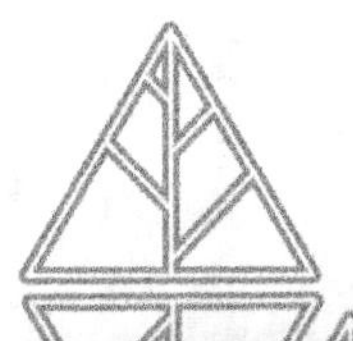

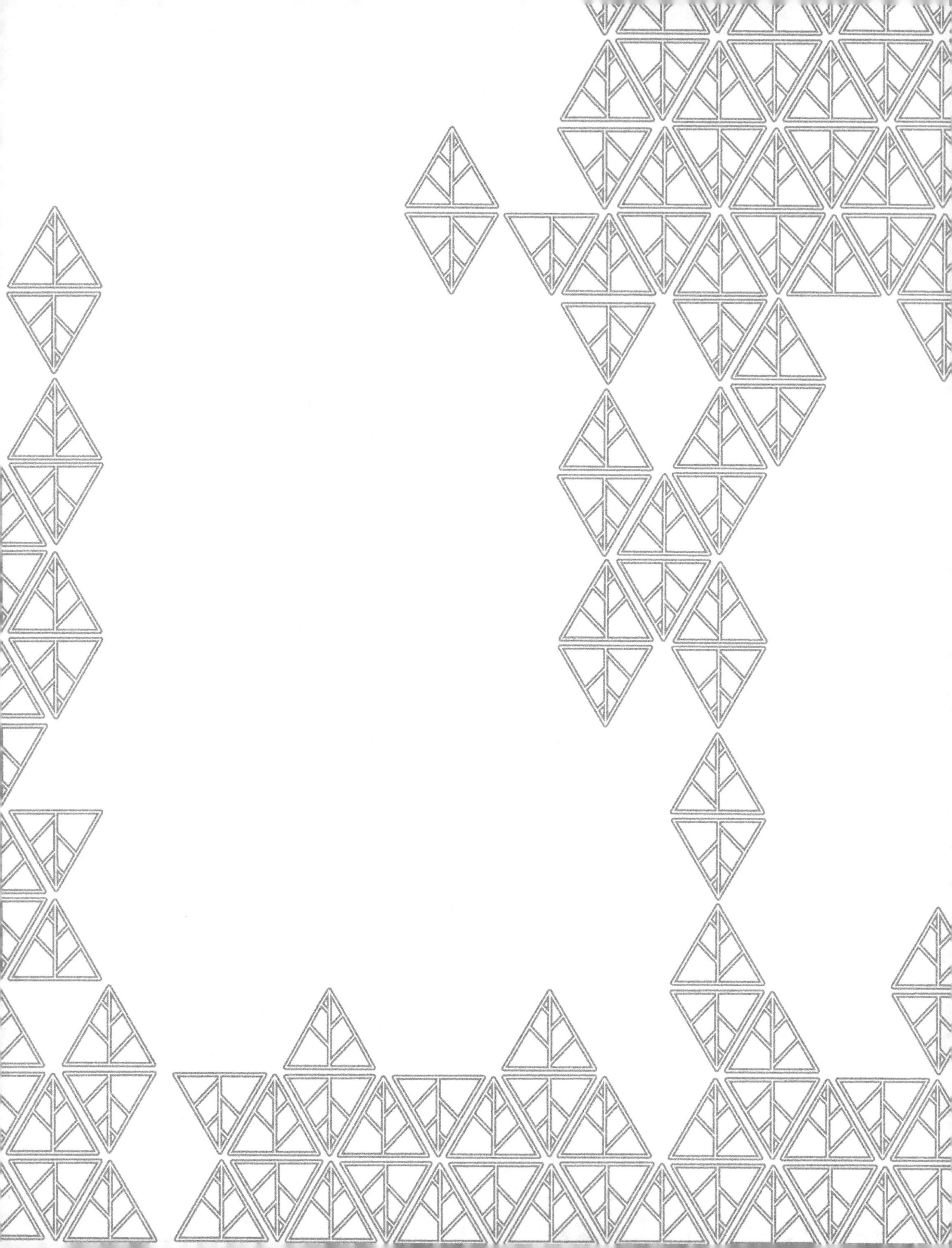

ABOUT THE AUTHOR

"We spend our days looking for the secret of life.
Well, the secret of life is art."

\- Oscar Wilde -

***Iréne de Brice, PhD, CHHP* | Iréne is a Costa Rican bioscientist, certified holistic health practitioner, budding herbalist, and self-taught artist. During her formal education, she completed graduate programs in biosciences. As a matter of personal interest, she also completed a MS in Natural Health and Lifestyles in 2011, where she concentrated in holistic nutrition, mind-body interactions, and holistic health modalities. She has taught classes ranging from molecular biology to genetics, artistic anatomy and meditation. She blends her 16 years of devotion to biosciences and alternative studies into her art and Contemplative Art Meditations™. Her calling has led her to merge all her skills into *art medicine*. Her work explores the mythology and science of the biosphere, space cosmology, the contours and fields of the human experience, and her personal ancestral mythos.**

Contributors

Vivia Astraia | Vivia has dedicated many years of research integrating the realms of science, art & spirituality. She has been teaching *Mudrā Workshops and Neurofeedback Interactive Meditation Installations* since 1999, including being featured at MIT Boston Cyberarts festival in Boston, MA. She studied at the Benson-Henry Institute for Mind Body Medicine at Harvard University, and earned her BA degree in Interactive Media at Massachusetts College of Art & Design. Gravitating towards music and movement as a medium for integration of somatic awareness, she has also studied a variety of martial arts, Qì Gong and Somatic Dance Psychology. A Vipassana practitioner for 20 years, she is also the creator and facilitator of *Dynamic Mudrā Flow* workshops in Sarasota, Florida, and worldwide. Vivia also designs *Zensoria Opulent Ambience* environments for events and *Sensory Awareness Installations,* where one's brain waves can interact with the pulse of light and sound, focusing in the creation of sacred space for awareness expansion through sensory perception and the awakening state of serenity, peace and illumination.

Louisa Wargo (Lotus Rising) | Louisa was born in New York City, and raised in England and South California. She wrote her first poem titled "The Ocean" at age 9 and has been writing ever since. She lives in Sarasota, Florida, with her three sons. She enjoys writing, yoga, good friends and eating her veggies as she strives to live a minimal lifestyle free of materialism.

Maricel Flores Díaz | Maricel is a Puerto Rican chemical and manufacturing engineer, with additional training in biology, psychology, comparative religions, and Egyptology. She became an accredited yoga instructor in 2007 at the Sivananda Yoga Centre in Canada. In 2013 she was certified in Regression and Past Lives Therapy by Dr. José Cabouli in Spain, and has received spiritual instruction from several teachers, among them, Magdaleno Calderón. Supplementary certifications include Therapeutic Reflexology, Neurolinguistic Programming, Autonomic Training, and Family Constellations. She received her first degree in Reiki from Josecarmelo Rodríguez, embarking afterwards in the healing techniques developed by Dr. Alba Ambert from Paramita Path, from whom she has received several initiations in different healing methodologies. She has participated in several women spirituality groups and workshops including Goddess Archetypes and being initiated as a Moon Mother by Miranda Gray.

We hope this book made you think, feel, and overall, love all a little bit more.

Thank you for supporting this work! Follow the link below to stay connected with art medicine.

Irène + team

www.ingramcontent.com/pod-product-compliance
Lightning Source LLC
LaVergne TN
LVHW061222100826
845148LV00004B/834
* 9 7 8 0 6 9 2 1 7 3 8 8 6 *